EMANUELE CASTAGNO

AUGMENTED INTELLIGENCE:

HOW AI ENHANCES YOUR CAPABILITIES AND SUCCESS.

FROM HISTORY TO STRATEGIES FOR TOMORROW: YOUR GUIDE IN THE AI WORLD

AUGMENTED INTELLIGENCE: HOW AI ENHANCES YOUR CAPABILITIES AND SUCCESS.

I Edition July 2025

To Daniela, a tireless companion in life; to Jade, Matthew and Peter, who illuminate my path with their curiosity and wonder; and to all those who, like you, cultivate a vision of a technology that, guided by responsible and ethical hands, becomes an instrument of genuine progress for humanity.

May this book inspire not only brilliant minds but also conscious hearts.

Table of Contents

INTRODUCTION

Today, generative artificial intelligence (AI) is no longer an option but a competitive necessity. With the integration of Copilot in Microsoft 365 *suites*, ChatGPT in browsers and Gemini in smartphones, AI has become an everyday collaborator for millions of people-from professionals seeking competitive advantages to ordinary people curious to explore new possibilities. This book was created to bridge the gap between theoretical potential and practical application. This book is not aimed at experts, already accustomed to constant experimentation, but at those who see technology as a tool for responsible progress and want to integrate it into everyday activities-from work to personal passions. I offer an accessible but comprehensive guide, requiring no specific technical expertise, just the ability to clearly communicate your needs.

Generative AI represents a revolutionary breakthrough: unlike traditional systems designed to analyze data and perform specific tasks, it can create original content - text, images, music, video, code - based on the requests (or *prompts*) we submit to it.

Its versatility ranges from developing and executing code from functional descriptions to synthesizing molecules for pharmaceutical research, from creating 3D models for industrial design to generating synthetic data for training other AI systems.

It is important to recognize that generative AI also has limitations: it can generate inaccurate information or "hallucinations" (plausible but false information, such as invented historical dates), it can reproduce biases present in training data, and it raises complex questions about intellectual property, privacy and content authenticity. We will take a balanced approach that recognizes both the transformative potential and the liabilities of using these technologies.

My personal journey with AI

My relationship with AI has deep roots. During my studies in electrical engineering, I delved into neural networks and the Lisp and Prolog languages for expert systems. I still keep some printouts of that code that remind me of the evolutionary path from symbolic reasoning to today's generative language models.

In my 30-year career in technology, I have observed the transformation of AI from a theoretical concept to a practical tool: from the first medical diagnostic systems in Italian web portals in the 2000s to advanced quality control applications in industries. During my management career, I promoted the adoption of innovative technologies such as *Robotic Process Automation* (RPA) and early applications of artificial intelligence.

Today, I implement generative AI with particular intensity, achieving outstanding results in automating the drafting of technical and economic documents, supporting the development of new services, and optimizing processes. Generative AI has also proven effective in marketing, personalizing B2B and B2C communication. *Machine learning* algorithms also allow us to optimize the scheduling of services by studying the optimal composition of teams.

This experience brings me back to the path I took years ago when I published a book on time management that explored the synergy between David Allen's GTD® (Getting Things Done) methodology and the emerging technology of the iPad. The key difference is that AI represents a quantum leap: we don't just optimize time management, we redefine personal productivity.

The structure of this book reflects my journey through different industries and technologies. In Chapter 1 I will share the evolution from neural networks to modern *Large Language Models* (LLMs). Chapter 2 presents *prompt engineering* techniques derived from my daily experimentation. Chapters 3 and 5 combine theoretical principles with real-world use cases. Chapter 4 is the heart of enterprise operational optimization, where I will look in detail at how nongenerative AI transforms planning and control across three key pillars: quality control in production with automatic defect identification systems, predictive maintenance to ensure business continuity, and optimization of service delivery-all applications I have implemented directly in my own executive experiences. In Chapter 6 you will discover how to use AI as a coach for personal development, in Chapter 7 we will explore career redesign in the AI era, and in Chapter 8 we will look at the future of generative AI and emerging agent systems.

Book pathway

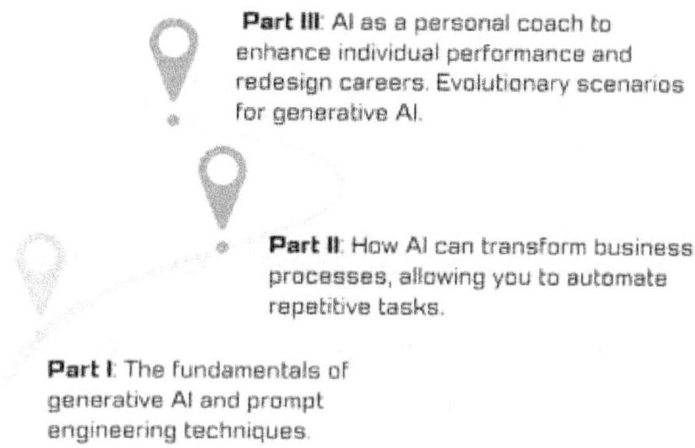

Part I: The fundamentals of generative AI and *prompt engineering* techniques-the strategic art of formulating precise instructions that guide AI toward optimal outputs.

Part II: The transformation of business processes by automating repetitive tasks and focusing on strategic decisions.

Part III: The use of AI as a personal coach to enhance individual performance and redesign careers, concluding with evolutionary scenarios of generative AI.

How to use this book: a flexible and modular handbook

This volume is designed as an everyday handbook that does not require sequential reading. You can start with the chapters most relevant to your needs, flipping through it like an encyclopedia to quickly find specific answers.

Theory always translates into practice through ready-to-use prompts-the instructions we provide to generative AI models. A good prompt combines task information, target context, desired format, and often examples. We will explore different types of *prompts* by learning how to construct, modify, and refine them through an iterative process.

Guide to *prompts* and practical tools

Throughout the book you will encounter blocks of text labeled "*Prompts*" followed or not by a web link. These are ready-to-use commands that can be inserted into AI assistants such as ChatGPT, Claude, or Gemini.

Prompt: **https://tinyurl.com/5x7yy22x**

> Provide a concise summary of the main points discussed in the podcast/video at [**URL**]. Include the most important insights, key points to remember, and any significant quotes or statistics mentioned.

Text [in square brackets] indicates content to be customized or blocks of instructions for the model. QR codes next to *prompts* simplify access to digital resources.

For particularly complex *prompts*, you will find tables structured with Name, Objective, Template, Prompt and Output, allowing you to understand how to formulate them and analyze the results obtained with different templates.

Prompt Name	Prompt Name
Objective	Purpose of the *prompt*
Template	Model on which the AI assistant used is based (e.g., Claude 4 Sonnet)
Prompt	Full text of the command with QR code/link
	https://tinyurl.com/5x7yy22x
Output	Result obtained (full version accessible via QR code/link if indicated with "CONTINUE...")
	http://tinyurl.com/5x7yy22x

This structure will allow you not only to understand how to formulate *prompts*, but also to easily use and modify them according to your needs. If the objective of the *prompt* were stated in the paragraph, the "Objective" section might be omitted from the table.

Within the book you will also find links that can be reached either from the link itself or by framing the relevant QR code:

https://tinyurl.com/5x7yy22x

Navigating examples and use cases

The examples in the volume represent concrete situations in which I have used these technologies to solve specific problems; consider them "starting points" rather than definitive solutions. Each *prompt* can be modified and customized to suit your context. The iterative approach will allow you to develop a deep understanding of how to communicate effectively with generative AI systems.

AI as a daily collaborator

In my daily life, AI has become a silent but effective collaborator. Microsoft Copilot prepares me for meetings and takes minutes, saving me over ten productive hours each week. Claude prepares me interactive dashboards, graphic elements for my slides, and supports me in creative sessions. On road trips, ChatGPT *Voice* is my companion for English practice and partner in numerous training and brainstorming sessions. AI also supports me in hobbies such as 3D printing and assists me in writing code, areas where I now cannot do without Google Gemini or Claude.

Disclaimer on the use of AI services

The versions of AI services I use are paid and/or enterprise versions, with advanced features that may not be available in the free versions. Before providing any personal data to an AI service, it is essential to carefully review the privacy and data confidentiality policies.

For each AI use, I formulate an initial prompt and continue with subsequent *prompts* until the desired result is achieved. Each *prompt* is shown along with the *Large Language Model*[1] that provides the best results:

- **Microsoft 365 Copilot**: integrated enterprise solution for collaborative and cloud-based Microsoft work environments.
- **ChatGPT 4.5:** versatile model for a wide range of prompts.
- **Gemini Advanced:** good for complex analytics and web content access.
- **Claude Opus 4:** effective for creativity and narrative content generation.
- **Perplexity**: perfect for quick searches and documented answers.

I am also experimenting with **Deepseek** (https://www.deepseek.com/en) and Alibaba's **Qwen** (https://chat.qwen.ai/), both Chinese models with advanced features. I encourage you to read their terms of use carefully, particularly regarding the use of data for model training.

It is important to note that the field of generative AI is rapidly evolving. The models mentioned might be updated or replaced, but the fundamental principles of interaction with AI and *prompt engineering* techniques remain valid regardless of the model used.

---

[1] The versions of the models listed here refer to the state of the art at the time of writing (June 2025) and are subject to rapid evolution. The principles described remain valid.

The use of these AI tools, especially in professional settings, carries significant responsibilities. Organizations must consider privacy issues, legal implications related to intellectual property, the need for human verification for critical results, and potential biases (biases) in the results. We will explore these issues in more detail in Chapter 8, providing concrete guidelines for ethical and responsible implementation.

In conclusion

This book is intended to be both a practical guide and a strategic reflection on generative AI. AI is not just a technology to be understood, but an ally to be integrated into our professional and personal lives.

In the next 2-3 years we will witness an unprecedented technological transformation. As we will see in detail in Chapter 8, the future moves along three basic dimensions of evolution that will completely redefine our approach to digital work.

The first dimension concerns the evolution of language models that manifests itself through:

- Computational efficiency: more compact and sustainable models that maintain advanced cognitive capabilities while significantly reducing hardware requirements.
- Domain-specific specialization: development of vertical models optimized for specific industries.
- Reduced latency: response times that approach natural human interaction.

The second dimension is the adaptive personalization of AI assistants. This evolution is realized through:

- **Continuous contextual learning**: assistants will develop the ability to dynamically adapt to the specific work context, learning behavioral patterns, communication preferences, and individual operating methodologies.
- **Advanced ecosystem integration**: the implementation of RAG technology is a crucial turning point. This methodology enables AI assistants to:
  - Access enterprise knowledge bases in real time.
  - Integrate information from databases, technical documentation and operational procedures.
  - Maintain consistency with specific organizational policies and standards.

The third and most revolutionary dimension is the convergence of LLM and *Robotic Process Automation* models. This technological synthesis is generating a new category of tools: collaborative digital agents. These can operate on different software, operating systems and platforms performing complex tasks that require context-specific decision making. They enhance and will increasingly enhance individual capabilities through human-AI collaboration.

These evolutions will radically transform organizational models, redefining processes and operational flows. The democratization of access to advanced analytical and operational capabilities will be the real turning point: no longer the exclusive preserve of technical specialists, these skills will become shared assets of the entire workforce. Enterprise knowledge management will evolve from static repositories to dynamic, natural-language queryable systems.

Do not consider this book an end point, but the beginning of an ongoing journey of learning and experimentation. True mastery comes from daily application and sharing experiences. I invite you to join me on LinkedIn where I regularly share new findings and innovative use cases:

https://www.linkedin.com/in/emanuelecastagno/

Try a first practical exercise now: open a generative AI tool and type, "Analyze this [short text/presentation/e-mail] and suggest three ways to improve it in terms of clarity, structure, and impact." Insert your own actual content and observe the results. It is through these first interactions that you will begin to build your familiarity with generative AI and sense its transformative potential.

Enjoy your journey!

PART I:

AI FUNDAMENTALS AND INTERACTION

CHAPTER 1

THE GREAT TRANSFORMATION OF AI: THREE DECADES OF TECHNOLOGICAL REVOLUTIONS

In this chapter we will trace the evolution of AI through three decades of innovations that have transformed a theoretical discipline into a revolutionary force. From my privileged vantage point of three decades in the world of applied technology, I have witnessed this metamorphosis: from the first expert systems in the 1990s to today's *Large Language Models* redefining the way we work. We will explore the key moments of this transformation, the technology architectures that made it possible, and the future prospects that are opening toward general AI (AGI), an AI that thinks like us about everything.

1.1 The history of AI: from pioneers to modern revolutionary breakthroughs

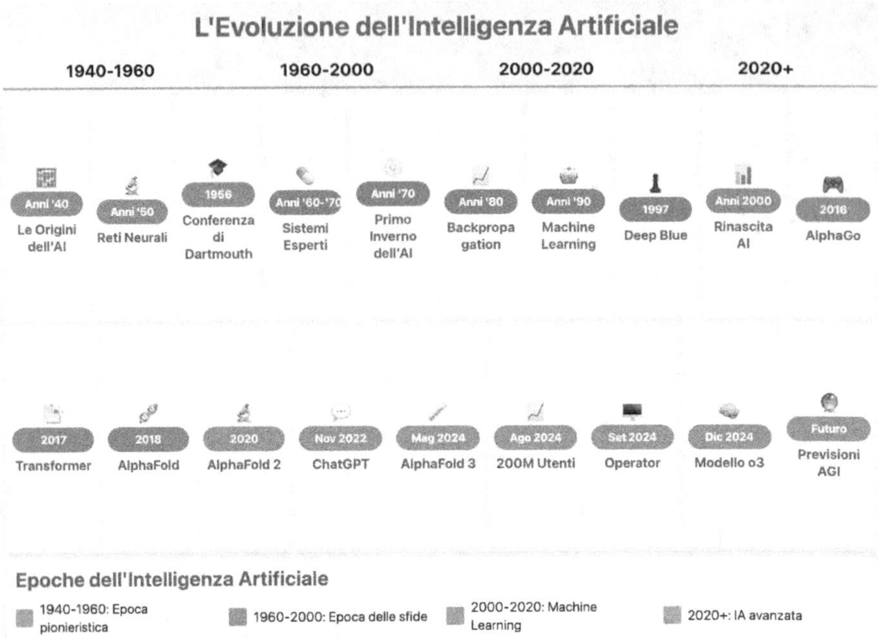

The founding fathers: Turing, McCarthy and the Dartmouth conference

The origins of AI date back to the 1940s, when the first experiments with machines capable of solving logical and mathematical problems were conducted. Alan Turing, often considered the father of modern computer science, made fundamental contributions to the concept of a machine capable of performing complex logical calculations.

In my early years of study at university, I was fascinated by the so-called "Turing Machine," one of the first abstract models demonstrating how a mechanical device could perform any algorithm. His famous "Turing Test," designed to determine whether a machine could exhibit intelligent behavior indistinguishable from human behavior, remains to this day a benchmark for evaluating AI capabilities.

During World War II, Turing developed decryption techniques for Enigma that demonstrated the potential of automated computation. This experience, combined with his earlier and later theoretical work, helped shape his vision of thinking machines and laid the conceptual foundation for AI.

Formal recognition of AI as an academic discipline occurred in 1956 at the Dartmouth Conference, which is often considered the official birth of AI. Professor John McCarthy, a key figure in the history of AI, defined it as the "science and engineering of creating intelligent machines," stressing that its methods should not be limited by biological analogies.

However, it is important to note that the evolution of AI has not been a linear path of steady progress. There have been periods of great enthusiasm followed by moments of stagnation, known as "AI winters." The first winter of AI occurred in the 1970s, when initial expectations were not met due to limited computational capabilities and difficulties in handling data. A second AI winter followed in the 1980s, when enthusiasm for expert systems waned due to high costs and limited practical capabilities. Only since the 2000s, with the advent of *big data*, advances in computing power, and the refinement of *machine learning* techniques, has AI begun to gain momentum again.

The field is inherently interdisciplinary. It draws from philosophy, mathematics, neuroscience, psychology, computer engineering, linguistics, economics, and control theory. All these different fields have contributed to the development of algorithms capable of mimicking human cognition and behavior. After the Dartmouth Conference, several strands of study developed, each with specific results. One of the main ones was the creation of the first expert systems in the 1960s and 1970s, designed to solve complex problems in specific fields such as medicine and chemistry.

Expert systems: the first generation of AI

Expert systems represent one of the first applications of AI to support decision making and have found successful application in complex diagnostic and decision-making tasks.

An emblematic example is MYCIN, an expert system developed to assist physicians in diagnosing bacterial infections and recommending antibiotic therapies. MYCIN used a set of rules based on expert knowledge to infer the most likely diagnoses and suggest appropriate treatments. Each rule followed the logical structure of "if a certain condition occurs, then perform a certain action." This approach was useful for simulating the thought process of a medical expert and providing immediate assistance in critical situations.

Other significant expert systems included DENDRAL for chemical analysis and PROSPECTOR for geological exploration. In industry, similar systems were used for fault diagnostics in production lines.

One of the main advantages of expert systems was their ability to encode specialized knowledge in an accessible and repeatable format. However, these systems suffered from some major limitations. The maintenance and updating of rules required continuous human intervention, especially as domain-specific knowledge evolved. This need for constant review and updating was burdensome and limited the scalability of the system.

Machine learning and *deep learning*: the turning point of the 1990s

An important strand in the development of AI was neural networks, which were introduced in the 1950s but initially hampered by the limited computing power available. Neural networks were designed to replicate to some extent the functioning of the human brain, using mathematical models to simulate biological neurons. However, the technology available at the time was not sufficiently advanced to support the computational load required by these models, and interest in neural networks declined until the 1980s.

It was not until the 1980s, with the introduction of backpropagation (literally "backward propagation") algorithms, that neural networks had a renaissance. *Backpropagation* allowed the training of more sophisticated models, updating the weights of connections between neurons as errors were found.

What are neural networks?

Neural networks are composed of units called "neurons," which are organized in layers and connected to each other. Each neuron receives input, processes it and transmits the result to the next neuron. Neural networks are used to "learn" to perform specific tasks, just as a human would learn from examples. The key concept of neural networks is that, through training, the weights of connections between neurons are updated so as to reduce the error between the predicted and actual result.

I recall with particular interest a neural network system for quality control. This system greatly improved the production process, first of steel and later of pasta. In the latter case, it eliminated waste and raised food safety standards. The two systems mentioned above used neural networks to process images from cameras in real time.

Backpropagation: how neural networks learn

Backpropagation, a fundamental algorithm for training neural networks, works similarly to an error-correction process. Imagine you have a neural network trying to recognize pictures of cats, but it makes a mistake in recognizing an image. *Backpropagation* allows the system to figure out where it made a mistake and correct the errors by adjusting the "weights" of the connections between the neurons.

The 1990s and machine learning

In the 1990s and 2000s, the focus of AI research shifted to *machine* learning and statistical learning. The increase in computing power and the availability of large amounts of data, known as 'big data,' allowed for increasingly meaningful results. This approach was based on mathematical models that could analyze historical data, extract *patterns* and make predictions with increasing accuracy, laying the foundation for the AI applications we know today.

During these decades, supervised and unsupervised learning began to spread. In supervised learning, the model is trained with matching input and output examples, trying to learn the relationship between the two.

A common example of supervised learning is Netflix's recommendation system. When a user selects "thumbs up" or "thumbs down" to indicate whether or not they liked a movie, they are providing feedback that Netflix uses to improve future recommendations.

Deep learning: the modern revolution

Finally, the recent *deep learning* revolution has brought further developments. *Deep learning* is a subcategory of *machine learning* that focuses on deep neural networks, that is, networks with many hidden layers (hence the term "deep"). These additional layers enable the model to learn data representations at increasingly higher levels of abstraction, improving performance in complex tasks such as image recognition, natural language understanding, and more.

From a technical perspective, what distinguishes *deep learning* from previous *machine learning* techniques is its ability to learn hierarchies of representations. In a deep neural network, each successive layer extracts increasingly abstract and complex features: the first layer might detect simple *patterns* such as lines and edges; the second will combine these lines into geometric shapes; the third will recognize parts of objects such as eyes or wheels; and deeper layers will recognize complete objects and their relationships. This hierarchical architecture is particularly effective for processing unstructured data such as images, audio and text, where relevant features are not obvious at the surface level but emerge from the organization of *patterns* at different levels of abstraction.

Deep learning has particularly revolutionized the field of *Natural Language Processing* (NLP)-the branch of AI dedicated to teaching machines how to understand, interpret and generate human language. In essence, NLP is what allows computers to "read" a text, extract its meaning and respond coherently, just as we are seeing today with ChatGPT or voice assistants like Siri. Before deep learning, NLP systems depended heavily on rule-based approaches. I remember working on an automatic categorization system for technical documents in the early 2000s: we had to manually code hundreds of grammar rules, create specialized dictionaries, and define syntactic patterns for each type of document. It was titanic work that produced acceptable results only in very narrow domains.

With the advent of deep neural networks, NLP underwent a radical transformation. Word2Vec (2013) demonstrated that words could be represented as dense vectors in multidimensional spaces, where semantic relations translated into geometric relations. Suddenly, mathematical operations on the vectors produced linguistically meaningful results: "king" - "man" + "woman" ≈ "queen." This mathematical operation on vectors demonstrated that the model had learned complex semantic relations, almost "reasoning" by analogy. This revolution in NLP set the stage for future *Transformers*, which would take language understanding to previously unimaginable levels, enabling machines not only to process text, but to generate it with amazing coherence and contextuality.

Thanks to *deep learning*, we have seen the emergence of technologies such as virtual assistants, autonomous vehicles, and machine translation applications, which are capable of handling and responding to complex scenarios almost autonomously.

I have had the opportunity to see up close the integration of *deep learning* systems for satellite image analysis that have revolutionized our capabilities. The implemented multilayer neural networks could identify and classify terrain features with unprecedented accuracy, providing critical information for both disaster response applications and environmental monitoring.

While these applications of *deep learning* represented significant advances, the real revolution in AI was about to come with the introduction of an entirely new architecture. Until 2017, most natural language processing models were based on recurrent (RNN[2]) or convolutional (CNN[3]) architectures, which showed limitations in processing long sequences and capturing long-term dependencies. A radically different approach was needed, which would come with the introduction of *Transformers*.

This evolution of AI, from early expert systems to modern *deep learning* architectures, has progressively expanded the computational capabilities of machines, enabling them to tackle increasingly complex challenges. To fully understand the transformative impact of these technological advances, it is illuminating to examine some historical moments when AI has concretely demonstrated its potential by directly confronting human intelligence in areas considered the exclusive domain of the human intellect. These "watershed moments" represent not just symbolic victories of technology, but true paradigm leaps in our understanding of the possibilities of AI.

---

[2] **RNNs**: Recurrent Neural Networks, represent a family of architectures designed specifically to process sequential data. Unlike traditional neural networks, RNNs incorporate recursive connections that create a form of "internal memory" within the network.
[3] **CNN**: Convolutional Neural Networks, are optimized for processing data with grid structure, particularly images. Their operation is inspired by the organization of the animal visual cortex, where individual neurons respond to stimuli in limited regions of the visual field.

1.2 Turning points in the development of AI.

Deep Blue (1997)

The Deep Blue supercomputer, developed by IBM, represented a milestone in the history of AI. It was an impressive machine for the time: it could analyze 200 million chess positions per second, using 30 RS/6000 SP processors and 480 VLSI chips specialized for chess play. Its victory over Garry Kasparov in 1997 was a historic moment: for the first time a computer beat the world chess champion in a regulation match.

It is important to note that Deep Blue could not calculate all possible chess moves-a mathematically impossible feat. The number of possible chess matches is estimated[4] at about $10^{(120)}$ (a 1 followed by 120 zeros), a number 40 orders of magnitude greater than the number of atoms in the universe (10$^{80)}$.

Deep Blue used clever shortcuts: instead of analyzing every single possible move, it immediately discarded the obviously losing ones and focused only on the most promising moves.

AlphaGo (2016)

Almost two decades after Deep Blue, DeepMind (a company acquired by Google in 2014) developed AlphaGo, an AI system based on deep neural networks and reinforcement learning algorithms. The Go challenge was even more complex than chess: the number of possible Go matches is estimated at about 10^{360}, a number so large that it exceeds the number of chess matches by 240 orders of magnitude.

---

[4] **Claude Shannon** calculated in 1950 that the number of possible chess games is approximately 10^120. This estimate, known as the "Shannon Number"

Given this astronomical complexity, AlphaGo could not rely on pure variant computation, but had to develop a more "intelligent" approach based on neural networks that "learn" to recognize promising moves. The victory over Lee Sedol[5] in 2016 was particularly significant because the "Move 37" in the second game - seemingly illogical by human standards but turned out to be ingenious - proved that AI could develop original and creative strategies, overcoming the limits of conventional human thinking.

AlphaFold (2018)

AlphaFold represents a rare example of AI capable of not only accelerating but also radically transforming a field of scientific research. Its ability to rapidly predict the three-dimensional structure of proteins, which traditionally took months or years, is profoundly changing biomedical research.

This technology is revolutionizing drug discovery by facilitating the identification of interaction points on proteins with new drugs. In rare diseases, AlphaFold makes it possible to study mutated protein structures in little-known diseases, opening up new therapeutic avenues. It also enables industrial biotechnology to create more efficient enzymes and personalized medicine to analyze individual genetic variants.

AlphaFold 1, introduced in 2018, showed for the first time that AI could compete with traditional methods by winning CASP13, an international competition on protein structure prediction. In 2020,

---

[5] **Lee Sedol:** Born in 1983 in South Korea, he is a legendary figure in the landscape of the game of Go. He retired in 2019 with this statement, "Even if I become number one, there is no entity that can surpass AI. I have become an insignificant existence."

AlphaFold 2 marked a true revolution, achieving accuracy comparable to experimental methods and radically transforming the field.

The democratization of structural knowledge was achieved with the creation of the AlphaFold Protein Structure Database by DeepMind, making more than 200 million protein structures freely accessible.

Announced in 2024, AlphaFold 3 represents a further step forward: it predicts not just isolated proteins, but whole protein complexes with DNA, RNA, and small molecules, thanks to the innovative use of *Transformer* and *Diffusion Model*, technologies already used in LLMs and DALL-E (the latter capable of generating realistic images from textual descriptions).

A practical example is from the University of Oxford, where AlphaFold 3 has made it possible to rapidly identify an emerging viral protein, test virtually thousands of candidate compounds, and significantly accelerate the search for new drugs. AlphaFold thus represents a fundamental breakthrough with direct implications for human health and the accessibility of scientific knowledge.

1.3 Architecture of *Large Language Models* (LLMs): from *Transformers* to neural networks

"All You Need Is Love," the *Transformers* and the Breakthrough

"All You Need Is Love," sang the Beatles in 1967. Fifty years later, eight Google Brain researchers unwittingly paraphrased this iconic song with "Attention Is All You Need," a *paper* published in 2017 that would redefine modern AI.

Before exploring this architectural revolution, it is essential to understand how language models "see" text.

Tokens: the alphabet of AI

Imagine having to teach a computer to read. You cannot simply show it words-you have to break them down into units it can process. These basic building blocks are called *tokens*.

A *token* is not necessarily a whole word.

It can be:

1) A common word ("house" = 1 *token*).
2) Part of a word ("extra-ordin-ary" = 3 *tokens*).
3) A symbol or number ("€" or "2025" = 1 *token* each).

Basically, for the Italian text:

- 1 *token* ≈ 3.8-4.2 characters.
- One page of a book like this ≈ 330-350 *tokens*.
- A complex prompt ≈ 500-1000 *tokens*.

Understanding *tokens* is crucial because they determine:

- **Processing capacity**: how much information the model can consider simultaneously (the "context window").
- **Computational costs**: AI services charge per *token* processed.
- **Practical limits**: a model with a window of 100,000 *tokens* can analyze about 250-300 pages of text.

With this basic understanding, we can now explore how *Transformers* have revolutionized the processing of these *tokens*.

The Transformer architecture: a conceptual revolution

The *Transformer* architecture represented a conceptual revolution in the way computers process language. The 2017 paper introduced a radically different approach that changed the field of artificial intelligence forever.

Before *Transformers*, recurrent neural networks (RNNs) processed text sequentially, as if they were reading one word at a time with their finger under each term. This approach had a fundamental limitation: by the time the system reached the end of a sentence, it risked having lost the initial context.

The Transformers solved this problem through the "attention" mechanism, which allows all *tokens to* be examined simultaneously. To understand this difference, let us consider a practical example:

"The certificate of compliance was issued after the full technical inspection of the system."

A sequential system (RNN) would read: "The" → "certificate" → "of" → ... → "facility." By the time it gets to "plant," it may have lost the initial context associated with "certificate."

A *Transformer*, on the other hand, operates differently. It first divides the sentence into *tokens*: ["The", "certific", "ato", "di", "conform", "ità", ...]. Then it simultaneously computes the relationships among all the *tokens*. Each word "observes" all the others to assess the degree of correlation, as if it were assigning a "friendship score" to each pair. To do this, each token generates three vectors: a Query (the question the token asks), a Key (the token's label), and a Value (the token's contents). The mechanism calculates how much each "Query" is related to each "Key" to determine these scores.

Let's take "certificate" as an example. This word evaluates its relationship with all the other terms in the sentence:

- With "compliance": uncovers a very strong relationship.
- With "inspection": identifies a medium-strong link.
- With "facility": detects a moderate bond.
- With "after": finds a weak link.

These correlation scores (which we technically callQK^T) are then transformed into "attention rates" through a function called softmax.

The result might be that "certified" decides to devote 60 percent of its attention to "compliance," 25 percent to "inspection," 10 percent to "facility," and 5 percent to "after."

Each word then enriches its meaning by combining the contributions of the other words according to these weights. The final meaning of "certificate" becomes a weighted mixture that includes mainly the context of "compliance" and "inspection," with smaller contributions from the other words.

Mathematically, this process is expressed by the formula:

$$\text{Attention(Q,K,V)} = \text{softmax}\left(\frac{QK^T}{\sqrt{d}}\right) \text{V}$$

Where Q (Query), K (Key) and V (Value) are vectors associated with each token, QK^T measures the relationship between each word pair, $\sqrt{d}$ is a normalization factor that stabilizes the calculation, and softmax converts raw scores to percentages.

To visualize this concept with a practical analogy, imagine a meeting where several experts must coordinate their assessments. Instead of speaking sequentially one at a time, everyone can simultaneously view each other's contributions on a shared whiteboard, focusing on the items most relevant to their area of expertise.

This simultaneous approach allows the system to maintain a comprehensive understanding of the text. Each word no longer retains only its isolated meaning, but is enriched by the full context of the sentence. The *Transformer* thus understands that "certificate," "compliance," and "inspection" are conceptually connected, regardless of their position in the sentence.

It is this capacity for parallel processing and global attention that makes *Transformers* so effective in processing complex text, enabling modern language systems to maintain coherence and context even in long and articulate conversations.

For an interactive visualization of this mechanism, I recommend Grant Sanderson's video:

https://tinyurl.com/39ewpkvh

From architecture to application: ChatGPT, the beginning of a new era

This parallel and contextual processing capability has paved the way for increasingly sophisticated models. When OpenAI launched ChatGPT on November 30, 2022, it showed the world what it means to combine:

- *Transformer* architecture scaled to billions of parameters.
- Training on trillions of text *tokens*.
- *Fine-tuning* to follow human instructions.

The result? A system that can maintain context over thousands of *tokens*, generating consistent and contextually appropriate responses- just as we are experiencing daily in our processes.

The success was immediate and unprecedented. The application reached one million users in the first week, expanding to over 200 million weekly active users in August 2024.

OpenAI, founded in 2015 by Sam Altman and Elon Musk, pursues the ambitious goal of developing general purpose AI (AGI) that is safe and beneficial to humanity. Unlike AIs that specialize in specific tasks, AGI aims to replicate the versatility of human intelligence.

This architectural revolution has not only improved linguistic capabilities, but has paved the way for unprecedented technological diversification, as we will explore in the next section.

1.4 From linguistic revolution to technological diversification

The evolution of language model architecture, particularly the introduction of *Transformers* and the success of ChatGPT, has been the catalyst for a veritable explosion of technological diversification in the field of AI. What made this structural evolution revolutionary was not only the improvement of language capabilities, but the creation of fundamental principles that were transferable to other application domains.

In the technology domain, we witnessed how attention mechanisms initially developed for natural language were gradually being adapted and applied to image analysis, understanding of time sequences in industrial data, and even optimization of automated decision making. This cross-fertilization between domains has generated an extraordinarily diverse technological ecosystem, where innovations in one area rapidly permeate and transform other disciplines.

The *Transformer* architecture, born to improve machine translation, has ended up redefining not only how computers understand language, but also how they interpret the visual world, predict complex behaviors, and interact with the physical environment. As we explore this diverse technological landscape in the next section, it is important to understand that AI is no longer a single technology, but an umbrella term encompassing a collection of specialized approaches, each with its own peculiarities, strengths and limitations.

1.5 AI: One term, many technologies

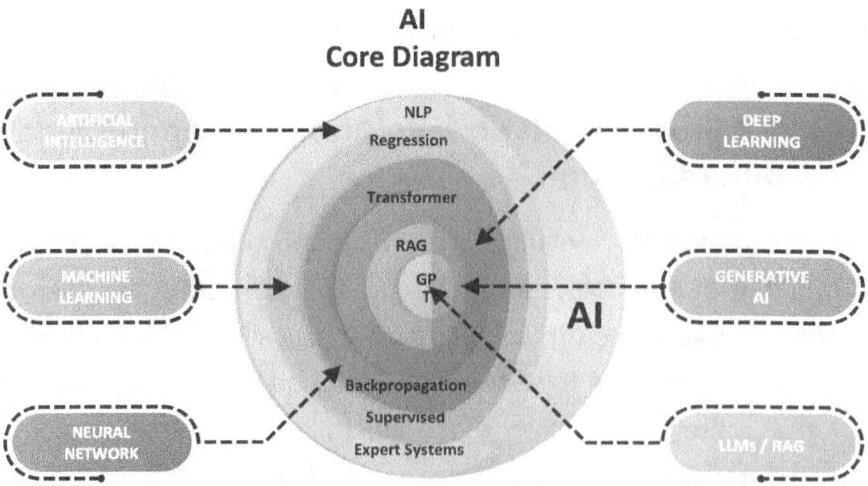

The term "AI" is often used loosely to refer to a vast array of different technologies. So far we have examined:

- Expert systems, which emulate human decision making through predefined rules.
- Neural networks, which are inspired by the workings of the human brain.
- *Machine learning*, which allows systems to learn from data.
- Deep *learning*, a specialization of *machine learning* based on deep neural networks.
- Natural Language Processing (NLP), which enables natural language processing and understanding.
- *The Transformer* Architecture, which forms the foundation of modern generative AI.

Before delving into further specific applications, it is important to understand the main categories of AI according to their scope and capabilities:

- Artificial Narrow AI (ANI): systems designed to perform specific tasks with great efficiency, but limited to those precise domains. All AI systems currently in use, from voice assistants to autonomous vehicles, belong to this category.
- Artificial General Intelligence (AGI): a system with human-like cognitive capabilities that can understand, learn and apply knowledge across domains. AGI remains a research goal, not yet realized.
- Artificial Superintelligence (ASI): a hypothetical intelligence that would far exceed human cognitive capabilities in virtually all domains. This currently remains in the realm of theoretical speculation.

The applications we will see in the following sections represent advanced examples of ANI, systems that excel at specific tasks while remaining limited to those particular domains.

We will now delve into three key domains:

- *Computer Vision*, which allows systems to interpret and analyze visual information.
- Robotics and humanoid robots, which integrate AI with physical systems.
- Generative AI, which enables the creation of new content.

ANI has great transformative potential when applied at scale, and Waymo driverless cabs are a prime example of this technology in action in the real world.

The travel experience with Waymo represents a watershed moment in the perception of the future of mobility. When the electric Jaguar I-PACE pulls up, completely empty, in front of the passenger, it offers a concrete view of innovation in action. From the back seat (or from the seat next to the driver), with a simple press of the "Start Ride" button, one watches the steering wheel move autonomously, smoothly and precisely, as the car pulls into the heavy traffic of Market Street (San Francisco, USA).

Onboard screens show how the AI "sees" the world around it: pedestrians highlighted in real time, predictions of other vehicles' trajectories, traffic lights recognized instantly. On the way, the car handles complex situations naturally: it elegantly gives way to ambulances, slows down early for pedestrians about to cross suddenly, navigates complex intersections with confidence.

The phenomenon is expanding: San Francisco, Phoenix and Los Angeles have already integrated these AI-guided vehicles into their streets, while Austin, Atlanta and Miami are preparing to do the same.

The impact of this technology is significant: as of August 2023, large-scale implementation of these autonomous systems has led to considerable environmental results. The fleet of electric Jaguar I-PACEs has already avoided the emission of 570,000 kg of carbon dioxide, demonstrating how AI can be a powerful ally in the fight against climate change. Here is the video of my experience in San Francisco with Waymo:

https://tinyurl.com/y4ybtjha

Computer Vision: the eyes of AI

Computer Vision is the discipline that gives computational systems the ability to "see" and interpret the visual world with a level of understanding comparable to that of humans. This technology is based on advanced image processing algorithms and specialized neural networks that transform visual data into meaningful, actionable information.

To better understand how *Computer Vision* works, let's consider a concrete example from everyday life: facial recognition from your smartphone. When you take a picture, the system does not see a face as you see it, but initially only a grid of pixels with numerical color values. The recognition process follows these steps:

1. Detection: The algorithm looks for specific *patterns* of pixels that could represent a face (such as ovals with certain proportions).
2. Normalization: Once a potential face is identified, the image is standardized to compensate for variations in illumination, angle and distance.
3. Feature extraction: The system identifies key points such as eyes, nose, mouth and their geometric relationship.
4. Recognition: These features are compared with a database of known faces.

This whole process happens in milliseconds, allowing your phone to automatically tag friends and family in photos or unlock when it recognizes your face.

Behind the scenes of *Computer Vision*, highly specialized neural networks operate. CNNs (Convolutional Neural Networks) use convolution filters as hierarchical detectors: first identify edges and textures, then complex shapes, and finally complete objects. A modern architecture such as EfficientNet uses a compound scalability principle, which balances depth (number of layers), breadth (number of neurons per layer) and resolution to optimize performance and computational efficiency. This approach has revolutionized the ability of systems to "see" with an accuracy comparable to-and in some contexts superior to-human vision, while using processing principles profoundly different from our biological visual system.

The applications of *Computer Vision* span several areas:

Medical Scope

- Diagnostic analysis of radiological images and MRIs.
- Early identification of pathologies through analysis of microscopic images.
- Assistance during surgical procedures with augmented reality.

Industrial Sector.

- Automated quality control in production lines.
- Predictive maintenance through visual inspection of machinery.
- Workflow tracking and optimization.

Mobility and Transportation.

- Autonomous driving systems.
- Real-time traffic monitoring.
- Assisted parking systems.

Security and Surveillance.

- Facial and biometric recognition.
- Detection of abnormal behavior.
- Access control in sensitive areas.

Retail.

- Automated checkout systems.
- Analysis of customer behaviors.
- Store layout optimization.

Robotics and humanoid robots

Robotics and AI often work in synergy to create machines capable of physically interacting with the environment. AI helps robots make decisions and adapt to new or complex situations. For example, an AI-equipped industrial robot can learn to manipulate objects of different shapes, adapting its grip based on what it "sees" through sensors.

The integration of AI into robotic systems occurs through a three-tier architecture: perception, planning and implementation. The perception subsystem fuses data from different sensors (cameras, LIDAR[6] , haptic sensors) to create a coherent representation of the environment. At the planning level, reinforcement learning algorithms enable the robot to optimize its actions through continuous feedback loops, improving through experience. Unlike traditional industrial robots, which are programmed with predefined paths, AI-driven robots use predictive models to dynamically adapt to unforeseen situations, balancing exploration (trying new strategies) and exploitation (using what has proven effective in the past).

The combination of AI and robotics is leading to major developments in manufacturing, logistics, and even assisted surgery. Today's robots are capable of performing increasingly complex and precise actions, and the integration of AI into decision-making processes enables them to continuously improve and learn from their mistakes, paving the way for a real revolution in automation.

Generative AI is now coming on board the first humanoid robots, helping to make these robots increasingly able to interact naturally with

---

[6] **LIDAR** is a remote sensing technology that uses laser pulses to accurately measure distances, creating detailed three-dimensional maps. The system emits laser beams, calculates the return time of the reflected signal from surfaces and generates high-definition point clouds, finding applications from autonomous driving to environmental modeling.

the environment and people. A prime example is the humanoid robot developed by Tesla, called Optimus. Optimus is designed to perform repetitive and potentially dangerous tasks, such as factory work or household chores, using advanced AI technologies to adapt to and interact with its environment.

While humanoid robots represent the physical embodiment of AI in the real world, there is another equally revolutionary dimension of AI that operates in the domain of knowledge and information. In my professional journey, I have observed how these two manifestations of AI-the physical and the informational-are rapidly converging. A robot like Tesla's Optimus is useful not only for its ability to manipulate physical objects, but also for its ability to process and apply knowledge in real time. This is where *Retrieval Augmented Generation (RAG*) systems come in, providing the bridge between powerful language models and the specific knowledge bases that organizations and individuals need on a daily basis.

Retrieval Augmented Generation (*RAG*) systems: the bridge between LLMs and corporate knowledge

LLMs represent one of the most advanced frontiers of AI, but their development requires colossal investments. To understand the scale of these investments, suffice it to say that Sam Altman, CEO of OpenAI, revealed that the training of GPT-4 alone required more than $100 million. However, once this massive training process is completed, the model becomes "frozen": it cannot be trained again to include specific new information, such as a company's documents or a proprietary knowledge base. This is where RAG systems come in, which solve this limitation brilliantly. When we use ChatGPT, Claude or Gemini with Internet access, we are already experiencing a RAG system in action:

the model consults external sources in real time to enrich its answers. The same principle can be applied to business documents. The RAG systems introduced here will be further explored in Chapter 4, where we will see concrete applications in operational process optimization and enterprise knowledge management. This architecture enables the creation of customized AI assistants that combine the power of language models with the specificity of proprietary information.

AI agents: when AI takes action.

If generative AI revolutionized the ability of machines to create content on demand, AI agents represent the next evolutionary step: systems that do not just respond passively, but act proactively to achieve complex goals. The AI agent is an advanced software system that operates with significant autonomy, demonstrating reasoning, planning and persistent memory capabilities while staying within defined operational parameters. The crucial distinction between pure generative models and AI agents lies in the "closing of the decision loop": while a traditional model generates outputs that require human interpretation and action, an agent completes the entire perception-decision-action cycle, adapting based on the results of its actions.

Architecture and core components

The architecture of an AI agent includes four fundamental components that interact cyclically:

- Sensors: enable perception of the environment (API[7] , web interfaces, cameras, microphones).
- Processors: constitute the "brain" of the agent, processing information and planning actions.
- Actuators: enable the execution of actions in the digital or physical environment.
- Learning systems: store experiences and continuously improve performance.

This functional architecture enables a continuous cycle of perception-reasoning-action that allows the agent to dynamically adapt to unexpected situations. Unlike traditional generative models, an AI agent maintains a persistent perception of the environment, reasons autonomously toward specific goals, plans sequences of actions with real-time adaptation, and can invoke deterministic functions inaccessible to a simple LLM.

Types of AI Agents

AI agents can be classified into several categories based on their decision-making ability:

- **Simple reflex agents**: act based solely on current perception following predefined rules (example: a thermostat).
- **Model-based reflex agents**: maintain an internal model of the world while also considering past actions (example: robot vacuum cleaner that memorizes the map of the environment).

---

[7] **API** (Application Programming Interface): is a set of rules and protocols that allows different software to communicate with each other, like a standardized "bridge" for exchanging data and functionality. ChatGPT's API, for example, allows developers to integrate artificial intelligence capabilities into their software by sending text requests and receiving model-generated responses.

- **Goal-based** agents: plan sequences of actions to achieve specific goals (example: navigation system).
- **Utility-based agents**: choose actions that maximize an expected utility by evaluating different consequences (example: traffic optimization system).
- **Learning agents**: improve performance over time by learning from experience (example: adaptive spam filter).

Examples of advanced AI agents.

The most emblematic example is OpenAI's Operator, released in September 2024. Based on a new model called Computer-Using Agent (CUA), Operator combines the visual capabilities of GPT-4o with a sophisticated reinforcement learning system. This architecture enables it to recognize and interact with graphical web interfaces through screenshots, performing mouse and keyboard actions in a manner quite similar to a human user. Operator can then perform tasks such as booking flights, filling out forms, searching for comparative information, and even creating content multimedia, dynamically adapting in the face of unexpected obstacles.

In order to use Operator, a subscription to OpenAI of $200 per month is currently required.

Web automation with AI agents: a hands-on experience with Browser Use

In my exploration of emerging technologies, I recently experimented with a particularly elegant solution for automating web tasks through AI agents: Browser Use (https://browser-use.com/). This platform represents a concrete example of how AI can interface directly with web applications, automating complex processes through natural language instructions.

Technical implementation

The installation of Browser Use from the GitHub repository[8] (https://github.com/browser-use/browser-use) proved to be straightforward. The strength of this solution lies in its simplicity of implementation, as demonstrated by this sample Python code[9] that I used to create a stand-alone agent:

```
from langchain_openai import ChatOpenAI
from browser_use import Agent
import asyncio

llm =  ChatOpenAI(model="gpt-4o").

async def main():
    agent = Agent(
        task="Find a one-way flight from Genoa to New York on
January 31, 2025."
        = llm,
    )
    result = await agent.run()
    print(result)

   asyncio.run(main())
```

Process execution and observations

The request, expressed in natural language in the task definition ("Find a one-way flight from Genoa to New York on January 31, 2025"), triggered a surprisingly sophisticated automation process. The agent

---

[8] **GitHub:** cloud-based collaborative development platform that enables developers to host, share and manage source code for software projects, facilitating collaboration and version control.

[9] **Python**: a high-level programming language characterized by simplified syntax and application versatility, particularly popular in areas such as artificial intelligence, automation, data analysis and web development.

integrated ChatGPT-4o capabilities through my OpenAI license, demonstrating how modern AI technologies can be orchestrated for practical tasks.

During execution, I was able to observe the agent autonomously navigate between different flight booking sites. Particularly interesting was its ability to handle complex and unexpected interface elements: informational pop-ups, cookie consent requests, and other interactive elements were processed autonomously, always keeping the focus on the primary goal.

Transparency of the decision-making process

One aspect I particularly appreciated was the operational transparency: throughout the process, colored boxes highlighted on the browser the content the agent was analyzing to make decisions. This real-time visualization offered a unique window into the AI's decision-making process, allowing me to understand the logic underlying its actions.

This experience demonstrates the concrete potential of AI agents for automating complex business processes, opening up interesting scenarios for optimizing workflows that require interaction with multiple web interfaces and management of articulated decision logics.

You can see the agent in action here:

https://tinyurl.com/wmk2723k

The most popular AI agent *frameworks*

There are a large number of AI agent frameworks, some general and some vertical, below are some examples that are by no means meant to be an exhaustive list:

Category	Name Framework	Key Features / Provider
Enterprise and Cloud Frameworks	Google Cloud Automotive AI Agent	Optimizes voice assistants for vehicles / Google
	Microsoft Security Copilot Agents.	Eleven specialized agents for cybersecurity / Microsoft
	Microsoft Copilot Studio	Develop AI agents that can be integrated with Microsoft 365 / Microsoft
	Salesforce Agentforce	Autonomous agents for services, sales, marketing (formerly Einstein Copilot) / Salesforce
	AWS Bedrock Agents.	Building AI agents with foundation models and AWS integrations / Amazon Web Services
	IBM watsonx Assistant	Platform for advanced conversational virtual assistants / IBM
	Oracle AI Agent Studio	Integrated platform in Oracle Fusion Cloud Applications for enterprise AI agents / Oracle
	SAP AI Agents (Joule & SAP Build)	Autonomous agent capabilities in SAP, orchestrated by Joule, developed with SAP Build / SAP
	NVIDIA Agent Intelligence Toolkit & AI-Q Blueprint.	Open-source toolkit and blueprint for orchestrating AI agent teams, focus on NVIDIA / NVIDIA acceleration
	Intel AI Assistant Builder	Framework for creating custom AI assistants on Intel AI PCs, extendable to enterprise / Intel clusters
	Microsoft Semantic Kernel	Open-source SDK (C#, Python, Java) to integrate AI into existing apps and build AI agents; enterprise middleware / Microsoft
Development and Programming Frameworks	Anthropic Claude Code	Agent for software development (code management, debugging) / Anthropic

	OpenAI Assistants API	Building AI agents with code interpreter, retrieval, function calling / OpenAI
	GitHub Copilot	AI assistant integrated into IDE for code suggestions / GitHub (Microsoft)
Open Source and Research Frameworks	LangChain	Modular framework for building applications with LLM (agents with memory, tools, chain reasoning) / Open Source
	AutoGPT	Autonomous agent system for complex tasks with minimal supervision / Open Source (Significant Gravitas)
	CrewAI	Framework for orchestrating teams of collaborative AI agents / Open Source
	Microsoft AutoGen	Open source framework for multi-agent applications with complex conversations / Microsoft (Open Source)
	Hugging Face Agents	Toolkit for creating agents with different templates and tools / Hugging Face (Open Source)
	LlamaIndex	Framework to build AI agent applications with enterprise data (advanced RAG, agents) / Open Source
	LangGraph	Library for creating agentic and multi-agent stateful and cyclic workflows (based on LangChain) / Open Source (LangChain)
Specialized Frameworks	BabyAGI	Autonomous task management system (creates, prioritizes, executes tasks) / Open Source
	AgentGPT	Web platform for deploying autonomous AI agents in the browser / Open Source
	Rasa	Open-source framework for conversational AI (advanced AI assistants, Rasa Studio no-code) / Open Source (Rasa Technologies)
	Agno (formerly Phidata)	Lightweight, high-performance library for multimodal agents; focus on speed, low memory usage, model-agnostic / Open Source
Visual Builders / Low-Code / No-Code	Rivet	Open-source visual programming environment for complex LLM prompt graphs; remote debugging / Open Source (Ironclad)
	FlowiseAI	Open-source visual tool (drag-and-drop, no-code) for LLM flows; multi-agent, HITL, enterprise-ready / Open Source (supported by YCombinator)

	Langflow	Low-code builder for AI apps with visual flows; integrated with LangChain; rapid iteration / Open Source

Applications in enterprise ecosystems

AI agents are being used in many organizations to automate tasks characterized by high repetitiveness and low value-added. Such tools are capable of autonomously handling tasks such as creating and updating standardized reports, filling out forms and documents based on predefined parameters, and performing preliminary analysis to support decisions. This approach reduces execution time and minimizes errors resulting from manual intervention, while ensuring large-scale operational consistency.

Another particularly effective area of application concerns the automation of the receivables management cycle: AI agents can analyze payment history in real time, identify delays or anomalies, and generate customized reminder notices, calibrated to the borrower's profile and contract terms. In addition, by continuously monitoring due dates and adopting predictive algorithms, timely action can be taken to mitigate default risks, optimizing cash flow and improving the quality of customer relationships.

The adoption of intelligent automation solutions promotes process standardization, contributing to a significant reduction in variability and operational errors. As a result, more skilled human resources can be reallocated to highly consultative and strategic activities, where experience and critical judgment are an indispensable value. The result is a more efficient and resilient business ecosystem, where routine operations are entrusted to algorithmic procedures and human capital is enhanced according to growth and innovation objectives.

Applications of AI agents extend to numerous strategic sectors, below is a non-exhaustive list:

- **In the health sector**: they assist in diagnosis by analyzing symptoms and lab results, monitor patients remotely by sending alerts when abnormalities occur, and facilitate matching patients to clinical trials by analyzing medical records.
- **In finance**: they monitor transactions in real time to identify fraudulent schemes, provide investment advice by analyzing market trends, and automate regulatory compliance by tracking financial activities.
- **In process automation**: they orchestrate complex workflows, optimize supply chain management by predicting demand and coordinating logistics, and implement predictive maintenance by analyzing sensor data.
- **In customer service**: they handle multiple requests simultaneously, analyze[10] *sentiment* in real time to tailor responses, and automatically categorize and assign support tickets.

Future implications and ethical considerations

The crucial distinction between pure generative models and AI agents lies in the "closing of the decision loop": while a traditional model generates outputs that require human interpretation and action, an agent completes the entire perception-decision-action cycle, monitoring and adapting based on the results of its actions.

The increasing autonomy of these systems raises important ethical issues concerning:

---

[10] **Sentiment analysis**: technology that automatically identifies emotions (positive, negative, neutral) in customer messages by analyzing the language used.

- Potential bias and discrimination in automated decision-making processes.
- Transparency and logical process of decisions made by AI agents.
- Legal accountability for the actions of autonomous agents.
- Impact on the labor market with the potential disappearance of some professions.

Considering the simple agent example I ran on my computer to find an airline ticket, a fundamental issue emerges: I have no way of knowing whether the algorithms that made it select those ticket-selling agencies over others applied bias or discrimination, for example, by excluding web domains related to countries considered high risk for fraud. This issue is not unlike that of the search engine algorithms we routinely use, which may have these biases "inherent" in their AI algorithms. In addition, questions of liability arise: if the agent instead of buying one ticket buys 10, whose legal responsibility is it? A final consideration, no less important, concerns the employment impact: if the number of repetitive or otherwise replaceable tasks with evolved agents grows at the current speed of this technology, will we have enough opportunities in high-value-added activities, such as strategic ones, to relocate the people replaced by these agents? The future of AI agents is promising, with the convergence of advanced *machine learning, edge computing*[11]

[11] ***Edge computing***: a data processing system that moves computational computing closer to the source of the data (the "edge" or "edge" of the network) rather than into centralized data centers or the cloud. This approach reduces latency, improves response times and preserves bandwidth, proving crucial for AI applications that require real-time processing such as autonomous vehicles, IoT devices and smart video surveillance systems.

and Internet of Things (IoT)[12] setting the stage for a new generation of even more sophisticated agents.

It is expected to evolve toward collaborative multi-agent systems where several specialized agents work together to tackle complex problems, and increasingly deep integration with the physical world through robots and IoT devices.

As the evolution of the field shows, AI agents are rapidly transitioning from research to practical applications, radically transforming decision-making and automation in the enterprise and beyond. The challenge for the future will be to balance technological innovation with ethical and governance frameworks that ensure that these powerful systems remain safe, reliable, and aligned with human values.

AI agents vs agentive AI systems: a fundamental distinction

For explanatory simplicity, I have used the term "agents" in the text both to refer to AI agents proper and to refer to agentic AI systems. However, it is incumbent on me to clarify the fundamental distinction between these two concepts, as understanding them is essential to properly implementing effective AI solutions.

In the rapidly evolving AI landscape, the terms "AI agents" and "agentic AI systems" are often misused as synonyms, generating conceptual and operational confusion. This terminological overlap is not only a semantic issue, but can significantly undermine the design and implementation of effective AI solutions.

AI agents are discrete, autonomous software entities designed with a specific operational structure - perception mechanisms (sensors),

[12] **Internet of Things (IoT)**: a network of physical devices equipped with sensors, software and connectivity that collect and exchange data via the Internet such as home appliances, wearable devices and industrial sensors that communicate autonomously.

reasoning capabilities (processors) and execution modules (actuators) - that operate within defined parameters to achieve specific goals. They function as independent units with their own decision cycles, similar to "specialists" focused on narrow domains.

In contrast, **agentic AI** refers to the broader characteristic or quality of *agency* embedded in AI systems - the ability to act autonomously on behalf of users across multiple domains and contexts without being confined to a single operational *framework*. It represents a higher level of autonomy and integration, characterized by more generalized and adaptive intelligence.

To simplify with an analogy, an 'AI agent' is like a single skilled craftsman (e.g., a carpenter), while an 'agent system' is like the site manager orchestrating the carpenter, electrician, and plumber to build an entire house.

A concrete example: in digitization processes, isolated AI agents can automatically check document compliance according to predefined parameters. These agents, while effective in their specific domain, operate as "islands" of automation. Agent-based systems, on the other hand, simultaneously orchestrate entire processes-from planning to report generation to the proposal of corrective actions-while maintaining contextual memory between different interactions and dynamically adapting their behavior as regulations and goals evolve.

The transition from agent-based to truly agentic systems marks a profound paradigm shift: from the automation of individual tasks to the implementation of intelligent infrastructures that integrally reshape decision-making and operational processes.

We will explore agentic systems in Chapter 8 where we will analyze their impact on *knowledge work*.

1.6 General AI and Superintelligence: future prospects

The latest developments in the field of AI are greatly accelerating the path toward AGI. With the release of OpenAI's o3 model in December 2024, there has been significant progress in logical reasoning and complex problem solving.

In my professional experience, I have learned that we cannot improve what we cannot measure. This simple truth applies perfectly to AI as well. To assess how closely these systems are really approaching human-like cognitive capabilities, the scientific community has developed standardized *benchmarks* that serve as "cognitive Olympiads" for AI.

Tokens: the fundamental unit of language processing

To fully understand the capabilities and limitations of advanced AI, it is essential to become familiar with the concept of tokens-the atomic unit of text processing for these systems, which we have already explored in Section 1.3.

Tokens represent more than just units of text: they deeply influence how we interact with AI across three fundamental dimensions. The first is the context window, which determines how much information the model can process simultaneously, essentially defining the limits of its "working memory." The second concerns the economic structure, establishing the billing model for AI services where each token processed has a specific cost. The third dimension touches on computational efficiency, directly affecting the energy impact and resources required for processing.

During the development of this volume, I personally experienced the importance of the context window in a particularly illuminating way. With a manuscript of about 400 pages, equivalent to a range of 130,000 to 150,000 tokens, I tested the capabilities of leading AI models. Claude and ChatGPT showed limitations in processing the entire document simultaneously, while Gemini proved to be the only tool capable of handling the entire text corpus, thanks to its context window of one million tokens, extendable up to 2 million for developers through the Gemini and Google AI Studio software libraries.

This firsthand experience highlighted how the size of the context window is not just a technical specification, but a determining factor in choosing the most suitable tool for large, complex projects. The ability to keep the entire context of a book in memory while working on its revision is a qualitative advantage that goes far beyond mere operational convenience.

Key benchmark: measuring AI

SWE-Bench Verified represents the ultimate test for practical programming. This *benchmark* assesses a model's ability to act on real software code, implementing functional bug fixes or developing new features. Imagine a hands-on exam for a senior software engineer: not solving theoretical exercises, but navigating existing code *repositories*, understanding complex systems, and making functional changes. A model with a high score in SWE-Bench could significantly replace or assist professional programmers.

ARC-AGI is considered the most challenging *benchmark* in the industry, designed specifically to assess generalization to completely unknown problems. If SWE-Bench measures competence in a specific domain, ARC-AGI assesses adaptive intelligence-the ability to transfer knowledge to contexts never encountered before. It is the difference between preparing for an exam with known questions and dealing with unexpected situations that require original reasoning. A system that excels in this *benchmark* demonstrates a form of intelligence closer to human intelligence.

AIME and MATH-500 assess structured mathematical reasoning. AIME, based on problems from the American Invitational Mathematics Examination, simulates a mathematical Olympiad for AI, requiring not only calculation of correct answers, but demonstration of the logical path. MATH-500 extends this assessment over 500 problems of varying difficulty. I have personally observed how models with high capabilities in these *benchmarks* can assist structural engineers in optimizing complex designs, solving problems in minutes that would require hours of manual calculations.

GPQA Diamond focuses on specialized scientific understanding by presenting physics questions at the postgraduate level. It is like submitting an AI to a doctoral exam, requiring not only specialized knowledge, but the ability to connect concepts across domains and apply them to novel situations. Models with high GPQA scores have demonstrated an amazing ability to suggest innovative approaches to complex scientific problems.

Benchmark models and comparative performance

The table below compares performance on the described *benchmarks*:

Model	SWE-Bench	ARC-AGI	AIME 2024	MATH-500	GPQA Diamond
OpenAI o3	**71.7%**	**87.5%**	N/A	N/A	N/A
Claude 3.7	70.3%	0.7%	80.0%	N/A	**84.8%**
Gemini 2.5 Pro	63.8%	~15-20%	**92.0%**	N/A	84.0%
Deepseek-R1	~49%	~15-20%	79.8%	**97.3%**	71.5%
QwQ-32B	N/A	N/A	50.0%	90.6%	65.2%

It can be seen from the table that there is no overall winner but practically each one excels in a specific field with the exception of ChatGPT o3 which excels in the first two *benchmarks*.

Summary of comparative results

To put these numbers in context: a score of 50% is comparable to the abilities of a college student, 70-80% is close to a seasoned professional, while scores above 90% represent excellence that exceeds most humans who specialize in that domain.

The most significant gap appears in ARC-AGI, where o3 reaches 87.5 percent while other models lag far behind. This highlights how, despite impressive progress, generalization to completely new situations-considered the quintessence of intelligence-remains a largely unexplored frontier for most current systems.

A system with high generalization capability can quickly adapt to unexpected scenarios in manufacturing, while models with excellent mathematical capabilities but less flexibility require frequent human adjustments when operating conditions change.

Perspectives on AGI: a landscape of contrasting forecasts

Time forecasts on the development of AGI show significant variations among industry leaders, reflecting different technological and philosophical views on the future of AI:

- **Ray Kurzweil** (Google's Director of Engineering, world-renowned inventor and futurist), predicts the advent of AGI by 2029. His vision, rooted in the theory of technological acceleration and singularity, is based on a historical analysis of the exponential development rates of information technologies.
- **Sam Altman** (CEO of OpenAI) stated that systems that can match human intelligence in economically relevant tasks could emerge by 2025-2027. He stressed that o3 represents a significant "step forward" toward AGI, with the ability to perform "a single-digit percentage of all economically relevant tasks in the world."
- **Dario Amodei** (CEO and co-founder of Anthropic) predicts the emergence of "powerful" AI as early as 2026, although he calls AGI a "marketing term" and prefers to focus on developing systems with transformative practical capabilities rather than theoretical definitions of generality.
- **Ben Goertzel** (CEO of SingularityNET and pioneer of AGI research) places the development of AGI on a more cautious time horizon, between 2030 and 2040, emphasizing the need for fundamental advances beyond current deep learning paradigms.
- **Nick Bostrom** (Oxford philosopher and author of "Superintelligence: Paths, Dangers, Strategies[13] ") takes the more conservative perspective, with a timeline that spans the

[13] https://www.amazon.com/gp/product/0198739834

century. His cautiously analytical approach emphasizes epistemic unknowns and possible theoretical obstacles that could slow progress toward true general intelligence (https://nickbostrom.com/).

This spectrum of predictions reflects the inherent uncertainty in mapping an unprecedented technological frontier. Despite these divergences, a consensus on direction emerges: recent advances represent substantial advances toward systems with increasingly human-like cognitive capabilities.

What seemed impossible just five years ago is now part of our everyday professional lives. As we potentially approach AGI, the priority must be the parallel development of ethical frameworks and governance structures that ensure that these powerful technologies remain tools of positive progress, aligned with human values and serving the common good.

Chapter Summary

This chapter traces the path of AI from its inception as a mathematical abstraction to its current role as a transformative force in industrial and social sectors. Through the lens of my 30 years of professional experience, from undergraduate education to leadership of advanced technology divisions, I outline the evolution of a technology that has repeatedly pushed the boundaries of the possible.

From origins to modern architectures

AI arose conceptually in the 1940s with the pioneering work of Alan Turing, finding formal recognition at the 1956 Dartmouth Conference, where John McCarthy defined it as the "science and engineering of creating intelligent machines." meaning systems capable of perceiving the environment, reasoning about complex information, and acting to achieve specific goals. This evolutionary path has not been linear, but characterized by cyclical periods of great enthusiasm followed by "AI winters"-phases of stagnation caused by technological limitations and unfulfilled expectations.

The early expert systems of the 1960s-1970s, such as MYCIN for diagnosing bacterial infections, represented first-generation AI: effective in specific domains but limited by the rigidity of predefined rules and onerous manual maintenance. The real breakthrough came in the 1980s with the *backpropagation* algorithm, which revitalized neural network research by enabling the training of more sophisticated models.

Decisive moments and technological revolutions

Three moments radically redefined the capabilities of AI:

- **Deep Blue (1997)**: the IBM supercomputer's victory over world chess champion Garry Kasparov demonstrated the ability of machines to excel in complex strategic domains.
- **AlphaGo (2016)**: victory over Lee Sedol in the game of Go - with mathematical complexity 240 orders of magnitude greater than chess - revealed the ability of AIs to develop original and counterintuitive strategies.
- ***Transformer* (2017)**: the revolutionary architecture introduced in the scientific article "Attention Is All You Need" transformed natural language processing, forming the basis of all modern *Large Language Models*.

The commercialization of ChatGPT in November 2022 marked the beginning of a new era of democratization of AI, reaching 200 million weekly active users in less than two years.

The Contemporary Technology Ecosystem

Modern AI is divided into several specialized technologies:

- ***Computer Vision***: gives systems the ability to "see" and interpret visual information through advanced convolutional neural networks, with applications from medical diagnostics to autonomous driving.
- **Robotics and Humanoid Robots**: integrates AI into physical systems capable of interacting with the environment, coordinating perception, planning and action through continuous feedback loops.
- ***Retrieval Augmented Generation* (*RAG*) systems**: act as a bridge between powerful language models and proprietary knowledge bases, enabling customized applications without requiring costly model retraining.

- **AI Agents and AI Agent Systems**: represent the most recent evolution from reactive systems to proactive entities with complete perception-reasoning-action cycles, capable of operating autonomously to achieve complex goals.

In my experience, implementing AI agents to automate repetitive tasks such as preparing standard bids and handling payment reminders has freed up skilled human resources for higher-value tasks, simultaneously improving standardization and operational efficiency.

Future prospects: toward AGI?

Recent advances, exemplified by models such as OpenAI o3 and Claude 4 Sonnet, show increasingly sophisticated reasoning capabilities. Specialized *benchmarks* reveal significant progress, with o3 reaching 87.5 percent in generalization tests (ARC-AGI), suggesting an acceleration toward general AI (AGI).

Time predictions on the emergence of AGI vary dramatically: Ray Kurzweil places it by 2029, Sam Altman between 2025-2027, while other experts such as Nick Bostrom adopt more conservative perspectives. This divergence reflects the inherent uncertainty in assessing an unprecedented technological frontier.

In my career, I have observed how initially theoretical technologies have quickly become transformative operational tools. As we potentially approach AGI, the priority must be the parallel development of ethical frameworks and governance structures that ensure that these powerful technologies remain an instrument of positive progress for humanity.

CHAPTER 2

HOW TO COMMUNICATE WITH GENERATIVE AI: *PROMPT ENGINEERING*

2.1 Introduction to *prompt engineering*

Prompt engineering is the art of formulating effective questions (input) to elicit useful responses from a generative AI model. With a well-formulated prompt, the user can guide the AI toward an accurate and relevant response. The difference between a generic *prompt* and a well-constructed one is often the difference between getting generic information and getting exactly what you need.

What is *Prompt Engineering* and why it is critical

Prompt engineering enables structured and guided conversations to be constructed. This type of communication becomes essential to make the most of the model's capabilities and optimize decision-making and information.

Here is a practical example of how we can evolve a *prompt*:

- **Basic Prompt**: "How can I retrieve my account password?"
- **Enhanced *Prompt***: "How can I retrieve the forgotten password for my Gmail account using an Android device? Provide a step-by-step guide by including necessary screenshots and possible common problems."

Ultimately, *prompt engineering* allows us to maximize the value of each interaction with AI by reducing ambiguity and increasing the quality of the information provided. Moreover, because of the iterative nature of this process, each interaction becomes a learning opportunity, both for the user and for the AI system itself.

My path of experimentation with different LLMs

The effectiveness of a *prompt* or structured sequence of *prompts* is closely related to the specific characteristics of the Large Language Model we are using. Through intensive experimentation and numerous hours of practical use, I have developed a thorough understanding of the peculiarities of each model, allowing me to predict which LLM offers optimal performance for certain types of *prompts* and specific use cases.

For example, I have noticed that some models excel in technical analysis and programming, while others demonstrate particular skill in creativity and narrative content generation. Some LLMs stand out for their ability to maintain a coherent and contextualized conversation, while others shine in developing precise and concise responses.

It is critical to note, however, that these observations represent a snapshot of a very rapidly changing landscape. My conclusions about which model is most effective for specific activities can vary dramatically over weeks or even days, given the dizzying speed with which these systems are being updated. Competition among the major players in the field - OpenAI, Anthropic, Google and Meta - drives an almost daily evolution of the capabilities of their respective models, making any *benchmarking* a temporary measurement.

The evolution of the model ecosystem

Each LLM allows us to select specific models to target our *prompt*. In the case of ChatGPT, as this chapter is being written, the user with a Plus subscription ($20/month) can choose from several options optimized for specific scenarios.

GPT-4o: Comprehensive multimodal model that excels at everyday tasks such as brainstorming, summaries, e-mails, and creative content. Supports almost all features (GPTs, data analysis, web search, image generation, *Canvas*, advanced voice) and accepts diverse input (documents, images, CSV, audio and video). Ideal for tasks such as summarizing meeting notes, follow-up email drafts, or real-time brainstorming with sketch and screenshot uploads.

GPT-4.1: Specializes in precise coding and following detailed instructions. It excels at web development and debugging, producing more robust code and following complex requirements with greater fidelity. It is a favorite of developers and advanced technical users for debugging Python scripts, benchmarking reports or explaining complex code.

GPT-4.1-mini: Fast version that replaces the previous GPT-4o mini, offering significant improvements in code generation and general intelligence while maintaining low latency. Ideal for those who need better answers on technical and programming questions with fast response times.

GPT-4.5: The model best suited for creative tasks, with superior emotional intelligence, clear communication and a more collaborative approach to brainstorming. Perfect for creating engaging LinkedIn posts, product descriptions or letters with an empathetic tone. Limited to 20 weekly requests.

OpenAI o-series: For in-depth analysis requiring deductive, inductive or inferential skills, specialized models are available:

- **o3**: The most powerful engine for complex multi-step analysis, strategic planning, extensive coding and advanced mathematical/scientific reasoning (100 requests/week).

- **o4-mini**: Fast and efficient reasoning for code, math and visual tasks (300 requests/day).
- **o4-mini-high**: Enhanced version of o4-mini with greater depth for more comprehensive technical answers (100 requests/day).
- **o1-pro mode**: Legacy model for complex reasoning in high-risk analytical tasks requiring maximum accuracy (5 requests/month).

The proliferation of specialized models inevitably creates confusion for the user, who must manually select the most suitable option and decide whether to enable additional features such as Web search or *Deep Research*. It is likely that OpenAI will soon resolve this fragmentation by implementing a system that automatically directs *prompts* to the most appropriate template, while also optimizing the consumption of computational resources.

Google is no different with its Gemini, which currently numbers the 2.5 Flash and 2.5 Pro models, within which we can further choose whether to activate the Vero 2 feature to generate video from text, upload attachments, start the *Canvas* collaboration mode and/or the *Deep Research* feature.

Anthropic's Claude also presents this complexity, allowing us to choose between Claude Haiku 3.5, Claude Opus 3, Claude Sonnet 3.7, and for the 4 series, Claude Sonnet 4 and the more powerful Claude Opus 4 model. For the latter two models, the *Extended* Thinking option could not be missed to activate their full potential.

I am sure that when the first among the 4 dominators of the LLM market introduces a single model that can invisibly route the user to the appropriate model the others will also introduce it for the benefit of all users. I hope this will happen as soon as possible both for the environment and for us users.

Comparative strategies: testing the same *prompt* on different platforms

In my experience, there is currently no single model that universally excels at all tasks. Claude may shine in complex textual analysis today, while tomorrow GPT may surpass it after an update; Gemini may excel in mathematical reasoning this month, only to be surpassed the following month. This "competitive dance" between models makes continuous study and systematic experimentation the only truly effective approach.

It might seem inefficient to test 3-5 different models for each specific need, but this seeming "waste" of time turns into a valuable investment that deeply stimulates our ability to interact with AI. Through this comparative process, we deepen our understanding of the limitations of these systems, develop a sensitivity to their peculiarities and, most importantly, concretely verify that the human being must always remain at the center of this interaction process-as guide, interpreter and ultimate decision maker.

However, despite this evolutionary fluidity, I always adopt a methodical and comparative approach: I systematically subject the same *prompt* to three or four different LLMs. This parallel testing strategy allows me to:

- Objectively assess the quality of the responses generated.
- Identify different nuances and perspectives of the same problem.
- Discover potential innovative approaches that I had not considered.

- Verify the consistency and accuracy of the information provided.
- Select the most appropriate response for the specific needs of the project.

Although this method requires a greater investment of time, it guarantees more reliable results and allows me to continually refine my understanding of the capabilities and limitations of each model, progressively improving the efficiency of my work with LLMs.

In rare cases only the combined use of 4 models has allowed me, partially, to achieve my goal. The case I am referring to was the attempt to use these models as proofreaders of the present book, especially for grammatical, syntax and punctuation errors. Even by dividing the book into sub-chapters only by submitting to Claude, ChatGPT, Gemini, and Deepseek I was able to find as many errors as possible. The individual found only a subset of them.

The continuous practice of comparing different models has also helped me develop a kind of "professional intuition" about what combination of *prompts* and LLM might work best in certain situations, while always maintaining an experimental approach and open to unexpected results. It also often happens to me to use the output of one LLM as input for another to refine or enrich the result as I did for the correction in this volume.

The figure below provides a comparative overview of the capabilities of the major AI tools available as of June 2025, highlighting the areas in which each platform excels (indicated with a star) or simply meets requirements (indicated with a check mark):

Capabilities of the Most Popular AI Tools

	ChatGPT	Claude	Gemini	Perplexity
Everyday answers	[illegible]	✓	✓	✓
Writing	✓	[illegible]	✓	✓
Coding	✓	✓	[illegible]	✓
Math	[illegible]	✓	✓	✓
Reasoning	[illegible]	✓	✓	✓
Web search	✓	✓	✓	[illegible]
Deep research	[illegible]	×	✓	✓
Voice chat	[illegible]	×	✓	✓
Image gen	[illegible]	×	✓	×
Video gen	✓	×	[illegible]	×
Live camera	[illegible]	×	✓	×
Computer use	[illegible]	✓	×	×

The table is my elaboration of what Peter Yang (Product lead at Roblox) realized in his blog:

https://tinyurl.com/j77tspa2

2.2 Why is *Prompt Engineering* Important?

Prompt engineering is a crucial skill for anyone wishing to exploit the full potential of AI. The quality of the *prompt* significantly affects the accuracy, relevance, and creativity of AI responses. An effective prompt can lead to a higher level of interaction with AI, offering responses that are not only relevant but also detailed and useful. The ability to formulate high-quality *prompts* becomes even more important when using language models for professional, educational tasks, or in areas where accuracy and quality of information are critical. In a business context, a well-formulated prompt can reduce work time, improve efficiency, and support decision making by providing accurate and operational responses. A well-constructed prompt enables AI to drive results that not only meet immediate demands, but can also anticipate future needs and provide added value.

A well-constructed *prompt* also improves the accuracy of AI-based analysis and decision support tools. For example, in health care, a well-constructed *prompt* such as "Describe possible diagnoses for a patient with high fever, persistent cough, and difficulty breathing" enables targeted responses that can be used as support for health professionals. These analysis tools not only provide useful information, but can also be used to develop personalized care plans. Providing accurate *prompts* allows AI to focus on the most relevant elements and propose effective solutions to improve the quality of health care.

The continued development of AI agent environments that can perform complex tasks on our PCs in a similar way to how we perform them through the appropriate use of our everyday tools such as the Web, e-mail, and office tools requires the development of precise and accurate *prompts*.

Another example involves the creative use of AI: if the goal is to generate original content, such as a story, a detailed *prompt* ("Write a short story about a child who finds an ancient magical book in a forest and discovers that it has the power to change the past") will lead to a much richer result than a generic *prompt* ("Write a story"). The details provided in the *prompt* allow the AI to craft a more vivid and interesting narrative, rich in description and with a coherent narrative structure. This ability to personalize content is extremely useful in the creative environment, where the quality of the narrative is critical to engaging the reader. Providing AI context and specific details allows for stories that resonate emotionally and are able to convey deeper, more meaningful messages.

In addition, *prompt engineering* can help reduce the risk of bias in AI responses. When *prompts* are worded accurately and in detail, the possibility of AI providing responses that reflect stereotypes or biases is minimized. This is especially important in sensitive contexts such as social communication or training. For example, a *prompt* such as "Describe the role of women in the technology sector over the past two decades, highlighting major changes and successes" allows AI to focus on positive contributions rather than falling into stereotypes. A well-structured *prompt* that incorporates historical, cultural, and social aspects allows AI to craft a response that recognizes and values the contributions of diverse groups, promoting an inclusive narrative. This aspect is particularly useful when AI is used to develop educational content or when it needs to interact with heterogeneous audiences.

Experimentation and iteration are critical to arrive at a deep understanding of how to effectively drive the AI model.

2.3 Anatomy of an effective *prompt*

The structure of a good *prompt* is based on a few key elements: clarity, context, specificity, and a thorough understanding of the desired outcome. These elements not only improve the quality of the response, but also allow the AI model to be directed toward a response consistent with the user's goal. Let's look at each element in detail.

The four pillars: clarity, context, specificity, and expected outcome

- **Clarity**: a clear *prompt* is simple and unambiguous. Avoiding vague wording allows the model to understand the prompt exactly and reduces the margin of error in the response. For example, a *prompt* such as "Explain how electricity works" can lead to very broad and different responses, while a more detailed *prompt* such as "Explain how electricity works in a residential circuit" provides clearer context and limits the scope of the response. In addition, it is helpful to ensure that the language of the *prompt* is accessible and understandable, avoiding terms that are too technical unless strictly necessary. This increases the likelihood that the AI output will be relevant and centered on the required goal.

  A rarely considered aspect of clarity is the economy of language. Sam Altman, CEO of OpenAI, revealed that courtesy formulas such as "please" and "thank you" in ChatGPT *prompts* cost the company tens of millions of dollars annually. This is because each additional word results in increased computational and energy load on the servers and GPUs[14] that process the prompts. Although Altman considers these costs "well spent" on maintaining respectful interactions, this finding highlights an important principle of *prompt engineering*: the balance between politeness and conciseness. An optimal *prompt* eliminates

[14] **GPU** (Graphics Processing Unit)**: A** specialized processor originally designed for graphics processing and image rendering, but now widely used in artificial intelligence because of its ability to perform mathematical calculations in parallel.

unnecessary words while maintaining all the essential elements to properly guide the model. My advice is not to use these formulas for the benefit of sustainability.

- Context: providing context helps the AI respond more accurately and consistently with the user's expectations. An effective example might be, "Describe the impact of the Industrial Revolution in England in the 19th century in terms of social and economic changes." This *prompt* provides temporal, geographic, and topic context, allowing the model to develop a response rich in relevant detail. When you provide context, you create a "frame" in which the AI can operate, reducing the possibility of generic or off-topic responses. Specifying further, such as the target audience ("Describe the impact of the industrial revolution for high school students") can help the AI calibrate the tone and depth of the response, making it more appropriate and useful.

- **Specificity**: the more specific *a prompt* is, the more precise and relevant the response will be. For example, "What are the advantages of Agile methodology in software development versus the Waterfall model?" gives the model the opportunity to answer in a much more accurate and focused way than a generic "What are the advantages of Agile?" A specific *prompt* allows the model to avoid digressions and focus on the salient points that exactly answer the question. For example, adding additional details such as "in terms of project flexibility and customer engagement" can make the AI response even more focused and useful to the user, as it directs the AI toward particular aspects of a broad topic.

- **Understanding the desired** outcome: defining the desired outcome from the *prompt* helps to further reduce ambiguity. For example, if a concise or detailed answer is desired, it should be specified, "Explain concisely how the process of photosynthesis works." This information allows the model to modulate the level of detail in the answer, making it more useful to the user. In addition, it is important to consider the format of the response; for example, if the desired outcome is a bulleted list or narrative explanation, it should be made explicit in the *prompt*: "List the security benefits of blockchain in the form of numbered bullet points." This kind of specificity makes the answer easily usable for the user without the need for further editing.

From generality to specificity: examples of *prompt* transformation

Here are some concrete examples illustrating how to evolve a *prompt* from generic to specific and detailed:

- Generic: "Describe digital marketing."
    - **Output**: A general description of digital marketing, which can include various aspects such as SEO[15] , social media, e-mail marketing and more. The output could be quite broad and cover various topics without going into the specific details of each aspect.

[15] **SEO** (Search Engine Optimization) is the practice of optimizing websites and content to improve visibility in search engine results by generating organic traffic through meeting the needs of users and search engine algorithms.

- **Specific**: "Describe how *content marketing* can increase user engagement for a tech startup."
    - **Output**: A targeted response that explores the role of *content marketing* for a startup, explaining how creating valuable content can attract and retain users, building trust in the brand. This *prompt* allows the AI to focus the response on a specific context, avoiding irrelevant information.
- **Additional context**: "Describe the best SEO strategies for a blog about international travel."
    - **Output**: AI will respond with travel-specific strategies, such as the importance of localized keywords, content creation evergreen content, and optimization for specific destination searches. Adding context makes the output much more relevant to the specific case, helping to focus attention on what is most useful to the blog owner.

Another example of a good *prompt* might be, "List the main benefits of using blockchain technology in the financial sector, including security and transparency." This level of specificity helps the AI provide more timely and relevant answers, reducing the need for clarification. Adding additional details such as "include examples of real-world use in the banking and insurance sectors" can provide an even more useful answer that can be immediately applied to better understand how blockchain is revolutionizing these industries.

While the four pillars form the basis for a single effective prompt, in practice rarely is a single prompt sufficient to achieve complete results. Let us therefore look at how to construct structured sequences of *prompts*.

Structured sequences: when a single *prompt* is not enough

One hardly gets the desired result with a single prompt, especially if the prompt involves complex reasoning, such as a market analysis for a new product launch. In such cases, one generally proceeds through a sequence of successive *prompts* to progressively refine the output and arrive at the final goal.

A structured sequence may follow this pattern:

- **Initial *Prompt***: define the overall objective and context.
- **In-depth *Prompt***: request specific details on areas of particular interest that emerged from the first response.
- **Refinement *Prompt***: provide feedback on the previous response and request improvements or changes.
- **Synthesis *Prompt***: ask the AI to integrate all previous information into a cohesive and finalized format.

This iterative approach enables a productive dialogue with the AI, guiding it toward increasingly accurate and personalized results.

2.4 Types of *prompts* for different applications

Prompt types vary depending on the goal, and knowing how to use the right type for each scenario is critical to achieving the best result. Different types of *prompts* offer distinct approaches to stimulate AI to provide responses that best meet the user's needs. Each type can be adapted depending on the context and the user's goals, providing greater versatility in interacting with AI models.

Creative Prompts: stimulating imagination and innovation

These *prompts* stimulate AI to produce innovative content by stimulating imagination and imagination. For example, "Imagine a world in which machines can read people's minds. Write a short story about how this affects human relationships."

This type of *prompt* is especially useful for:

- Writing short stories and narratives.
- Creating futuristic business ideas.
- Developing movie scripts.
- Exploring hypothetical scenarios with potential real-world applications.

Another example of a creative *prompt* might be, "Imagine a future in which humanity colonized Mars. Describe what daily life would be like in one of the Martian colonies." Such a *prompt* encourages AI to develop a detailed and engaging picture of a possible future, exploring the psychology, emotions and challenges of life on another planet.

The Descriptive *Prompts*: painting detailed scenarios

These *prompts* are used to describe scenarios, objects or concepts in detail. An example is, "Describe a typical day in the life of an astronaut on the International Space Station."

Descriptive *prompts* are particularly effective when trying to:

- Paint a clear and detailed picture of an environment.
- Explain scientific phenomena vividly.
- Depict historical scenarios in detail.

- Create immersive descriptions that engage multiple sensory modalities.

For example, "Describe how a person who is swimming in the ocean during a storm feels" is a *prompt* that encourages AI to explore the senses-sight, hearing, touch-and generate an emotional, immersive description. This approach makes descriptions more vivid and meaningful, helping the reader feel part of the described experience.

Narrative prompts: building stories and communicative pathways

These *prompts* are designed to construct stories or anecdotes. An example might be, "Tell the story of a private detective who solves a case through a clue found in an ancient book."

Narrative *prompts* are ideal for:

- Developing complete narratives with a narrative arc.
- Creating complex, developed characters.
- Producing narrative marketing content.
- Developing case studies or training scenarios.

A more articulate *prompt* might be, "Tell the story of a young inventor who builds a robot to help his community and discovers something unexpected about himself in the process." This helps the AI develop not only the story but also the character of the protagonist, exploring his dreams, challenges, and inner journey, thus creating a narrative that not only entertains but also inspires.

Logical and technical prompts: getting precise analysis

These *prompts* seek precise and analytical answers, and are particularly useful for obtaining technical information or detailed explanations. For example, "Explain how the TCP/IP protocol[16] works in computer networks."

Logical and technical *prompts* are essential for:

- Solving mathematical or computational problems.
- Obtain detailed technical analysis.
- Understand complex scientific concepts.
- Generating technical documentation.

A more detailed *prompt* might be, "Describe the main steps in the operation of the TCP/IP protocol, including how it is broken down into packets and reassembled." These *prompts* require the AI to come up with coherent, structured responses that are useful to anyone who needs to understand complex processes without having advanced knowledge on the subject.

Instructional prompts: guiding through complex processes

This category of *prompts* is designed to teach or provide information in an educational way. For example, "Explain step-by-step how to plant a tree, including materials needed and precautions to take."

Instructional *prompts* are great for:

- Creating tutorials and practical guides.
- Developing educational content.
- Describe step-by-step procedures.
- Provide clear instructions for complex tasks.

Another example might be, "Teach how to make a simple chocolate cake, including all ingredients and cooking timings." The AI will provide

---

[16] **TCP/IP**: is the set of network protocols that forms the foundation of the Internet. It divides data into numbered packets, manages their reliable transmission across different networks, and provides a universal addressing system that allows communication between any connected device.

a well-structured response that guides the user step by step, making the instructions practical and easily applicable.

Each of these *prompts* can be improved by adding additional details or specifications. For example, a descriptive *prompt* such as "Describe a futuristic city" can become more detailed with the addition of items such as "Describe a futuristic city nestled in a jungle with skyscrapers made of natural materials and powered by renewable energy." This helps the AI build a richer, more coherent picture with details that make the description more interesting and visually engaging. Similarly, in technical *prompts*, adding the target audience-for example, "Explain how TCP/IP protocol works to a high school student"-can improve the quality of the output, ensuring that the level of detail is appropriate for the *audience* and that the explanation is more accessible and clear.

After exploring the basic types of *prompts*, it is important to understand how these elements can be combined into more complex architectures.

Layered contextual *prompting*: layered architecture

In complex technology projects, layered organization of information greatly improves both understanding and execution.

The same principle applies to *prompt engineering*, where a well-defined layered architecture can radically transform the effectiveness of interaction with AI.

The layered architecture of prompts

A complex prompt can be structured into four distinct layers, each with a specific role:

- ***System Layer***: defines the fundamental purpose, operational constraints, and general framework of the interaction.

- ***Context Layer***: provides the *task-specific background* information, the "ground" on which to build.
- ***Role Layer***: assigns a "professional personality" to the model, guiding its approach and style.
- ***Instruction Layer***: specifies the immediate *task* with clear parameters and defined expectations.

Here is an example of a layered *prompt:*

Prompt Name	content_marketing_strategy_layered
Objective	To generate a quarterly content marketing strategic roadmap for a SaaS startup[17] project management. Structured into four key components (system, context, role, instruction), it guides AI to create a detailed plan with 5 essential content pillars, each defined in terms of strategic goals, formats, distribution channels, creation processes and success metrics. The strategy is specifically calibrated to convert IT managers and CTOs of *mid-size* companies (50-200 employees) into enterprise customers, optimizing a quarterly budget of €30,000 to reach the goal of 100 new customers in 6 months. The *prompt* balances educational and commercial content, turning channels with limited engagement into an effective lead generation *pipeline*.
Model	Claude-3-7-sonnet with Extended Thinking
Prompt	[SYSTEM] You are a consultant specializing in B2B digital content marketing with a particular focus on the technology industry. You base your answers on recent industry data and established best practices, highlighting the relationship between KPIs and business objectives. [CONTEXT] The client company is a SaaS startup that has developed a project management solution for distributed teams, with 25 employees and an active customer base of 50. They have a quarterly marketing budget of €30,000 and aim to acquire 100 new enterprise customers within 6 months. Their

[17] **SaaS**: A business model where a company develops software that is accessible via the Internet via subscription.

	primary audience is IT managers and CTOs of companies with 50-200 employees. Their current channels include a corporate blog with moderate traffic (5,000 visits/month) and LinkedIn and Twitter profiles with limited engagement. [ROLE] Act as Head of Content Strategy for a digital marketing agency specializing in SaaS, with specific experience in creating *lead generation pipelines* through high-value content and a particular sensitivity to balancing educational content with commercial materials. [INSTRUCTION] Develop a quarterly content roadmap that includes 5 essential content pillars, specifying for each: strategic objective, format and distribution channels, creation process, success metrics, and potential obstacles to anticipate. Include a high-level editorial calendar for the first month.
	https://tinyurl.com/54bm66u2
Output	Quarterly Content Roadmap: SaaS Strategy for Distributed Teams. Strategic and Methodological Overview. Analyzing your SaaS startup's current situation and reflecting on acquisition goals (100 new enterprise customers in 6 months), I developed a content-driven roadmap that balances three key dimensions: brand visibility, market education, and conversion. This strategic triangulation, which I have refined in similar projects for other B2B SaaS platforms, has proven particularly effective when the target audience is technical decision-makers such as IT managers and CTOs. The €30,000 budget requires an extremely targeted approach, where each piece of content must serve multiple objectives within the conversion funnel. My experience with startups at a similar stage suggests that the optimal ratio of awareness content to conversion is 60:40 at this stage of growth. The 5 Essential Content Pillars 1. Authored Whitepaper: "Distributed Project Management 2025: Maturity Model and Quantifiable ROI" **Strategic Goal**: Position yourself as a thought leader and create a high-value *lead generation* asset.

	Format and Channels: Downloadable PDF (25-30 pages) with professional design and consistent visual identity Dedicated landing page with progressive lead capture form Distribution: LinkedIn Ads (targeting by role), newsletters, blogs, and partnerships with technical communities **Creation Process**: Proprietary research: interviews with 5-7 current customers to extract quantitative data on benefits Maturity Framework: development of a proprietary 4-level model Collaborative drafting between marketing and product teams (3 weeks) Professional design and technical review (2 weeks) **Success Metrics**: Downloads: target 350+ in first 45 days Form completion rate: >30%. Qualified leads (MQL → SQL): conversion >20%. Referrals in sales processes: >40% of sales calls **Potential Obstacles**: Differentiation in a market saturated with white papers Solution: Include unique proprietary data and original evaluation frameworks 2. Interactive Webinar Series: "Masters of Remote PM" **Strategic Goal**: Nurturing leads and indirect product demonstration through concrete use cases. **Format and Channels**: Series of 3 connected webinars (45 minutes + Q&A session) Format: customer interview + hands-on demonstration Recordings available on-demand with content segmentation Promotion: email marketing, industry media partnerships, retargeting campaigns CONTINUE...
	https://tinyurl.com/4y4m9rkd

Advantages of the layered approach:

- **Clarity of purpose**: Each layer has a distinct and well-defined role.
- **Operational flexibility**: ability to edit individual layers without rebuilding the entire *prompt*.
- **Reusability**: creation of effective templates for recurring contexts.
- **Traceability**: facilitation of the documentation process and *prompt* optimization.

The layered architecture described here is applied concretely in the decision-making processes discussed in Chapter 7, where it becomes a tool for strategic prioritization.

Prompts for code generation: democratizing software development

The silent revolution in software development

The software development landscape is undergoing a radical transformation thanks to *Code Prompting*. This seemingly simple technique is redefining the boundaries between developers and end users, creating a new "conversational programming" paradigm accessible to anyone who can clearly articulate their operational needs.

Looking at the historical trajectory of development technologies, a consistent path toward democratizing access to innovation emerges. In the early 1990s, visual programming represented a significant first attempt in this direction. This approach replaced traditional lines of textual code with manipulable graphical elements, allowing developers to drag and connect visual components instead of writing complex syntax. Tools such as Visual Basic, LabVIEW, Delphi, and HyperCard allowed software to be built through graphical interfaces, reducing (but not eliminating) the need for specialized technical skills. Although these development environments brought more people closer to software creation, they still required an understanding of the underlying programming principles.

Today, with generative AI, we are finally seeing the fulfillment of that vision: the ability to create software through natural language rather than through formal programming languages or visual interfaces. This evolution represents not just a technical change, but a profound reorientation of the relationship between humans and technology, where the ability to clearly communicate a need becomes more important than syntactic knowledge of a programming language.

Fundamentals of Code Prompting

Code *Prompting* represents the art of formulating structured prompts that guide AI in the creation, interpretation, conversion or optimization of code. Unlike generic *prompts*, this category requires:

- **Accuracy in functional requirements**: what exactly the code must do.
- **Clarity in expected inputs and outputs**: what data will be processed and what is to be achieved.
- **Contextualization of the technological environment**: in what system the code will run.
- **Performance parameters**: what efficiency, safety or maintainability constraints are prioritized.

The effectiveness of this technique lies in its ability to translate operational needs expressed in natural language into working technical solutions, bridging the gap between idea and implementation.

The four application dimensions

We can identify four main ways of using Code *Prompting*, each with specific applications:

1. Code generation from scratch

"Develop an Excel VBA macro that automatically extracts data from columns A-G of the 'Monthly_Sales' sheet, calculates quarterly trends by region (column C), and generates comparative charts in the '*Dashboard*' sheet. The code must handle up to 10,000 rows of data and include error handling for empty cells."

This approach is ideal for quickly turning an idea into a working solution, bypassing the learning curve of a new programming language.

2. Understanding and documenting existing code

"Analyze this Excel macro I inherited from the previous team and explain in detail what each section does. Identify potential inefficiencies and suggest improvements:

[existing VBA code]"

Especially useful when acquiring code developed by others, this mode turns the AI into a "translator" between technicalities and operational language.

3. Translation and migration between platforms.

"Convert this Excel VBA macro to Google Apps Script while maintaining exactly the same functionality." The code handles extracting data from multiple sources and integrating them into a consolidated report:

[original Excel macro]"

4. Debugging and optimization

"This Excel macro works correctly with small *datasets* but crashes with 'Out of memory' message when processing more than 5,000 rows. Analyze the code, identify the problem and optimize it:

[problem code]"

This last dimension turns the AI into a technical collaborator who can identify and solve problems in existing code, even for those without advanced programming skills.

A real-world case: from manual routines to automation

A particularly enlightening example that I am observing on a daily basis concerns my wife. Every week, she devoted almost an entire workday to manually extracting data from multiple sources to prepare PowerPoint presentations for management. The process was tedious: downloading Excel spreadsheets from various systems, consolidating data, calculating KPIs, manually creating charts and then inserting them into slides.

This personal experience fits into the larger debate about the evolution of AI in the context of software development. As pointed out by Sam Altman of OpenAI, AI is emerging primarily as a productivity multiplier, potentially increasing productivity by up to 1000%. It is not about completely replacing human skills, but rather strategically amplifying them-exactly what happened in my wife's case.

Through a targeted sequence of AI *prompts*, my wife developed a macro solution in Excel VBA that transformed this workflow. The first prompt asked for a macro to automatically extract data from different files based on specific time parameters. Next, he iterated with *prompts* to add functionality for automatic trend calculation, dynamic chart generation, and even direct export to PowerPoint format with preset layouts.

This dynamic represents on a small scale what Meta's Mark Zuckerberg predicted would happen at the professional level: the emergence of AI systems with skills comparable to "mid-level engineers" capable of writing and debugging code independently. In my wife's case, although she had no programming skills, she was able to achieve results that previously would have required a developer.

The result has exceeded expectations: a process that used to occupy 6-7 hours per week has been reduced to about 40 minutes, mainly devoted to reviewing and strategically interpreting the data, not mechanically processing it. The quality of presentation has greatly improved due to the consistency of calculations and standardization of visual formats.

This scenario reflects Bill Gates' view that programming remains too complex an activity for complete algorithmic automation. In fact, human input in defining requirements and verifying results remains crucial. My wife continues to oversee the process, making changes and improvements when necessary.

The most surprising aspect of this transformation has been to observe how, starting with user-level knowledge of Excel and no programming experience, my wife has progressively refined its *prompts*, adding features such as automatic comparison with historical data from the same period in the previous year and the generation of trend-based forecasts. What initially required my technical support has become a process she manages independently, periodically modifying the *prompts* to adapt the solution to new reporting needs.

The Evolution to Artifacts: from generation to execution.

A significant evolution in the Code *Prompting* landscape is the introduction of the *Artifacts* feature in Claude. This innovation marks a fundamental shift: from AI generating code to AI creating applications that are directly executable and accessible via the Web.

I experimented with this feature by developing an interactive *dashboard* to monitor performance metrics: starting with a natural language description, Claude generated a complete interactive web application that was immediately runnable and accessible to everyone via a browser, with no need for server configuration or complex *deployment*.

With a *prompt* like the following we can create the interactive *dashboard* in seconds:

Prompt Name	Interactive_dashboard
Objective	The *prompt* aims to transform natural language instructions into a fully functional business analytics application without requiring programming skills. It systematically defines visualization requirements, interaction models, and data structures to enable Claude's Artifacts feature to autonomously generate a complete dashboard solution that presents complex performance metrics through interactive charts, maintains a professional aesthetic, and demonstrates how sophisticated Web applications can be created through conversation rather than traditional software development processes.
Model	Claude-3-7-sonnet with Extended Thinking
Prompt	Create a comprehensive interactive web application that implements a modern interactive dashboard to monitor business performance metrics. The dashboard should have the following features: ## Layout and Structure - Header with logo, title "Analytics Dashboard" and navigation icons (search, notifications, settings, profile)

	- Main area divided into sections with responsive design (grid system) - Tab navigation system for different views of data - 4 KPI cards at the top showing key metrics with trends ## Data views 1. Line graph for financial trends (turnover, expenses, profit) 2. Pie chart for customer acquisition channels 3. Bar graph for monthly conversions 4. Horizontal bar chart for performance indices ## Interactive Features. - Time range selection (1 month, 3 months, 6 months, 1 year) - Tab to navigate between different views (Overview, Turnover, Conversions, KPIs) - Tooltips on charts for details on mouseover - Option to export reports ## Sample Data - Create fictitious data for 6 months showing positive trends for revenue and conversions - Include data by acquisition channels (organic, social, email, referral, direct) - Add KPI metrics for operational efficiency, customer satisfaction, delivery time and product quality ## Visual Appearance. - Use a modern palette with a primary color and accents for different types of data - Clean design with white cards on a light gray background - Use Lucide icons for interface elements - Add visual trend indicators (up/down arrows) for key metrics ## Libraries to Use. - Recharts for data visualizations - Lucide for icons - TailwindCSS for styling

	Make sure the dashboard is fully functional, with realistic interactions and a clean code structure. The design should be professional and elegant, suitable for a business environment. **https://tinyurl.com/3wp78vme**
Output	 CONTINUE... **https://tinyurl.com/bdft89zc**

This approach offers three key advantages:

Immediacy: from conception to implementation in a single step.

Accessibility: applications that can be used by anyone via standard browsers.

Iterability: ability to quickly modify the application by reformulating the *prompt*.

Strategic considerations for the future of programming.

This technological evolution raises profound questions about the future of software development. The most transformative perspective is articulated by Dario Amodei of Anthropic, who predicts how AI will be responsible for 90 percent of code production within a few months, with the possibility that it will come to handle "all code" within a year.

If this prediction comes true, we would see a radical redefinition of:

- **Job roles**: with developers shifting to architectural and supervisory tasks.
- **Core competencies**: where the ability to communicate clear requirements becomes more important than syntactic knowledge.
- **Development cycles**: drastically accelerated and more iterative.
- **Accessibility of innovation**: with an unprecedented democratization of the ability to create software solutions.

Conclusion: a new development paradigm.

Code *Prompting* is not simply making programming more accessible-it is redefining the very meaning of software development. We are transitioning from a paradigm where code was the exclusive domain of specialists to one where technical implementation becomes a natural extension of operational thinking.

This transformation democratizes technological innovation, enabling anyone with a clear vision of their needs to translate it into workable solutions. As I have personally observed, this does not diminish the value of professional developers, but redirects their skills to more complex challenges, freeing them from the repetitive tasks that can now be delegated to AI.

2.5 The revolution of Canvas interfaces

With the introduction of Canvas modes in major generative AI platforms, we are witnessing a radical transformation in *prompt* writing and processing.

This mode is an interactive space within the application itself (web and mobile) that allows documents, images or code to be created, edited and formatted in real time with the support of AI. It functions as a digital "canvas" where changes are displayed immediately and one can interact with the AI to refine the content.

This evolution represents a fundamental shift from the one-way conversational paradigm to a more flexible, visual and iterative approach.

From linear *prompts* to interactive *workspaces*

Traditional *prompt* writing was based on a sequential model: formulate a complete request, wait for a response, and then possibly refine it with subsequent *prompts*. Operating daily with these tools, I observed how this approach had significant limitations, especially for complex or creative projects.

With the introduction of Canvas interfaces, the dynamic changes dramatically:

- **Spatial structuring of ideas**: we can now arrange different sections of *prompts* in a nonlinear way, visually organizing them as we would on a physical whiteboard.
- **Simultaneous Iteration**: it is possible to work on multiple components of a project simultaneously, editing individual sections without having to reformulate the entire *prompt*.
- **Visual contextualization**: relationships between different elements become explicit through their spatial arrangement.

Comparison of implementations: ChatGPT, Gemini and Claude

The different Canvas mode implementations offer distinctly nuanced *prompt engineering* experiences:

- **ChatGPT Canvas**: favors freedom of spatial placement. When preparing technical presentations, I can create *prompt* blocks dedicated to different aspects-one for conceptual content, one for graphical visualizations, one for code examples-all visible at the same time and mutually influential.
- **Gemini Canvas**: is distinguished by its real-time visualization and interactivity. When writing technical documentation, I can immediately see how HTML or React[18] code is rendered, iteratively modifying both the *prompt* and the result in a continuous feedback loop.
- **Claude Artifacts**: while not explicitly labeled as Canvas, it introduces a programmable *prompt* model through specific update commands. This approach, which I have found extremely effective for detailed technical documents, allows surgical changes to specific sections without regenerating the entire content.

The new paradigm of human-AI collaboration.

This evolution of interfaces requires a rethinking of traditional *prompt engineering* techniques:

- **Modular thinking**: effective *prompts* are now those that recognize and take advantage of the composable nature of work.

---

[18] **React** is a JavaScript library for creating interactive user interfaces

- **Directional language**: new ways of expressing spatial relationships and connections between elements emerge.
- **Visual feedback**: *prompt* formulation becomes a more interactive process, driven by immediate visualization of results.

Canvas mode represents a natural evolution in human-AI interaction, aligning these tools with human cognitive processes that are inherently nonlinear and visual. We are seeing a gradual abandonment of the "conversation" metaphor in favor of the "creative workshop" metaphor, where the AI becomes a collaborator in a shared environment rather than just an interlocutor.

In my experience working with these systems, this evolution has led to a significant improvement in the quality of the results achieved and the fluidity of the creative process, bringing interaction with AI closer to the natural way we develop and organize our ideas.

Chapter Summary

Prompt engineering represents a fundamental art and science in interacting with generative AI models. This chapter explores the principles, methodologies, and advanced techniques needed to achieve optimal results from *Large Language Models*.

Fundamental Principles

Prompt engineering is based on four essential pillars: **clarity** in prompts, appropriate **context**, **specificity** in details, and **definition of the expected result**. A good *prompt* structured according to these principles can transform generic responses into precise and highly personalized content, maximizing the value of each interaction with AI.

Types of Prompts

The chapter identifies five main categories of *prompts*:

- **Creative**: to stimulate imagination and generate innovative content.
- **Descriptive**: to paint detailed and engaging scenarios.
- **Narrative**: to build stories and develop complex narrative arcs.
- **Logical and Technical**: to achieve precise analysis and structured explanations.
- **Instructional**: to guide through complex processes and procedures.

Evolution of interfaces

The shift from linear conversational interfaces to the new Canvas modes (ChatGPT, Gemini, Claude) represents a paradigm shift, allowing non-linear spatial organization of *prompts* and facilitating simultaneous iteration on different components of a project.

Prompts for code generation

An important application of *prompt engineering* is the democratization of software development, enabling even non-programmers to create, understand, and modify code through natural language prompts, with use cases ranging from script generation to the creation of complete applications.

Methodological Approach

To maximize the effectiveness of interactions with AI, the chapter recommends an experimental and comparative approach, testing the same *prompt* on different models to identify nuances, different perspectives and innovative approaches, confirming the central role of the human as guide, interpreter and ultimate decision maker in the process.

Conclusion

Prompt engineering, as we saw in section 2.2, is the key to unlocking the full potential of generative AI. This chapter has provided the practical tools-from the four fundamental pillars to layered architectures, from prompt types to new Canvas interfaces-to transform this skill from theory to everyday practice, remembering that continuous experimentation and human guidance remain the true success factors in the era of augmented intelligence.

PART II

AI IN BUSINESS AND PRODUCTIVITY

CHAPTER 3

EFFICIENT COMMUNICATION IN THE AI ERA: E-MAIL AND BUSINESS COMMUNICATION

3.1 *Framework* for optimizing digital communication.

Business communication in the digital age is both a challenge and an opportunity. This chapter offers a progressive path to transform e-mail management from a time-consuming activity to an optimized process through generative AI.

The *framework* that will guide our exploration consists of three interconnected phases:

1. Content analysis and optimization.
    - Assisted creation of effective messages.
    - Quality improvement of existing communications.
    - Synthesis and simplification of complex information.

2. Process automation.
    - Intelligent routing of communications.
    - Automated management of responses.
    - Integration into existing workflows.

3. Human-machine balance.
    - Balance between efficiency and skill development.
    - Human supervision in automated processes.
    - Continuous evaluation of quality and effectiveness.

This systematic approach makes it possible to deal with information overload by turning it into an opportunity to improve not only efficiency, but also the overall quality of business communication.

In today's fast-paced and competitive professional world, productivity is no longer just about working harder, it is more about working smarter. Generative AI has burst onto the scene as the office companion you never knew you needed, capable of revolutionizing every aspect of daily work.

AI not only helps you complete tasks, but also enables you to reprioritize, identifying the tasks with the greatest impact and providing support to achieve goals more efficiently.

From automating repetitive tasks to providing insights that spur innovation, AI is radically transforming the way we work, collaborate and thrive in our careers.

In addition, AI is an ally in managing work stress, helping us avoid *burnout*[19] through tools that improve our ability to organize and plan.

In my career as a consultant and still today, I meet clients and colleagues resigned to having to spend not hours but entire days each month scrolling through and editing Excel files with thousands of rows. It is, therefore, natural for me, as a consultant, to propose a reengineering of the process, the introduction of a new workflow as well as to evaluate possible automations. All this, in organizations, takes time and investment, and in the meantime, months pass and the stress and resignation of colleagues increases. While waiting for digitization and process reengineering projects to take hold, a quick and immediate solution is precisely the use of AI.

In this way, technology becomes a key resource for ensuring a healthy balance between personal and professional life. AI's ability to adapt to each worker's needs, providing customized solutions, is an

[19] ***burnout***: a syndrome caused by chronic work stress that is not effectively managed, characterized by emotional and physical exhaustion, cynical detachment from one's work and reduced professional effectiveness. It occurs when demands consistently exceed available resources and recovery time.

additional benefit that contributes to a more enjoyable and satisfying daily work. Ultimately, AI is not just a technological tool, but a real strategic resource that allows us to expand our limits, opening up new scenarios for innovation and creativity.

3.2 Email, communications and business documentation: write faster, better and with less effort

The problem of e-mail overload

I recently decided to take a day out of my schedule to count e-mails received and sent (I actually asked Microsoft Copilot to do this for me) and the result was 64 e-mails received and 20 sent. This led me to reflect on the workload associated with managing e-mail primarily for internal organizational communications that I might call "service" and how much time this activity takes away from other strategic activities. The amount of e-mail I receive every day, especially on busy days, has prompted me to look for more effective ways to handle them while still maintaining the quality of responses and without sacrificing work efficiency.

If, for whatever reason, you have not opened your mailbox for an entire workday you will surely share my words.

So it became increasingly urgent to find an approach that would allow me to optimize the management of electronic correspondence.

Email can be useful for collaboration, but I am observing a growing trend toward hyper-communication, which often turns email into a tool for "dumping the ball" on others. Email is often used as a kind of virtual proxy, allowing the writer to pass on responsibilities or tasks without fully considering the impact of that communication on the recipient. In many situations, this leads to information overload that reduces the ability to respond effectively and timely.

AI solutions for email management

These thoughts prompted me to implement AI on a daily basis to better manage e-mail, reduce the stress and frustration associated with trying to achieve *zero-inbox*[20] ". These tools have allowed me to be more productive, respond faster and be more courteous, even being able to respond to requests that I would not normally be interested in. AI's ability to speed up the creation of email drafts or the response to particularly long messages has allowed me to reduce the time spent on email and devote more time to higher value-added tasks.

Thanks to the far-sighted decision of our CIO[21] , who as early as May 2023 led our company to be among the first 600 in the world to adopt Microsoft Copilot in early access-before the official launch in November 2023 and subsequent extension to the entire organization-I can today:

- Summarize lengthy e-mails, regardless of language: in the case of poorly summarized senders, this saves me several minutes per e-mail. Also very useful in the case of complex message sequences. Imagine having to deal with a series of concatenated messages, with dozens of replies and updates; summarizing them with AI allows a clear and immediate view of the situation.

---

[20] ***zero-inbox***: is an e-mail management methodology that aims to keep the inbox consistently empty or nearly empty. The concept, developed by Merlin Mann, is based on the principle that the inbox should function as a temporary processing point rather than a permanent repository, requiring immediate decisions on each message received: delete, archive, delegate, reply, or schedule.

[21] **CIO**: Chief Information Officer, the person in charge of information systems.

- Generate a draft response that I then adapt to my own style. Even with the necessary revisions, I can save several minutes per email. In particular, this function proves essential when it is necessary to respond quickly to numerous messages without compromising the quality of communication.
- Create draft e-mails to send. Drafting a formal e-mail from scratch, especially in a non-native language, can be a time-consuming and painstaking task. AI allows me to start from a solid base that I then customize according to the recipient.

The benefit of Microsoft Copilot is obvious if you are in the Microsoft ecosystem, thus using MS Outlook, but these features are also available with other generative AI systems. In that case, will require only one additional step: copying the produced text into your e-mail *client* for sending. This flexibility allows you to take advantage of AI regardless of the specific platforms you use, helping to improve mail management across the board.

AI can help us with email in many ways:

1. Compose the best content based on the recipient and the message we want to convey.
2. Providing an opinion on the tone and content of our email, as well as suggestions on how to improve it.
3. Take advantage of AI's advanced linguistic capabilities for quick translations or to verify those already made.
4. Improve clarity and synthesis of e-mails.
5. Synthesize very long e-mails, whether received or written by us.
6. Routing the e-mail to the best recipient based on its content.
7. Automatically reply to the e-mail for us with or without our supervision.

Let us analyze them in detail one by one.

1. Compose the best content according to the recipient and the message we want to convey.

Assisted composition represents the first level of AI integration into the communication process. This feature analyzes the context, the recipient, and the goal of the communication to suggest optimized content that complies with the principles of communicative effectiveness. Particularly useful in situations that require persuasiveness and precision, such as *lead generation* or strategic communications, this approach significantly reduces preparation time while maintaining high message quality.

For example, in business and marketing circles, AI can prepare the text for an e-mail in which we ask for a meeting to present a service/product, or create customized content for *direct e-mail marketing* campaigns based on the characteristics of the target *audience*. This results in an increased chance of getting positive responses, thanks to the ability to adapt the tone and content of the message according to the context and audience.

If we needed support to set up a meeting with a potential client via e-mail, we could use a *prompt* such as the following:

***Prompt*: https://tinyurl.com/43uvkyjc**

> Create a *lead generation* e-mail for our NIS2 (Network and Information Security, European Cyber Security Directive) assesment service targeting maritime container shipping companies. The e-mail must:
> 1) Begin with an impactful headline about the impending NIS2 deadline and risks of non-compliance.
> 2) Include a short paragraph (3-4 lines) highlighting:
> - Our successes with the previous NIS directive
> - Our integrated approach (cybersecurity + compliance + sector expertise)
> - A concrete figure on our achievements with other clients
> 3) Briefly (maximum 3 points) present the specific benefits for maritime operators
> 4) Close with a direct call-to-action for a free 30-minute consultation
> Tone: professional but conversational, maximum 15 lines total, separate email subject line

A model like Claude Sonnet 4 with *Extended Thinking* will produce the following result:

Subject: [NIS2 DEADLINE] Protecting Your Container Fleet from Cyber Risks: Complimentary Consultation

NIS2: Don't Wait Until October 2024 to Ensure Compliance - Non-compliance Risks Could Cost Up to 2% of Global Revenue

Dear [Name],

Our team has successfully guided over 40 companies through the transition to the previous NIS directive, achieving a 68% reduction in compliance gaps through our integrated approach. We combine cybersecurity expertise, regulatory compliance knowledge, and specialized understanding of the maritime container sector – an integration that makes a direct impact in the consulting landscape.

Why Choose Our NIS2 Assessment:

- **Rapid Assessment** (7 days) of your current compliance level with personalized action plan
- **Supply Chain Operations Profiling** focused on terminals and tracking systems
- **Compliance Solutions** aligned with ISPS Code and other maritime regulations to optimize your investments

Shall we schedule a virtual coffee? I'm offering a complimentary 30-minute consultation to evaluate your NIS2 readiness level. Simply reply to this email or call me at [number] to schedule an appointment.

We understand the unique challenges facing the maritime transport sector, and our proven track record in both cybersecurity and maritime compliance positions us to help you navigate the NIS2 requirements efficiently and cost-effectively.

Best regards,

[Signature]

Retry

Claude can make mistakes. Please double-check responses.

If I were to send this e-mail, I would not send it as it was generated from the first *prompt*. In part because it does not reflect my communication style with a very consumer approach in tone not appropriate for the interlocutor to whom it is addressed. It refers to a date in the past i.e., when NIS was repealed and NIS2 came into effect. He invented from scratch the fact that he has successfully supported 40 organizations to be compliant as well as 65% time optimization. When I asked him to explain why he had invented this information first he claimed it was a *placeholder* to remember to put in the exact number but then admitted it was a hallucination. He made up these numbers to satisfy my request "- Our successes with the previous NIS directive" and "- A concrete figure on the results achieved with other customers." If I had specified this information while also remaining generic, he would not have invented this information. The tone not appropriate to the interlocutor also continues in the "*call-to-action*" section where he proposes a virtual coffee, which is too informal and colloquial for an initial B2B communication aimed at management figures. A second *prompt* like this was sufficient:

"Use a more professional tone, do not refer to the October 2024 date but remain more generic. Don't make up the number of organizations supported or even the 65 percent compliance timeframe. Also the *call to action* section make it more professional."

To get a better result:

Subject: NIS2 Directive: Compliance Solutions for Maritime Container Transport Sector

New NIS2 Requirements: Preparing to Avoid Significant Non-compliance Risks in the Maritime Sector

Dear [Name],

Our expert team boasts proven experience in implementing compliance solutions for the previous NIS directive. We offer an integrated approach that combines advanced cybersecurity expertise, regulatory compliance, and specialized knowledge of the maritime sector – a synergy that represents the distinctive value of our consulting.

Benefits of Our NIS2 Assessment:

- **In-depth Assessment** of current compliance status with development of a personalized action plan
- **Protection of Critical Supply Chain Operations** with particular attention to tracking systems and terminals
- **Implementation of Solutions** compliant with both NIS2 and international maritime regulations

To Learn More: We invite you to contact us to schedule a complimentary 30-minute virtual consultation session dedicated to the preliminary assessment of your NIS2 directive readiness.

Best regards,

[Signature]

Retry

Claude can make mistakes. Please double-check responses.

While content generation provides a solid foundation, stylistic and tonal refinement is a next level of optimization. Moving from creation to critical evaluation, AI can act as a communication consultant, offering objective analysis that complements our subjective perception of the message.

2. Providing an opinion on the tone and content of our email, as well as suggestions on how to improve it.

Tone and style analysis represents a higher level of assistance, where AI does not just generate content, but acts as a communication consultant. This functionality is particularly valuable when communicating complex messages to diverse audiences or in multicultural contexts, where linguistic and cultural nuances can significantly influence the perception of the message. The goal is to identify and correct potential ambiguities or inconsistencies before they reach the recipient.

Over the years, I have learned that when writing to a very large number of recipients (in my case to nearly 1,000 colleagues), it is critical to curate every sentence and word to avoid misunderstandings. Especially if it is addressed to colleagues from different languages and cultures. AI can help us strike a balance between formality and clarity, ensuring that the message is well understood by all.

Assume we have written an email like the following:

"*Subject: Q1 Activity Update.*

Dear colleagues,

with reference to recent organizational developments and to what has emerged in recent cross-departmental meetings, an update of the previously shared operating procedures is necessary.

As anticipated by some contact persons, the new guidelines will impact the planned deliverables. We therefore ask you to proceed with the appropriate adjustments, taking into account the agreed timelines, albeit with due flexibility.

As far as priorities are concerned, the broad guidelines remain unchanged, without prejudice to the possibility of assessing any exceptions on a case-by-case basis, which will still have to be handled according to standard procedures.

It is also recalled that, as per previous communications, what has been established regarding deadlines remains valid, unless different arrangements may emerge in the coming days.

For any clarification needs, you can refer to your direct managers or relevant focal points. "

The following *prompt* helps us identify ambiguous or unclear parts, any omissions of information, vague language, inappropriate tone, and suggests an alternative:

***Prompt*: https://tinyurl.com/538bxybm**

Carefully analyze this e-mail and identify:
1. **AMBIGUOUS PARTS**: Highlight phrases or terms that could generate multiple interpretations or misunderstandings.
2. **CRITICAL OMISSIONS**: Identifies information that is missing but necessary for understanding or required action (dates, deadlines, responsibilities, operational details).
3. **VAGUE LANGUAGE**: Detects generic expressions, imprecise adverbs ("soon," "a lot," "some") or non-specific adjectives that make the message unclear.
4. **INADEQUATE TONE**: Assesses whether language is appropriate for the professional context and the recipient (too formal/informal, passive-aggressive, overly urgent).
5. **PROBLEM STRUCTURE**: Examines whether the order of information is logical and whether the main points are easily identifiable.
Then:
- Specifically list each identified problem with a brief explanation
- Propose an optimized version of the entire e-mail that solves all identified problems
- Maintain the same communication objective but with greater clarity, precision, and appropriate tone.
E-mail to analyze: [INSERT E-MAIL HERE].

Using Claude Sonnet 4, the response we receive is as follows:

"Email Analysis.

1. AMBIGUE PARTS:

- "recent organizational changes" and "what transpired in the last cross-cutting meetings" do not specify what changes or decisions were made.
- "new guidelines will impact deliverables" does not clarify which guidelines and how they will affect the work.
- "Appropriate adjustments" does not specify what changes to make concretely.

- "Agreed timelines, albeit with due flexibility" creates confusion as to whether deadlines are rigid or flexible.
- "Broad directions" and "standard procedures" do not describe the specific instructions to be followed.

2. CRITICAL OMISSIONS:

- Specific dates for deadlines are missing.
- Specific deliverables required are not listed.
- Names of managers or *focal points* to contact are not given.
- It is not specified by when to make adjustments.
- Lack of details on what the "new guidelines" mean in practical terms.

3. VAGUE LANGUAGE:

- Expressions such as "recent," "some focal points," "appropriate adjustments," "due flexibility," and "coming days" are imprecise.
- "Possible exceptions" and "broad guidelines" do not provide clear parameters.

4. INADEQUATE TONE:

- Overly formal and bureaucratic style.
- Impersonal language ("it becomes necessary," "you are reminded") that appears detached.
- Lacks a collaborative tone that acknowledges the commitment required.

5. PROBLEMATIC STRUCTURE:

- Absence of bullet points or lists to highlight key information.
- Lack of clear logical sequence (situation → changes → required action → support).
- Important information diluted in paragraphs without adequate highlighting.

Optimized Email.

"Subject: Q1 activity update - Actions required by May 10.

Dear Colleagues,

I am writing to inform you of operational changes as a result of the reorganization of the Marketing department announced on April 15 and discussed at the cross-functional meeting on April 22.

What changes:

- *Market analysis reports will have to follow the new template (attached).*
- *The frequency of updating changes from monthly to biweekly.*
- *Priority KPIs are now: conversion, retention and CAC (no longer sales volume).*

Actions required by May 10:

- *Update your reports using the new template.*
- *Revise Q2 forecasts according to the new KPIs.*
- *Schedule a checkpoint with your manager by May 5.*

Deadlines:

- *May 5: Completion of checkpoint with manager.*
- *May 10: delivery of updated reports.*
- *May 15: presentation of results to leadership team.*

Support available:

- *For operational questions: contact Marco Rossi (m.rossi@azienda.com).*
- *For clarification on new KPIs: contact Giulia Bianchi (g.bianchi@azienda.com).*
- *Q&A session: May 2, 2 p.m., Meeting Room 3 or via Teams.*

We understand that these changes require rapid adaptation. Your manager is available to support you in this process and assess any specific needs together.

Thank you for your cooperation, [Your Name]."

The example email was purposely written with ambiguous parts, omissions, vague language, etc., but on a daily basis AI manages to improve even the email I write with great care, and the result above is a clear demonstration of this.

Claude's "style" feature allows us to get very similar results to our own style, once properly instructed.

Optimizing style and tone is a critical step for monolingual communication, but the challenges multiply when operating in multilingual contexts. AI's ability to handle not only stylistic correction but also accurate translation opens up new possibilities for organizations operating in international environments.

3. Leverage AI's advanced linguistic capabilities for rapid translations or to verify those already made.

Multilingual management represents one of the most immediate and high-impact applications of AI in the globalized business environment. This feature overcomes the limitations of traditional machine translations by preserving not only literal meaning, but also stylistic nuances and context-appropriate register. It proves essential for organizations with international operations, not only for external communications but also for the cohesion of internal communication in geographically distributed groups.

For quality translation we can use a *prompt* such as:

***Prompt*: https://tinyurl.com/63x33uu6**

> Translate this e-mail from Italian to English, maintaining the same level of formality and a professional tone. Please:
> 1. Preserve any opening and closing formulas typical of formal e-mails
> 2. Keep the original formatting (paragraphs, bulleted lists, etc.)
> 3. Ensure that technical or industry-specific terms are accurately translated
> 4. In case of Italian idioms, use appropriate English equivalents
>
> Original e-mail: [INSERT E-MAIL HERE]

If, on the other hand, we already have an English text, either written by us or previously translated, we can ask AI to proofread it. By prompting it to point out errors and suggest corrections, we not only get a better text, but we use the interaction as a training opportunity to improve our language skills. To do this we can use a *prompt* similar to the following:

***Prompt*: https://tinyurl.com/mwm6f3ys**

Analyze this e-mail written in English and highlight in bold any:
1. Grammatical or spelling errors
2. Unnatural or non-idiomatic expressions
3. Problems with punctuation or formatting
4. Terms not appropriate for the professional context
5. Inconsistencies in tone or language register

For each item highlighted in bold, provide:
1. An explanation of the error or problem
2. A proposal for the most appropriate correction
3. If applicable, suggestions to further improve the fluency of the text

Email for review: [INSERT E-MAIL HERE].

These communication management techniques fit into the *Personal Knowledge Management framework* of Chapter 6, creating a holistic system for information management.

Language management solves the barriers of multilingual communication, but even within the same language significant challenges persist related to the structure and organization of information. Clarity and synthesis are the next step toward truly effective communication, regardless of the language used.

4. Improve email clarity and synthesis.

Structural optimization of communication addresses one of the most common problems in organizations: messages that are too complex, disorganized, or overly verbose. This feature applies principles of information design and cognitive psychology to restructure content, making it easier to identify and assimilate key points. The result is more accessible communication that reduces cognitive load for the recipient and accelerates decision making based on the information conveyed.

Not all of us are adept at simplifying content, and emails (especially those written in a hurry) often come across as unclear or too verbose. AI helps us achieve more effective and streamlined communication.

An example of a *prompt* to achieve this goal is as follows:

Prompt: **https://tinyurl.com/4exnrr4n**

Analyze this e-mail and turn it into more effective communication:

STEP 1: DIAGNOSTIC

- Identifies ambiguities, vague language, and unexplained technical terms
- Detects redundancies, digressions, and phrases that do not add value
- Highlights critical missing information (who, what, when, how)
- Evaluates the effectiveness of the subject line and overall structure

PHASE 2: OPTIMIZATION

Creates an improved version that:

1. STRUCTURE
- Organizes content into logical blocks with clear visual hierarchy
- Uses bulleted or numbered lists for actions, deadlines, and options
- Places the most important information at the beginning
- Creates an information object that communicates the main purpose

2. CONTENT
- Eliminate redundancies and non-essential phrases
- Replace vague terms with precise, quantifiable information
- Retain all essential dates, deadlines, requirements, and operational details
- Add missing but critical information (if inferable from context)

3. TONE
- Adapt level of formality to context and recipient
- Maintain professional but accessible language
- Use an active voice and a direct approach
- Ensures that requests and expectations are clearly phrased

STEP 3: ANALYSIS RESULTS
Provide:
1. The optimized version of the email
2. A list of key information retained
3. An estimate of the percentage of text reduction
4. A brief explanation of the key improvements made

EMAIL TO BE OPTIMIZED: [INSERT EMAIL HERE]

Structural optimization significantly improves communication effectiveness, but what happens when faced with high volumes of information requiring rapid analysis? The ability to effectively synthesize extended communications is a natural progression, particularly critical in business environments characterized by intense information flows.

5. Synthesizing very long e-mails, whether received or written by us.

Information distillation represents an evolution of simple summarization, focusing on the hierarchical extraction of critical information from high volumes of content. Unlike traditional summaries that uniformly compress text, this capability automatically identifies actionable items, deadlines, and required decisions and presents them in a structured format. This capability becomes indispensable in information-intensive environments, where decision-making efficiency depends on the rapid identification of truly relevant information.

It is often difficult to extract key information from a long and detailed e-mail, especially when under pressure or short on time. We are helped by a *prompt* such as the following:

Prompt: https://tinyurl.com/36jypy9w

Turn this e-mail into a structured executive summary:

STRUCTURE:
1. ESSENCE (1 sentence): Captures the main message and intent

2. KEY POINTS (maximum 5 bullet points):
-Required actions (what to do)
-Critical deadlines (when to do it)
-Necessary decisions (what to choose)
-Essential context (why it is important).

3. NEXT STEPS (maximum of 2 bullet points).

4. TIMING (precise date format or range)

SELECTION CRITERIA:
- Priority to items with tangible consequences
- Focus on what requires immediate action or decision
- Complete elimination of courtesy formulas and digressions
- Conversion of extended paragraphs into concise single points

FORMAT:
1. ESSENCE:
- [Main message in 10-15 words].

2. KEY POINTS:
- [Point 1]
- [Point 2]
- [...]

3. NEXT STEPS:
- [Action 1]
- [Action 2]

4. TIMING:
- [Dates and deadlines in DD/MM/YYYY format].

E-MAIL: [Insert e-mail here]

So far we have explored how AI can optimize the content of communications-from creation to evaluation, from translation to restructuring and synthesis. These approaches significantly improve the informational quality of individual messages, but do not address systemic inefficiencies in the communication flow. The next step in the evolution of digital communication is to automate not only content generation, but the entire information management process. By moving from message optimization to communication system optimization, we can apply AI to automatically route communications, creating a more efficient and responsive information ecosystem.

6. Routing email to the best recipient based on its content.

Information flow optimization shifts the focus from content optimization to intelligent management of the communication process. This advanced feature uses semantic analysis to determine not only subject matter but also communicative intent, automatically routing messages to the most appropriate resources to handle them. The result is significantly faster response times and more efficient distribution of the communication workload within the organization.

Automatic email routing represents one of the most practical and useful applications of generative AI in the business and organizational context. Every day, companies and institutions receive an enormous amount of e-mail, many of which need to be assigned to the person or department best suited to respond. Manual assignment is often inefficient, error-prone and delayed. This is where generative AI comes in, capable of analyzing the content of emails, understanding their meaning and sorting them to the most appropriate recipient in real time.

Most popular customer service management platforms have or are integrating generative AI capabilities to improve their content recognition capabilities and thus the proper routing to the contact person who can respond faster and more effectively to the email.

If we have a need to automatically interpret the content of an e-mail we receive to route it to another mailbox, we can experiment with this functionality with several solutions even less complex and expensive than the platforms mentioned before.

The solution I will describe will obviously not have all the functionality of commercial platforms and integrations with *ticketing* and other platforms, which are often essential for large companies also for analyzing customer data, complaints and *customer base sentiment* in general.

But for experimental use, professionals or companies without the above-mentioned needs can already be an answer to their needs.

To create this automation we can get help from MAKE (https://www.make.com/en), a platform that allows the creation of automations by also accessing external resources such as ChatGPT. The platform also has a free subscription plan. We can use the platform's AI Assistant to enter the following *prompt*:

***Prompt*: https://tinyurl.com/yp5paw2y**

I need to develop an automated e-mail classification and forwarding system that leverages ChatGPT capabilities to analyze incoming e-mail content and intelligently route messages to the appropriate department mailbox.

System requirements:
-The system should analyze the complete e-mail (subject + body) to determine its primary purpose.
-Based on content analysis, each e-mail should be categorized into one of three classifications:
1.Claims/Support issues (e.g., complaints, refund requests, product issues)
2.Technical inquiries (e.g., specifications, integration questions, troubleshooting)
3.Commercial matters (e.g., pricing requests, sales inquiries, partnership opportunities)
-Once classified, each e-mail should be automatically forwarded to the corresponding departmental mailbox:
-claims@company.com
-technical@company.com
-commercial@company.com
-The system should maintain a log of all classifications for quality assurance
Edge cases with uncertain classification should be flagged for human review and forwarded to human@company.com mailbox

This *prompt* requires the platform to create an automation that starting from the received e-mail, using the capabilities of an LLM such as ChatGPT analyzes its content and subject matter and depending on this categorizes it as an e-mail intended for the company's e-mail handling complaints (claims@company.com) or technical issues (technical@company.com) or the commercial department (commercial@company.com) and forwards it to the correct mailbox.

The automation will need to keep track of what it handles and if it has doubts about the classification, it should ask for human intervention by sending the e-mail to human@company.com.

Make's assistant, despite having next to its name the words BETA letting us know that it is in experimentation has achieved at the first shot without the need to refine the *prompt* the desired automation, minus the log functionality, which it has graphically represented very clearly as follows:

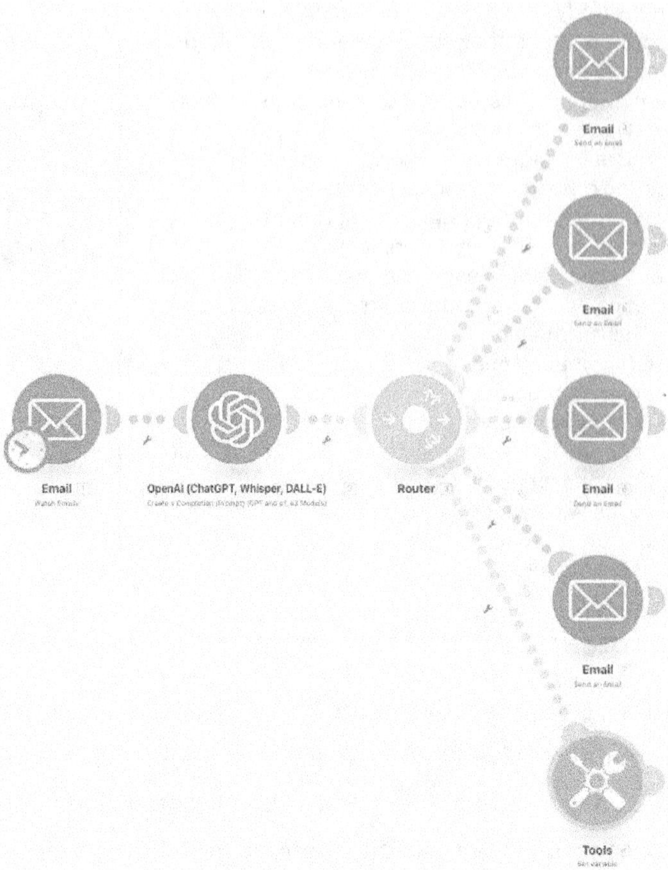

To complete the automation, all we have to do is to click on each icon and enter the necessary parameters in a simple and intuitive way: in the first icon on the left, "E-mail" we will have to enter the data of our e-mail provider (e.g., Gmail), in the icon with the ChatGPT logo the API of OpenAI should be entered, which is obtained by subscribing to at least "Plus". In the four icons labeled "E-mail "on the right we will need to enter the data of the destination mailboxes. The "Tools" icon is the system's attempt to create a variable to be used for storing the forward operations performed.

The result of the *prompt* is very good, all that remains is to refine the unfinished parts without the need to write any lines of code.

There are numerous examples and tutorials within the platform itself that make this work quick and easy.

Automation like this can also be done with other platforms such as Zapier.com.

If you are in a Microsoft ecosystem you are helped by Power Automate, which among its ready-made automation templates has one that suits us "Classify and route e-mails using GPT."

In this case you do not need to have a ChatGPT subscription to use its libraries (API) because Power Automate already has a component that interfaces with ChatGPT.

In the following image the flow diagram created with the template, ready-made:

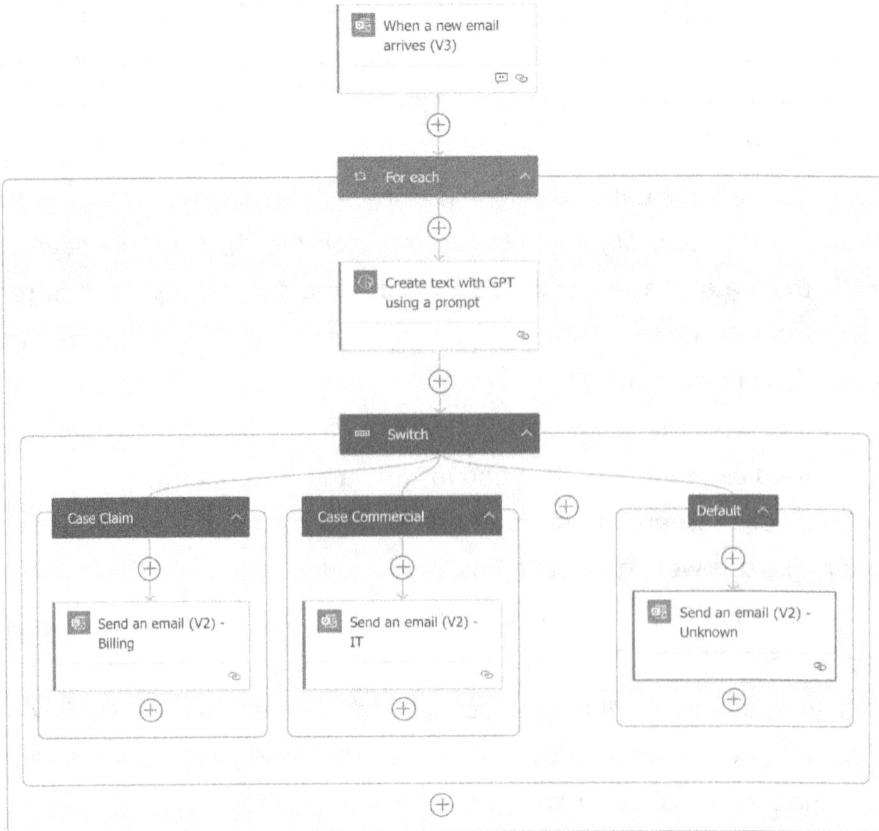

Automated routing represents a significant step forward in optimizing communication flows, ensuring that each message reaches the resource best suited to handle it. However, there is an additional level of automation that can radically transform individual productivity: automatic response generation. This evolution completes the cycle of communication automation, from analysis to action, with varying degrees of human oversight.

7. Automatically responding to e-mail for us with or without our supervision

Response automation represents the most advanced level of AI integration into the communication process, where the system not only analyzes and routes, but autonomously generates appropriate responses. This feature, which can operate with varying degrees of human supervision, is particularly effective for recurring communications or communications that follow predictable patterns. Stylistic and contextual personalization ensures that the responses generated maintain the authenticity of the communicative voice of the organization or individual.

The idea of an AI capable of relieving me of the task of responding to so-called "service" emails-those that require only a few minutes of my attention to formulate a response-is particularly appealing.

To meet this need, I have implemented a system, currently in the experimental stage, that requires my approval before sending. This tool, based on my communication style, automatically prepares possible responses to e-mails. Soon it will be able to offer me multiple options to choose from, making *task* completion as simple as giving an OK or selecting the preferred alternative.

The main challenge has been teaching the AI my writing style, both in Italian and English, so that it can faithfully replicate it in its responses.

Although I have taken out numerous subscriptions to the most renowned generative AI systems and have access to Copilot in Enterprise environment, when it comes to handling extremely sensitive data, I prefer to use *open-source* versions of LLM running locally on my computer, equipped with processors specifically for parallel computing, accepting its inherent limitations.

I therefore exported years of correspondence in Italian and English from my e-mail *client* into several PDF files, providing them as "*training data*" to the LLM installed on my device. The goal was to create a *prompt* capable of accurately describing my writing style and, consequently, my characteristic communicative approach.

The system successfully produced the following *prompt*:

***Prompt*: https://tinyurl.com/mr7hwx33**

Compose an e-mail response that reflects my communication style as Executive Vice President. The response must be in the same language as the original e-mail (Italian or English).

The main characteristics of my style are:
- Efficiency and conciseness: Short but complete messages that get straight to the point without prolixity
- Results orientation: Constant focus on business goals, metrics and performance
- Direct tone but always professional and respectful
- Opening with "Hello [name]" and closing with "Thank you, hello" or English equivalent
- Analytical precision, especially when dealing with financial data
- Strategic thinking that goes beyond immediate issues
- Constructive feedback with concrete suggestions when needed
- Formulation of clear requests with specific timelines
- Pragmatism in approaching problems
- Appropriate use of priorities and sense of urgency

The typical structure of my e-mails is:
1. Informal but professional opening
2. Direct and logically organized message body (with bulleted lists for complex information)
3. Conclusion with any requests or expected actions
4. Short and cordial closing

For English-language e-mails, maintain the same direct and concise style, with a slightly more formal but still approachable tone.

I then used a template within Power Automate called "Replay to a customer using GPT," modifying it specifically for my needs.

The workflow works like this:

1. When a new e-mail arrives on my Outlook account ("When a new e-mail arrives"),
2. the system retrieves my full profile on Office 365 ("Get my profile") and
3. generates a response text by processing both the subject and the body of the received e-mail, using the *prompt* mentioned above in the form "Create text with GPT using a *prompt*."
4. Next, an e-mail is sent to me with the prepared draft response ("Start and wait for an approval text"), allowing me to check it and, if satisfactory, approve it with a simple OK, after which it is immediately sent ("Reply to e-mail").

Below is the flow just described:

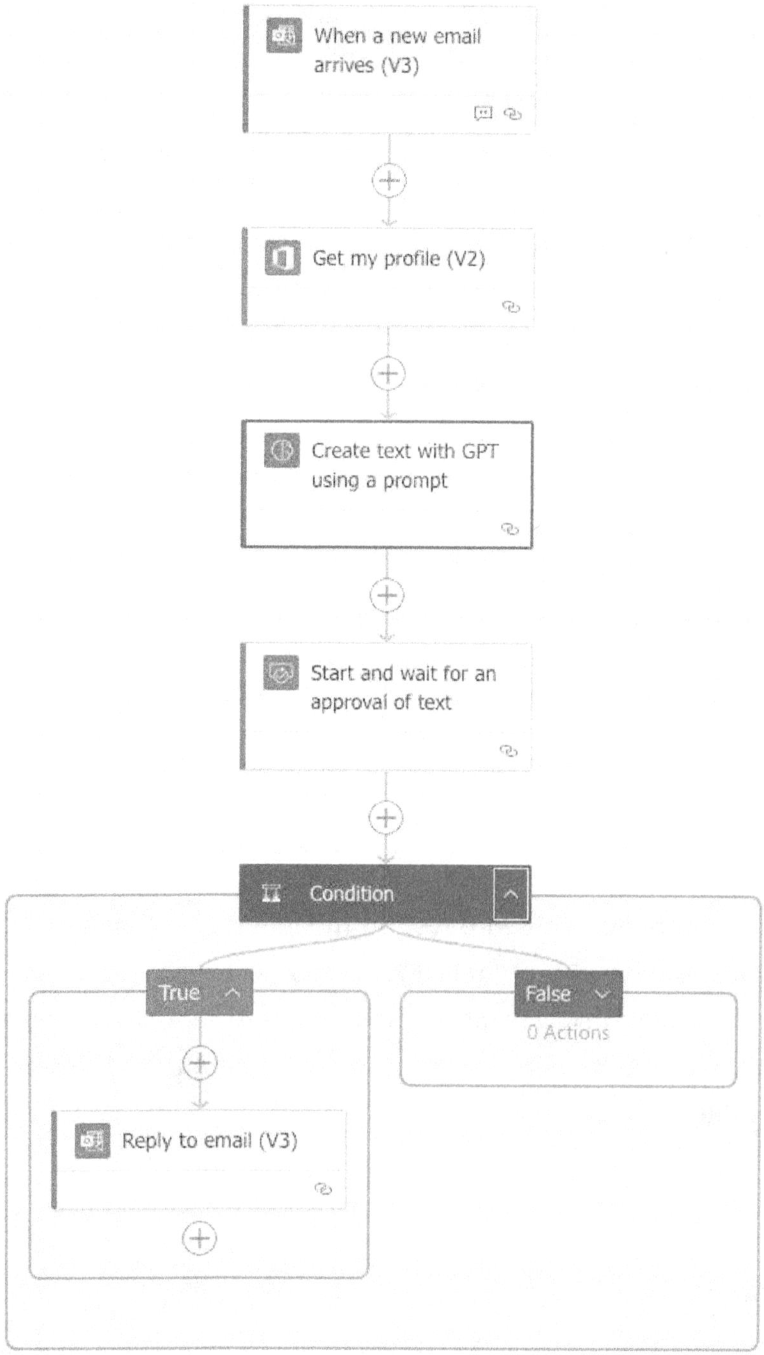
When a new email arrives (V3)
Get my profile (V2)
Create text with GPT using a prompt
Start and wait for an approval of text
Condition
True
False
0 Actions
Reply to email (V3)

It is possible to further refine this automation by providing the form preparing the reply not only with GPT's libraries but also with the historical database of my replies in PDF format. This approach produces higher quality responses that are extremely more faithful to my style, although it requires Power Automate to have access to the aforementioned PDF files.

Alternatives to the Microsoft ecosystem, such as Make.com, Airtable, Zapier, and a properly configured GPT, achieve similar results, with the added benefit of being able to easily set up the system to generate multiple response options to choose from.

Privacy, security and governance considerations in communication automation

The integration of AI into business communication processes, while offering undeniable benefits in terms of efficiency and quality, raises important issues related to data management, privacy and corporate governance.

Using proprietary cloud-based AI models (e.g., ChatGPT, Claude, Gemini, Deepseek, Perplexity, etc.) to process business communications involves the transmission of potentially sensitive data to external systems. This practice requires careful risk assessment achievable through:

1. **Classification of communications:**

- Public communications: low risk, manageable with any solution.
- Generic internal communications: moderate risk, evaluate vendor's data retention policies.
- Strategic communications or those containing intellectual property: high risk, favor "in-house" solutions.
- Personal or sensitive data: critical risk, require fully controlled solutions.

2. **Layered deployment model**

The previously described case of using locally executed *open source* models is a prudent approach for highly sensitive communications. A complete *framework* should include:

- Tier 1: generic low-risk communications -> cloud-based systems but guaranteeing in their terms of use/privacy the ability to inhibit the use of our data to train their models (option usually available for paid usage plans).
- Level 2: Internal communications with moderate sensitivity -> use of enterprise solutions (e.g., MS Copilot) with detailed terms of use/privacy that ensure maximum levels of confidentiality to our data.
- Level 3: communications containing proprietary information -> use of local solutions without Internet access (*on-premises*).

- Level 4: communications with highly sensitive or regulated data -> I do not recommend its inclusion in generative AI systems, to possibly evaluate solutions as for Level 3.

3. **Regulatory compliance.**

Communications automation must operate in compliance with applicable regulations:

- Privacy (e.g., GDPR (EU)):
    - Ensure that *prompts* do not contain unnecessary personal data.
    - Implement *data minimization* mechanisms in integrations.
    - Ensure that data subjects' rights (access, rectification, deletion) can be exercised.

- Retention:
    - Maintain records of all automatically generated communications.
    - Document decision making and approvals.
    - Ensure availability for internal and external audits.

4. **Governance and Oversight.**

An effective governance system should:

- Include clear policies.
    - Define which communications can be automated and at what level.
    - Establish minimum human supervision requirements for each category.

  - Document escalation processes for ambiguous cases.

- Training and awareness:
  - Educate staff on the limitations and potential of AI systems.
  - Develop critical skills for evaluating generated outputs.
  - Promote a culture of shared responsibility.

- Continuous monitoring and improvement:
  - Implement random quality audits.
  - Periodically analyze the effectiveness and appropriateness of automated communications.
  - Update processes and policies based on feedback and technological evolution.

The experience described using locally executed *open source* LLMs for sensitive communications is a concrete example of applying the principle of proportionality in balancing innovation and protection. This approach demonstrates how advanced technologies can be integrated into communication processes while maintaining adequate control over the associated risks.

Decision-making framework: how much and how to automate communication

The effective implementation of AI in business communication requires a structured approach to determine the right level of automation for each communication context. The following decision-making *framework* offers practical criteria to guide these choices.

COMMUNICATION ASSESSMENT MATRIX

Dimension	Manual Management	AI Assistance	Supervised Automation	Complete Automation
Criticality	Strategic, legal communications or those with significant impacts	Important communications with predefined templates	Standard communications with limited variability	Highly predictable routine communications
Personalization	High personalization required and recipient knowledge needed	Personalization needed on predictable structure	Minimal personalization and few elements	Minimal or no personalization necessary
Frequency	Rare or unique	Occasional	Regular	Frequent and repetitive
Complexity	Multidimensional, non-standard or variable on multiple levels, comparison and structuring required	Moderate, with moderate structural variability	Structured with few variables	Highly structured and standardized
Sensitivity	Highly confidential and sensitive	Moderately confidential	Low sensitivity	Not sensitive

Structured Decision Making.

- Communication analysis:
    - Classify the type of communication according to matrix dimensions.
    - Identify recurring patterns and potential templates.
    - Assess the risk-benefit ratio of automation.

- Define the appropriate level:
    - Level 0 - Manual handling: strategic, highly personalized or sensitive communications.
    - Level 1 - AI assisted: AI proposes drafts that require substantial revision.
    - Level 2 - Supervised automation: the AI generates complete responses that require approval.
    - Level 3 - Sample-supervised automation: automated responses with periodic checks.
    - Level 4 - Full automation: *end-to-end* management without human intervention.

- Progressive implementation:
    - Always start at the most conservative level.
    - Monitor quality and appropriateness.
    - Gradual evolution to more automation when justified by results.

- Continuous review:
    - Periodic analysis of communication effectiveness.

- Evaluation of feedback from recipients and *stakeholders*.
- Adjustment of automation level based on results.

APPLICATION EXAMPLES

Communication Type	Recommended Level	Rationale
Product information requests	Level 3-4	Standardized information, high frequency, low sensitivity
Follow-up after meetings	Level 2	Predictable structure but variable content, requires accuracy
Project update communications	Level 1-2	Moderate complexity, personalized elements but common structure
Commercial negotiations	Level 0-1	High criticality, requires context understanding and strategy
Complaint management	Level 1-2	Emotional sensitivity, but with predictable elements and recurring patterns

This *framework* enables a rational, phased approach to communication automation, maximizing efficiency benefits while maintaining control over the quality and appropriateness of interactions.

AI as an empowering tool, not a replacement: the right balance between automation and personal development

If we pay attention to the wording in the lower right corner that Claude brings up after responding to one of our *prompts*, we will read that Claude can make mistakes and suggests double-checking his answers.

This wording reminds us that it is always critical to review content created, edited, or corrected by AI, and it is even more important when it comes to email content.

By the same token, we must be careful that this valuable help from AI does not diminish our abilities-English is not my native language and I have not had the opportunity to live in English-speaking countries for long periods of time, and keeping myself practiced with English on a daily basis is crucial for me. Therefore, I usually write almost all of my e-mails in English in my own hand, and then ask the AI for a grammar check, requesting that he point out errors and suggested corrections. Later, I also ask for its version for purely educational purposes.

AI must enhance our capabilities, not deplete them; we must be the ones to strike the right balance between automation and "human touch," consciously choosing when and how to use AI support.

AI, if used properly, can transform the way we handle our electronic correspondence, freeing up valuable time to focus on what really matters: collaboration and goal achievement.

Metrics

My strain as an engineer leads me to measure everything, and since introducing AI into my e-mail management I have gone from about 3 hours a day devoted to mailbox management to about an hour, going from an average response in 24 hours to a response in the same (calendar) day.

I have no metrics to share on quality but I am convinced that my communication has improved. I infer this from two factors: I am receiving fewer requests for clarification and, at the same time, getting results more in line with my expectations. Once we produce efficiency and save time it is up to each of us, day by day, to decide where to direct this gained time. Some days it may be going back to the family earlier, going for an extra run a week or greater volume of work managed. For this there is no AI that can help us; it is our choice alone.

Evolution of corporate communication: future prospects

The corporate communication landscape is undergoing a radical transformation thanks to AI. By looking at current trends and projecting them into the near future, we can outline an evolution that will profoundly change the way we interact in professional settings.

Stylistic customization represents perhaps the most promising frontier in this evolution. Tools such as Claude's "Styles" feature and the persistent memory systems implemented in both ChatGPT and Claude are creating a new communication paradigm. During my experimentation with these systems, I have noticed how communicative effectiveness increases significantly when AI learns and replicates our personal style. It is not simply copying words or phrases, but capturing nuances, tone, and argumentative structures that characterize our professional voice. These systems continually observe and learn, refining their ability to mirror not only our vocabulary, but also our conceptual approach to communication.

In parallel, we are seeing the integration of AI generative features directly into everyday content production tools. Adobe has introduced its Firefly throughout the Creative Suite, while Canva has implemented Magic Studio - systems that are democratizing the creation of integrated visual and textual content. In my daily workflow, the use of these tools has dramatically reduced the time it takes to go from concept to final communication while maintaining stylistic consistency across different channels and formats.

The barrier between communication channels is gradually dissolving, replaced by fluid conversational ecosystems where interaction proceeds seamlessly between e-mail, collaborative documents, and messaging platforms. AI assistants are evolving from simple reactive tools to proactive communication partners, capable of suggesting not only responses but also strategic communication opportunities based on observed patterns and organizational goals.

The real potential of this evolution lies not so much in operational efficiency-already significant-as in the ability to free up cognitive resources to focus on uniquely human aspects of communication: empathy, strategic creativity, and authentic relationship building. Organizations that can integrate these technologies while simultaneously developing hybrid skills in their teams will create a substantial competitive advantage, transforming communication from an operational necessity to a strategic lever of innovation.

Chapter Summary.

Generative AI has revolutionized digital communications management, offering concrete solutions to convert information overload into competitive advantage. This chapter explored a comprehensive *framework* for implementing these technologies in everyday communication.

Main applications and benefits

- Content optimization:
  - Assisted generation of personalized and contextually appropriate emails.
  - Stylistic and tonal analysis for consistent and culturally sensitive communications.
  - Advanced multilingual support that preserves nuance and communicative register.
  - Restructuring to maximize clarity, synthesis and communicative impact.
  - Informational distillation from extended and complex communications.

- Process automation:
  - Intelligent routing based on semantic content analysis.
  - Supervised generation of responses consistent with personal style.
  - Integration with existing platforms through *no-code/low-code* solutions.
  - Progressive implementation system adaptable to different levels of complexity.

- Documented success metrics:
    - 66% reduction in time spent on e-mail management (from 3 to 1 hour/day).
    - Significant improvement in response time.
    - Reduction in clarification requests due to more effective communications.
    - Increased time available for high-value strategic activities.

Critical considerations.

- Human-machine balance:
    - AI as a tool for enhancing, not replacing skills.
    - Strategic human oversight in automated processes.
    - Use of automation as an opportunity for professional development.

- Privacy and security:
    - Differentiated approach based on sensitivity of communications.
    - Critical evaluation of cloud models vs. on-premise solutions.
    - Effective governance to ensure compliance and control.

Recommended implementation path.

- Initial phase: introduce composition assistance and analysis tools.
- Intermediate phase: implement automated synthesis and structural optimization.
- Advanced phase: develop process automations for routing and response.
- Ongoing governance: continuously monitor, evaluate and refine integration.

This evolution in corporate communication management represents not only an increase in operational efficiency, but a strategic rethinking of how information flows within and outside the organization, with significant impacts on the quality of decisions, customer and employee satisfaction, and work-life balance.

CHAPTER 4

AI FOR OPERATIONAL OPTIMIZATION: PLANNING AND CONTROL

AI represents a valuable ally in the organizational and planning spheres. With the ability to analyze large amounts of data, generate action plans, simulate alternative scenarios and, produce content, these models support practitioners and managers in developing more informed, faster and more focused strategies. Implementing generative AI in a business or institutional setting means enabling more advanced forms of collective intelligence, optimizing processes ranging from logistics to administration, from production to human resource management.

With proper human oversight, the technology can contribute significantly to achieving tangible results, reducing the risk of error and maximizing overall efficiency. The gradual and conscious adoption of such solutions, coupled with a corporate culture that values continuing education and interdisciplinary collaboration, will enable the full potential of AI to be exploited at every stage of organization and planning.

The real breakthrough will come with the availability of easily accessible and configurable AI agent systems.

As AI expert Kavita Ganesan states in her book "The Business Case for AI"[22] we need to analyze the context where we want to adopt AI and understand, if necessary with expert support, whether AI is indeed the solution or is it sufficient to apply "traditional" software engineering techniques[23] and/or Robotic Process Automation (RPA).

Below are some examples, not exhaustive but that I have had the opportunity to see up close of applications of AI, specifically

---

[22] https://kavita-ganesan.com/the-business-case-for-ai/

[23] **software engineering**: The discipline that applies systematic engineering principles to the design, development, testing, and maintenance of software, combining structured methodologies with technical creativity to create reliable and scalable applications.

applications of *machine learning*, *deep learning* and generative AI in the following areas:

- Production quality control/defect identification.
- Predictive maintenance.
- Optimization of service delivery.

4.1 Quality control in production and defect identification

The introduction of AI in industrial production is generating extraordinary benefits, with the peculiarity of being able to scientifically measure the return on investment.

During my professional experience, I have had the privilege of closely observing the evolution of quality control in manufacturing, following its technological path from the first neural networks to *deep learning*.

Innovation in the Steel Industry: AI revolutionizes Quality Control.

At the beating heart of the modern steel industry, AI is redefining quality control paradigms, bringing a silent but profound revolution to one of the most traditional sectors of heavy industry.

The system I will tell you about is a cutting-edge system that challenges the limits of technology, operating in hostile conditions that until recently seemed impossible to handle.

Imagine a production line where steel is hurtling along at dizzying speeds, exceeding 100 meters per second-faster than many high-speed trains. In this extreme environment, the AI system performs continuous and meticulous monitoring, maintaining accuracy at the millimeter level. It is like having thousands of expert eyes simultaneously scrutinizing every inch of material, never getting tired or losing focus.

The real magic of this technology lies in its ability to operate under extreme conditions. The system analyzes steel while it is still at temperatures approaching 1,000 degrees Celsius, an environment where most traditional technologies would instantly fail. To make this possible, the team developed a complex architecture that integrates specialized optical systems and dedicated lighting designed specifically for these extreme conditions.

But the real value of this innovation goes far beyond mere quality control. The system doesn't just identify imperfections: it classifies them in real time, enabling intelligent production management. Rather than having to discard entire batches of material or, even worse, stop production, the system allows non-conforming products to be automatically classified as second-rate material, optimizing resource use and reducing waste.

This innovative approach represents a significant step toward sustainability in a traditionally *energy-intensive* industry such as the steel industry. Reducing waste, optimizing processes and minimizing production interruptions contribute to more efficient use of energy resources, demonstrating how AI can be a valuable ally in the green transition in even the most challenging industries.

The implementation of this technology required a multidisciplinary approach, combining expertise in AI, advanced optics, materials engineering and steel process. The result is a system that not only improves the quality of the final product, but fundamentally transforms the entire production process, making it more efficient, sustainable and competitive.

The earliest implementations date back several years and were based on simple neural networks that could learn from their mistakes, and production cycles upon production cycles improved the ability to identify imperfections from images. With the availability of large amounts of images, the appropriate computing power has shifted to *deep learning-based* solutions with very high levels of reliability, close to 100 percent.

This solution demonstrates how AI, when applied with vision and expertise, can overcome challenges that seemed insurmountable, opening new frontiers in industrial process optimization. It is a concrete example of how technological innovation can reconcile productivity needs with sustainability imperatives, charting the way forward for the steel industry.

The migration of intelligence: how AI solutions evolve across industries, from steel to pulp.

The versatility of AI finds one of its most interesting expressions in its ability to transfer skills and solutions between seemingly distant industries. The same technology developed for quality control in the steel industry has found a surprising and highly effective application in the food sector, particularly in pasta production, demonstrating an outstanding example of technological "*cross-fertilization*."

In pasta production, the challenges are different but equally critical. Instead of monitoring imperfections in the glowing steel, the AI system oversees food safety by identifying potential contamination between different production batches. This is especially crucial in modern production lines, where different pasta formats are processed sequentially on the same machines. The risk of residues from one format becoming trapped in the machinery and then being released during the production of a subsequent batch poses a significant food safety challenge.

The most critical scenario arises when, for example, a larger pasta format could end up in a packet of pasta intended for infants-a situation that could have serious consequences for both consumer safety and brand reputation. The AI system addresses this challenge with the same millimeter precision developed for the steel industry, but adapted to the specific needs of the food industry.

The system implements a tripartite approach to quality management: it ensures food safety through constant monitoring, protects brand value by preventing potential incidents, and contributes to sustainability by optimizing the rejection process. When a noncompliant item is identified, an automatic ejection mechanism removes the problematic product along with a minimal amount of compliant product, perfectly balancing safety and sustainability.

The most recent evolution of this technology is manifested in the integration of generative AI, which takes automation and optimization to the next level. These advanced systems are not limited to quality control, but extend to the entire value chain, from production planning to resource management. Generative AI analyzes massive amounts of operational data, generates predictive scenarios and suggests optimization strategies, supporting managers in decision making with evidence-based insights.

This integrated approach to industrial management represents a qualitative leap in the evolution of collective business intelligence. Technology does not replace human judgment, but enhances it by providing analysis and forecasting tools that enable more informed and timely decisions. The key to success lies in the gradual and conscious implementation of these solutions, accompanied by a strong investment in staff training and the promotion of a corporate culture that values innovation and interdisciplinary collaboration.

The integration of AI in these different industry contexts demonstrates how technology can adapt and evolve to meet industry-specific challenges, while maintaining as a constant the ability to optimize processes, ensure quality and promote sustainability. It is a concrete example of how technological innovation can cross traditional industry boundaries, creating unexpected synergies and opening new frontiers of development.

Defect identification technologies applied in the automotive field

In the automotive industry, the detection and documentation of damage to new and used cars during storage has historically been a significant operational challenge. This issue has found a cutting-edge solution through the implementation of AI-based systems, transforming a traditionally manual process into an automated and objective workflow.

Before reaching dealerships, vehicles transit through vast outdoor storage yards, where they remain vulnerable to multiple types of damage: weather events such as hailstorms, accidental damage during handling, and other potential hazards that compromise the cars' integrity. When a car arrived at the dealer with damage that had not been previously documented, legal disputes and litigation were frequently triggered among the various actors in the distribution chain, generating inefficiencies and additional costs.

To address this critical issue in a systematic way, an intelligent monitoring system that acts as a "digital watchdog" was developed. Strategically placed at the exit points of forecourts, this system performs real-time multi-parameter analysis of each moving car, accurately identifying different categories of damage:

- Dents on the bodywork.
- Paint scratches.
- Damage to the wheels.
- Compromise to optical assemblies.
- Damage to windows.

A distinguishing feature of particular technological significance lies in its brandable configuration, similar to a conventional camera, which allows it to be used even by unskilled personnel. This feature gives the system extraordinary operational flexibility, making the inspection independent of the fixed infrastructure and significantly expanding its application scenarios: from manufacturers' yards to car rental fleets, from insurance processes to boarding/disembarking operations on car transporters, with the possibility of being operated directly by the drivers responsible for the transport.

A particularly significant application case involved the management of hail damage, which is a seasonal issue but one with considerable economic impact. During periods characterized by severe weather events, damage assessment centers frequently experienced operational overloads, generating significant slowdowns through the entire automotive supply chain.

To effectively address this specific need, an innovative tool based on two complementary technologies was implemented:

Deflectometry - This advanced methodology projects calibrated light *patterns* onto the vehicle surface and analyzes the resulting reflection characteristics. The operating principle can be conceptualized as observing the reflection of a grid on a metal surface: in the presence of deformation, the reflected *pattern* manifests characteristic distortions. The system exploits these physical principles to identify surface distortions even in the millimeter range.

Fish-eye camera - This specialized acquisition device features an extremely wide viewing angle, with optical characteristics inspired by fish vision (hence the name). This configuration allows simultaneous coverage of large portions of the vehicle, facilitating precise spatial localization of detected damage.

The overall system architecture has been optimized for portability and operational simplicity, enabling:

- Rapid assessments with high accuracy.
- Instant documentation of detected damage.

- Significant contraction *of assesment* times.
- High accuracy in economic quantifications.

The benefits of implementing this technological approach are multidimensional:

- Minimization *of inter-stakeholder* litigation.
- Acceleration of claims management flows.
- Increased transparency along the supply chain.
- Economic optimization for all stakeholders.
- Improved overall experience for the end user.

This system represents a paradigm case of applying AI to solving concrete problems in the *automotive* industry, transforming a process traditionally characterized by subjectivity and latencies into a fast, objective and highly accurate operational flow. The technology has not simply improved operational efficiency, but has helped build a relational ecosystem based on greater trust among all participants in the automotive supply chain.

The interface's portability and intuitiveness features have made the system particularly effective in critical emergency scenarios, such as in the immediate aftermath of intense hail events, when it becomes necessary to quickly assess damage on high volumes of vehicles. This timely response capability has demonstrated a substantial impact in managing crisis situations and minimizing the economic consequences of extreme weather events.

In insurance, the system incorporates an advanced component that involves entering vehicle information into the vehicle's *Digital Product Passport*. The *Digital Product Passport*, formalized in the EU's *Ecodesign* Regulation (ESPR 2022), is a strategic element of the European *Green Deal* within the *Circular Economy Action Plan*.

This "digital passport" constitutes a standardized *repository* that collects and tracks all relevant product lifecycle information, ensuring its authenticity and verifiability. In the context of vehicles, damage data, appropriately certified through the AI system, contributes to the reduction of insurance fraud (e.g., in cases where hail damage is declared, compensation is obtained from the insurance company without making the repair, and then a claim is reopened at the next hailstorm even in the absence of new damage).

For more details: https://www.qbt.ch/it/

4.2 Predictive maintenance: innovation and business continuity

The ability to schedule maintenance work in advance and accurately, minimizing the impact on business operations, is a tremendous competitive advantage in the industrial sector.

This capability translates into significant economic value for many industries, while ensuring business continuity of critical systems as well as positive impacts on sustainability.

From harmonic analysis to Edge Computing: evolution of predictive maintenance of uninterruptible power supplies

An exemplary case of this application concerns uninterruptible power supplies[24] . By combining decades of know-how from experts in the field with AI algorithms, a system has been developed that can predict with high accuracy the remaining time before a potential failure, based on the analysis of the harmonics[25] generated by the devices themselves. This innovation allows users of uninterruptible power supplies to anticipate potential malfunctions and plan for preventive replacement of critical equipment.

Unlike the previously mentioned cases in industrial production, where the main input was images, in this context the system is based on the processing of a considerable amount of data coming directly from the uninterruptible power supplies, integrated with environmental parameters of their operating environment.

---

[24] **Uninterruptible** Power Supply: Devices that provide *backup* power when the main power fails, protecting electronic equipment from sudden shutdowns and data loss.
[25] **Harmonics**: Distortions in the electrical waves that uninterruptible power supplies generate during operation. These *patterns* change specifically when components begin to deteriorate, serving as early signs of malfunction.

This project, developed several years ago, faced significant challenges related to the secure transmission of data outside the business contexts where the UPSs were located, which was necessary to access the computational resources required by the processing of large amounts of data by AI algorithms. This complexity was mainly due to the high security standards characteristic of enterprise infrastructures.

Currently, thanks to technological evolution, the solution has come to fruition with *AI edge computing*[26] , which allows a substantial part of the processing to be performed directly on the sensors used for data collection, leveraging processors with architectures specifically designed for AI applications.

This evolution represents a significant step forward in optimizing predictive maintenance processes by combining operational efficiency and data security.

From expert systems to deep learning: a quantum leap in rail maintenance

In the railway field, particularly in locomotives, I have had the opportunity to observe the evolution of predictive maintenance systems, starting from those based on expert systems (2005) to the current implementation based on *deep learning*.

The expert system implemented initially translated human experience into codified operating rules. For example, maintainers had

---

[26] **AI Edge Computing**: A system that runs artificial intelligence algorithms directly on local devices (such as sensors) rather than on centralized cloud servers, reducing latency and improving privacy and energy efficiency.

found that when a particular system manifested a malfunction, almost invariably, after a specific time interval, another related system would also show a failure.

This empirical heritage was translated by the expert system into a procedural rule that required preventive replacement of both devices within a defined time interval from the first manifestation of failure.

However, the expert systems approach showed significant adaptability limitations when some apparatuses were upgraded during the locomotive life cycle, a substantial rewriting of the rules and decision tree structures that characterized these systems became necessary, highlighting their inherent rigidity.

In contrast, the current *deep learning-based* approach has demonstrated significantly greater flexibility and adaptability. The system is able to automatically incorporate new data sources, maintaining or even improving its predictive capabilities after the installation of new apparatus, especially when these provide additional parameters useful for algorithmic analysis.

Innovation in real estate management: AI-based predictive maintenance system

In the dynamic landscape of modern property management, a revolutionary predictive maintenance system has been developed and implemented that is radically transforming the approach to property *asset* management. This innovative system integrates AI (*machine learning* and *deep learning*) technologies to create a comprehensive and sophisticated *data-driven* process.

The heart of the system lies in its ability to continuously acquire and analyze data from a distributed network of IoT sensors installed on the buildings' technical systems. This data is integrated with the history of previous maintenance and interventions, creating a rich information pool that feeds our predictive models. The system monitors critical operating parameters in real time, also considering environmental conditions and usage *patterns of* the facilities.

Through the implementation of advanced *machine learning* algorithms, the system creates customized predictive models for different types of plants, analyzing correlations between multiple variables and identifying anomalies and degradation *patterns* early on.

This predictive capability translates into automated planning of maintenance interventions, optimizing maintenance resources and costs, and ensuring intelligent management of spare parts inventory and efficient coordination of intervention teams.

The benefits of this innovative approach are tangible and significant: a 40-60% reduction in sudden failures and a 25-35% decrease in maintenance costs, accompanied by an optimization of the lifecycle of equipment and a better allocation of maintenance resources. On the sustainability front, the system contributes to the reduction of energy consumption by optimizing performance, minimizing waste and inefficiency, and extending plant life, resulting in a positive impact on the environment.

AI plays a key role in this system through *deep learning* algorithms for predictive analysis, self-adaptive models that improve over time, expert systems for fault diagnosis, and neural networks for performance optimization. The system integrates seamlessly with existing infrastructure, interfacing with *building management* systems (BMS)[27] and offering a cloud platform for remote access, complete with mobile

[27] **BMS**: Intelligent platforms that integrate and automate critical building systems (HVAC, lighting, security, energy) through a network of interconnected sensors, optimizing comfort and energy consumption.

apps for technicians and managers and customizable *dashboards* for different *stakeholders*.

The impact on business is multidimensional. Financially, the system delivers significant ROI in the medium term, accompanied by reduced operating costs and increased cost predictability. Operationally, it results in increased process efficiency, reduced plant downtime, and improved coordination of activities. Strategically, it provides a major competitive advantage in the marketplace, improves risk management, increases *asset* value, and enhances customer satisfaction.

This innovative approach to predictive maintenance represents not only a technological evolution, but a real transformation in the way real estate management is conceived. By combining cutting-edge technologies with a deep understanding of the needs of the industry, the system delivers concrete and measurable results, laying the foundation for smarter, more efficient and sustainable management of real estate assets.

4.3 Optimizing service delivery

In shipping, intelligent navigation: how AI optimizes routes and reduces environmental impact

The fusion of AI and maritime domain knowledge finds effective application in SERTICA Performance, a technology solution developed by integrating naval engineering expertise with advanced AI technologies. Designed specifically for commercial fleet operators, this platform represents a systemic approach to optimizing maritime operations.

Based on a scalable cloud architecture, SERTICA Performance captures and processes real-time data streams from shipboard systems, transforming them into actionable information through intuitive *dashboards*. Ship command thus gains immediate visibility into critical parameters:

- Energy performance with continuous monitoring of consumption.
- Dynamic assessment of operational and environmental risks.
- Functional status of systems and predictive maintenance planning.
- Comparative analyses between vessels in the fleet.

The solution is divided into specialized and complementary modules:

- ***Advanced Analytics***: supports decision-making processes through comparative analysis of fleet performance, monitoring of post-hull degradation, and tracking of Key Performance Indicators essential. The interface allows multiple data visualizations through scatter plots, trends, and histograms.

- ***Trim Assistant***: scientifically determines optimal trim considering speed, draft, trim angle and water depth, with expert support performing computational fluid dynamics simulations and custom analysis.
- Propulsion ***Assistant***: monitors propulsive efficiency by integrating hull, propeller and engine parameters, including functionality to build hydrodynamic models of the vessel.
- ***Geofencing & Rules Editor***: implements georeferenced virtual perimeters that can be configured directly on a map, with rule definition and automatic actions triggered when entering or leaving designated areas.
- ***Reporting & Dashboards***: visualizes fleet performance through reports and *dashboards* powered by real-time data, with instant notifications of anomalies for timely interventions.
- ***Data Collector***: manages information on components, locations, interventions, certifications and spare parts in a structured way, providing essential insight for maintenance and procurement processes.
- **Voyage**: offers advanced fuel consumption modeling with predictive capabilities even under varying conditions, supporting optimized route selection for energy efficiency and operating costs.

Implementation of this platform generates measurable benefits on three key dimensions:

- **Economy:**
    - Algorithmic optimization of fuel consumption.

    - Documented reduction in operating costs.
    - Predictive planning of maintenance interventions.
    - Rationalization of spare parts and service management.
- **Environmental:**
    - Targeted abatement of pollutant emissions.
    - Proactive compliance with international regulatory framework.
    - Reduction of overall ecological footprint.
    - Documented alignment with Environmental, Social and Governance goals.
- **Operational:**
    - Route optimization based on predictive algorithms.
    - Integrated navigational risk management.
    - Remote monitoring of on-board physical *assets*.
    - Continuous improvement through analytical *benchmarking*.

Developed in collaboration with leading maritime operators and installed on more than 2,000 vessels.

This convergence of naval expertise and advanced technologies offers a holistic approach to contemporary maritime transportation challenges, balancing economic optimization, environmental responsibility and operational efficiency.

For more information and a demonstration video:

https://www.sertica.com/performance/

In planning audit activities

Planning audit activities in the certification industry is a management challenge of considerable complexity. An audit is a systematic, independent and documented process designed to collect objective evidence and evaluate it objectively to determine the degree to which audit criteria (specific standards, business requirements or regulations) are met. Audits may be internal, conducted by the organization itself, or external, conducted by independent entities.

Certification bodies must orchestrate an intricate system of audits designed to ensure that organizations comply with all the requirements of specific standards in order to issue or maintain the relevant certifications.

This planning activity must take into account multiple and intertwining time constraints. On the one hand, there are the requirements of customers, who often need to obtain certification by specific dates dictated by tender requirements, business needs or regulations. On the other, there are the constraints imposed by the certification schemes themselves, which require annual surveillance audits to be conducted within well-defined time windows to maintain certification validity.

The complexity increases considerably when logistical aspects are considered. The goal of optimizing the movement of auditors across the territory clashes with the need to meet the specific qualifications required for each certification scheme. It is important to note that the certification landscape is extremely diverse: considering ISO standards alone, we are talking about several hundred different schemes, each with its own specificities and competence requirements.

Each auditor has specific qualifications for particular certification schemes, acquired through specialized training and field experience. This creates an additional level of complexity in planning, since not all auditors are interchangeable: for each audit it is necessary to identify a professional who possesses the appropriate qualifications for the certification scheme in question.

The planning process must therefore consider simultaneously:

- The deadlines required by clients.
- The time limits imposed by the certification schemes.
- The availability of qualified auditors.
- The optimization of local travel.
- The efficient management of human resources.
- The containment of operational costs.

Further complicating the picture is the need to manage frequent rescheduling due to several factors:

- Sudden client unavailability.
- Auditor impediments.
- Unforeseen events or force majeure (think events such as pandemic).
- Changes in business needs.
- Changes in operational priorities.

The daily management of hundreds of audits in different locations around the world highlights the considerable scope of this operational challenge. As one of the leading certification bodies (RINA.org), we faced a volume of activity that needed a systematic approach to planning, supported by an integrated technology ecosystem where different AI solutions work in synergy.

My direct experience in implementing an innovative AI-based system revealed how digital transformation can revolutionize audit planning.

The integration of *machine learning* algorithms, specifically through combinatorial optimization models and intelligent *scheduling*, enabled significant automation and refinement of this crucial process.

The implemented system was based on three main components that revolutionized our approach to scheduling:

- a predictive scheduling engine that used genetic algorithms for multi-objective optimization,

- an intelligent decision support system based on specialized LLMs for analyzing auditor qualifications and *matching* with certification scheme requirements, and

- a risk prediction and management module that anticipated potential *scheduling* conflicts based on historical *patterns*.

The implemented architecture consisted of three layers that have proven their effectiveness in the field:

- a centralized database that integrated all the necessary information,
- a *suite of* AI algorithms for optimization and prediction,
- and an intuitive user interface for real-time visualization and management.

The system maintains a critical level of human oversight at all times: each AI-generated schedule undergoes validation by planners, who can modify, approve, or reject proposals based on contextual factors that the algorithm may not fully capture. The architecture provides human review checkpoints at strategic moments: initial validation of constraints, review of high-risk allocations (e.g., audits in countries with security risks), and final approval before communication to clients and auditors.

Process governance ensures that each critical step remains under qualified human control, transforming AI from an autonomous decision maker to a sophisticated decision support tool. This balance between intelligent automation and expert oversight proved critical to the acceptance of the system by operators.

The results exceeded initial expectations, recording a 35 percent reduction in planning time, a 28 percent improvement in travel efficiency, a 55 percent decrease in urgent rescheduling, and an increase in customer satisfaction.

The implementation followed a modular approach that proved crucial to the success of the project. We started with a pilot phase in one geographic region, which allowed us to refine the system before gradually expanding it to other geographic areas.

Ongoing optimization based on user feedback led to significant incremental improvements, culminating in a system that now effectively manages audits in several locations around the world.

We will soon extend it to other types of audits/inspections.

This advanced technological approach has not only solved audit planning challenges, but also created a solid foundation for the future evolution of certification services, positioning our organization at the forefront of industry innovation.

Digital transformation has generated a measurable positive impact on both the quality of service provided to clients and internal operational efficiency, contributing significantly to improved economic performance.

Supporting decision-making processes in the area of Certification

Generative AI has proven to be a valuable tool for analyzing documents, tables and charts, verifying their compliance with specific regulatory requirements.

In the certification process according to ISO standards (such as the widespread ISO 9001, which defines Quality Management System requirements), a certification body's auditor verifies that the system implemented by the organization is actually operational, not just documented. The Quality Management System (QMS) represents the set of procedures, processes and resources that an organization uses to achieve its quality objectives and meet customer needs.

During the audit, the verifier examines the practical application of what is stated in the organization's quality manual. For example, if the company has established in its manual a commitment to develop annual training plans for employees, the auditor will request concrete evidence of this activity.

At the end of the audit, the auditor prepares a detailed report that includes:

- Audit findings.
- Recommendations for improvement.
- Any nonconformities classified by level of criticality.

This report, along with the documentation collected, is forwarded to the decision maker, an expert figure who:

- Examines the complete file.
- Evaluates the evidence collected.
- Decides on the issuance or maintenance of certification.

Maintenance of certification is done through:

- Surveillance audits: annual audits to confirm maintenance of requirements.
- Re-certification audits: in-depth audits every three years to renew certification.

Given the significant amount of paperwork to be evaluated, AI has been integrated into the decision-making process to support decision makers in analyzing documentation, speeding up the process without compromising the accuracy of the evaluation.

The system automatically analyzes the entire documentation package of each practice, including audit reports, evidence collected, and previous certification history. Through advanced text comprehension techniques, the AI quickly identifies critical points, verifies document completeness and compares collected evidence with applicable regulatory requirements.

The technological core of this system is based on a RAG architecture implemented on Microsoft's cloud (Azure), which represents a significant advancement in document processing. RAG combines the power of LLMs with a knowledge base specific to the certification domain (e.g., ISO 9001 and related customer documents).

In our secure Azure environment, we have implemented a workflow where each request from the decision maker triggers a contextual search in the relevant documents. The system uses the ChatGPT API through Azure OpenAI Service, which ensures that all data remains within our secure environment. This approach allows ChatGPT's advanced linguistic understanding to be combined with the specific document base, ensuring accurate and contextually relevant answers.

My direct experience implementing this solution has shown how the system is able to present the decision maker with a structured analysis that automatically highlights detected nonconformities, significant changes from previous audits, and items that require special attention.

Take, for example, the annual training plan requirement: the system identifies the relevant section in the quality manual (typically 7.2 "Competency"), automatically locates all related evidence-such as the current year's training plan, attendance records, and effectiveness evaluations-and presents it in an interactive screen where the decision maker can immediately verify the correlation between requirement and evidence. This approach transforms manual searching through numerous documents into a smooth and immediate verification.

The practitioner can interact with the system through simple natural language questions, getting immediate answers based on the analysis of available documentation, with the possibility of directly accessing the original documents where relevant points are already highlighted. This approach has led to a 60 percent reduction in analysis time per file, while maintaining high quality standards in decision making.

Importantly, the system does not replace the professional judgment of the decision maker, but serves as an intelligent support that allows the focus to be on the most critical aspects of the evaluation. The integration of this technology has transformed the decision-making process, making it more efficient and consistent, while ensuring complete traceability of the path leading to the final certification decision.

Chapter Summary.

Chapter 4 explores the transformative role of AI in business operational optimization, presenting concrete cases of implementation in different industries. Through an in-depth analysis of real applications, the chapter highlights how AI is revolutionizing planning and control processes, with measurable benefits in terms of efficiency, quality, and sustainability.

Quality Control and Defect Identification

The chapter illustrates the evolution of AI-based quality control systems, starting from the earliest neural networks to modern *deep learning* systems. Particularly significant are the cases of the steel industry, where AI monitors steel in motion in real time at temperatures approaching 1,000 degrees Celsius, and the food industry, where it ensures safety in pasta production. The technology also extends to the *automotive* sector for vehicle damage detection, with a focus on hail damage detection.

Predictive Maintenance.

The implementation of predictive systems for uninterruptible power units, locomotives and real estate is analyzed. The chapter effectively compares the traditional expert systems approach with modern *deep learning* solutions, highlighting how the latter offer greater flexibility and ability to adapt to changes in the operating environment. Modern systems integrated with edge computing represent a significant evolution that improves efficiency and data security.

Optimizing service delivery.

The final section delves into the application of AI in maritime navigation management (with the SERTICA Performance system), audit planning, and certification decision making. The latter case highlights how the RAG architecture implemented in Microsoft Azure is transforming document analysis in the regulatory environment, with a 60 percent reduction in case analysis time.

The chapter demonstrates how AI is evolving from an analytical support tool to a central element in operational decision-making processes, offering a concrete perspective on the opportunities for digital transformation in business operations.

CHAPTER 5

CONTENT GENERATION: FROM IDEA TO EXECUTION

5.1 Professional text generation and editing.

Text generation is undoubtedly the first generative AI feature we have collectively experienced, particularly since the public launch of ChatGPT in November 2022. It will forever remain etched in our memory that extraordinary moment when, after entering our first *prompt*, we witnessed words and sentences materialize on the screen, as if by magic. This moment marked a turning point in our perception of the potential of AI, transforming what was previously the exclusive domain of experts into a tool accessible to everyone.

This ability to generate textual content has proven to be one of the most powerful tools in our daily work, manifesting itself in two main ways: either through the processing of simple prompts or through the analysis of more complex *prompts* accompanied by external sources such as documents, videos, audio, images and web content. In either case, AI can operate from scratch or by processing specific user-supplied input and documents, demonstrating extraordinary versatility in adapting to different needs. The real revolution lies in the ability of these systems to understand context, interpret the nuances of natural language, and produce outputs that not only meet specific demands but often enrich them with innovative perspectives.

Text generation using AI is not a monolithic field, but has significant variations depending on the model used. In my practical experience, I have found substantial differences: ChatGPT (particularly in the GPT-4.5 version) excels in logical structuring and versatility of styles, proving particularly effective for technical and creative content; Anthropic's Claude stands out for its ability to handle complex documents and lengthy *prompts* with articulated instructions, offering more sophisticated responses in the conceptual and philosophical domains; Google's Gemini shows particular skill in integrating with external data and analyzing real-time information, proving valuable for content that requires frequent updates. These differences, while constantly evolving with rapid model updates, are a strategic element in choosing the tool best suited to the specific type of content we intend to generate.

Content synthesis and advanced document analysis

In my daily professional activities, I am often faced with the need to analyze and synthesize crucial information from multiple documents and sources in order to support in-depth decision-making processes and analysis. The effectiveness of this is largely dependent on the accurate formulation of the *prompt*.

To illustrate this concept with a practical example, consider the scenario in which we wish to create a comparative synthesis of multiple documents, highlighting both common and unique elements found in each source. A specific case might be the analysis of three separate reports that explore predictions of AI trends for 2025. In this context, after uploading the documents to the platform, the structuring of the *prompt* becomes crucial to obtain meaningful and usable results; a *prompt* that fits the bill is as follows:

***Prompt*: https://tinyurl.com/yzm8k9an**

For each document:
-Identify and extract the main AI trends projected for 2025.
- Highlight the rationale and data that support each trend
-Annotes any use cases or practical applications cited and specific benefits to maritime operators

After the individual analysis:
-Compares the trends identified in the three documents.
-Eliminates overlaps, keeping the most detailed source for each duplicate trend
-Identifies any complementary or related trends.

Creates a structured report that includes:
-An executive overview of key trends
For each identified trend:
-Detailed description
-Expected impact on the market/industry.
-Associated challenges and opportunities.
-Concrete examples of implementation
-An in-depth section with quantitative data and market forecasts.
-Eventual interconnections between the different trends

Conclude with:
-A critical assessment of the most promising trends.
-Potential implications for business and society
-Strategic recommendations

The analysis and synthesis of documents through major conversational AI models present both opportunities and limitations, which it is important to be aware of. Currently, the free versions of the leading AI assistants-ChatGPT, Gemini and Claude-allow direct uploading of documents for analysis, albeit with some restrictions on the number, size and type of files supported.

As for the free versions:

- ChatGPT allows files (such as PDFs, images and spreadsheets) to be uploaded directly into the chat, with a limit of 3 files per 5 hours.

- Gemini allows uploading of documents and images from both device and Google Drive, with a good variety of formats supported.

- Claude offers the ability to upload up to 5 files at a time (up to 10MB each) between documents and images.

These features make it much easier to parse even long texts without having to manually copy the content into the input area. However, some limitations remain, such as file size limits and maximum number of uploads, which may vary among platforms.

Chinese solutions, such as Deepseek and Qwen, also allow uploading of attachments from the *prompt*, but it is recommended to read the terms of use and privacy carefully, as highlighted in the Introduction.

Microsoft offers an interesting alternative through its Copilot subscription. Users who have subscribed to this service can access an advanced feature: direct parsing of documents stored in Microsoft's cloud ecosystem (OneDrive). This eliminates the need for manual uploading, greatly simplifying the analysis process for those using Microsoft tools.

In terms of processing quality, comparative tests showed particularly high performance by ChatGPT and Claude in document synthesis and analysis. These two models stand out for their ability to produce accurate, consistent and well-structured results, demonstrating a thorough understanding of the processed content.

It is important to note that the AI tool landscape is rapidly evolving, with frequent updates that may introduce new features or modify existing ones. For this reason, it is advisable to periodically review the features and limitations of each tool to optimize its use.

I often find myself needing to identify particular information within one or more documents, and often the traditional "find" function is too limited or ineffective when it comes to PDF document output from an image capture. With a simple *prompt*, the AI can find for me the content I am looking for and show me the specific paragraph that meets my query so that I can verify the result proposed by the AI. This capability goes far beyond simple keyword search, extending to a true semantic understanding of the content.

Application scenarios:

1. Analysis of legal documents

In the area of contracts, AI can quickly identify:

- Specific clauses and their variations between different versions.
- Expiration and renewal dates.
- Obligations and responsibilities of the parties.
- Special conditions and exceptions.

Example *prompt*:

"Analyze this contract and identify all clauses related to early termination. For each clause found, show the exact text and indicate the article of reference."

2. Review of technical documentation

In reviewing technical specifications, the IA can:

- Identify specific requirements.
- Find inconsistencies between documents.
- Locate references to standards and regulations.
- Extract crucial technical parameters.

Suggested *Prompt*:

"Review these technical specifications and find all references to ISO standards related to cybersecurity. For each reference, show the full context of the paragraph."

3. Analysis of financial reports

For financial analysis, AI can quickly:

- Locate key performance indicators.
- Identify significant trends and variations.
- Find specific explanatory notes.
- Extract particular financial statement data.

Effective *Prompt:*

"Analyze these quarterly reports and identify all paragraphs that discuss EBITDA changes greater than 10 percent. Show the full text and calculate the percentage change for each case."

4. Review of Audit Documentation.

In the context of certifications, the IA can:

- Identify nonconformities.
- Find evidence of corrective action.
- Locate references to specific procedures.
- Extract recommendations and observations.

Prompt recommended:

"Review these audit reports and find all major nonconformities. For each, show: the full description, proposed corrective actions and their deadlines."

5. Analysis of tender documents

For tender activities, the IA can:

- Identify qualification requirements.
- Find evaluation criteria.
- Locate deadlines and milestones.
- Extract critical technical specifications.
- Verify that we have produced all the documentation required by the tender.

Useful *prompt:*

"Analyze this tender document and identify: 1) all minimum qualification requirements, 2) key deadlines, 3) technical evaluation criteria with associated scores."

Advanced features

1. Contextual search

AI can:

- Understand synonyms and language variations.

- Identify indirect references.
- Consider the broader context.
- Correlate information between different documents.

2. Multilingual extraction

Ability to:

- Search for content in different languages.
- Translate results while maintaining context.
- Manage multilingual documents.
- Identify cross-lingual correspondences.

3. Temporal analysis

Ability to:

- Track the evolution of specific issues over time.
- Identify changes between versions.
- Analyze temporal trends.
- Correlate events and changes.

As already pointed out in Chapter 2, the quality of the *prompt* wording can make a difference in the result obtained, below are some typologies applied to document analysis:

- **Specificity**

"Find all mentions of ISO/IEC 27001 certifications in the document, include the full paragraph, and indicate whether they refer to existing or planned certifications."

- **Structuring**

"Analyze these reports and create a table with: 1) Date of *finding*, 2) Description of nonconformity, 3) Proposed corrective action, 4) Current status."

- **Contextualization**

"Review these documents considering the context of the *automotive* industry and identify all references to IATF 16949 standards, showing how they relate to manufacturing processes."

- **Comparison**

"Compare these three policy documents and identify: 1) Common elements, 2) Significant differences, 3) Any contradictions, providing the exact text for each point."

This intelligent search capability radically transforms the way we interact with business documentation, enabling us to:

- Dramatically reduce search time.
- Increase accuracy in identifying information.
- Facilitate comparative analysis.
- Support decision making with accurate and contextualized information.

Integrating these capabilities into business processes represents significant time savings.

Technical documentation generation.

The generation of technical documentation represents one of the areas where AI particularly excels. Starting from technical specifications or product descriptions, AI can generate:

- Detailed user manuals, complete with diagrams and interactive illustrations.
- Technical specification documents, with automatic updates as the product changes.
- Standard operating procedures that ensure consistency and clarity.
- Troubleshooting guides that use algorithms to identify common problems and provide quick solutions.
- API and software development documentation, optimized for developers of different skills.

If we wanted to make a user guide for a macOs application for storing cooking recipes, we would have to prepare a *prompt* that asks all the questions we need to complete the sections of the guide we wish to have:

Prompt Name	macos_recipe_manager_user_guide_format
Template	ChatGPT-o4-mini-high
Prompt	Create a detailed user guide for [a MacOs application for storing cooking recipes] that includes: -A product overview with complete technical specifications. -Step-by-step installation instructions with explanatory diagrams -Troubleshooting section with the 10 most common problems and their solutions -FAQs based on customer support data -Glossary of technical terms

	-Use clear language suitable for [BASE] level users and format the document according to the standard [DITA].[28] Ask me as many questions as you need to produce the detailed user guide.
	https://tinyurl.com/bdz24veh
Output	Here is the complete user guide for Mac Cooking, structured according to the DITA 1.3 standard and designed for entry-level users. Each topic is self-contained and reusable, and the DITA map (.ditamap file) defines the overall hierarchy. General Overview. Mac Cooking is a macOS (Sonoma onwards) application developed by Emanuele Castagno for storing, organizing, and sharing English-language cooking recipes. The current release is version 1.0, with a 150 MB package downloadable exclusively from the Mac App Store on Macs with Apple M1 processors or higher. The app allows you to import recipes via copy/paste, categorize them, plan meals (with calorie calculation), generate shopping lists, synchronize data to iCloud, and restore them if needed. DITA Map (maccooking.ditamap) <?xml version="1.0" encoding="UTF-8"?> <!DOCTYPE map PUBLIC "-//OASIS//DTD DITA Map//EN" "map.dtd"> <map id="maccooking-map" title="Mac Cooking User Guide"> <topicref href="concepts/introduction.dita"/> <topicref href="tasks/installation.fingers"/> <topicref href="tasks/usage.dita"/> <topicref href="troubleshooting/troubleshooting.dita"/> <topicref href="references/faqs.dita"/> <topicref href="glossary/glossary.dita"/>

[28] **DITA** (Darwin Information Typing Architecture) is a technical documentation standard that uses XML, a universal coding language that organizes information in a structured way

	</map> *(Example of a modular DITA map) (DITA: Specializations (task, concept, reference)?)* 1. Concept: Introduction to Mac Cooking (concepts/introduction.dita) <?xml version="1.0" encoding="UTF-8"?> <concept id="introduction" xmlns="http://docs.oasis-open.org/dita/ns/architecture"> <title>Introduction to Mac Cooking</title> <shortdesc>General overview of the application for storing cooking recipes</shortdesc> <conbody> <p><b>Mac Cooking</b> is software for macOS (Sonoma+) that allows you to manage English-language cooking recipes.</p> <p><b>System requirements:</b> Mac with Apple M1 processor or higher, macOS Sonoma or later; 150 MB free space.</p> <p><b>Main features:</b> import via copy/paste, recipe categorization, meal planning with calorie calculation, shopping list generation, iCloud synchronization, backup and restore.</p> </conbody> </concept> (Basic structure of a "concept" type topic) (*The DITA Style Guide - Oxygen XML Editor*) CONTINUE... (5 A4 Pages)
	https://tinyurl.com/29dyxm3b

As can be seen from the output above, ChatGPT's 04-mini-high template does its job very well after asking us numerous questions necessary to have the content to write the guide.

In the output we also find which specification document of the DITA standard it used and also recommends us software to use to edit the DITA content.

If you try this *prompt* with Google Gemini and the Deep Research with 2.5 Pro template it will start doing a web search for similar applications and will draft in text format (no DITA) an extensive guide making up the functionality, requirements and any other information because it will not ask us any questions before it starts on the fourth.

It will produce a template that we can use by radically modifying it.

The same *prompt* on Claude Sonnet Extended Thinking will produce a result similar to the ChatGPT template (after asking us a dozen questions) but with a graphical representation of the XML text that is not as curated as ChatGPT.

Perplexity also performed well but without matching ChatGPT.

The two Chinese models, Deepseek and Qwen did not match the response quality of ChatGPT, Gemini and Claude.

Even using ChatGPT's model, the result will not be a publication-ready guide but a draft from which to make the final one. The more precise we are and the more content we produce in each of our responses, the more complete the guide will be.

The technique of asking the AI to ask the questions for the information you need is very useful when the request is complex, and we can use this technique in multiple occasions/scenarios.

Corporate **communication**

In the context of corporate communication, AI supports the creation of:

- Press releases and briefing notes, tailored to different distribution channels.

- Customized corporate newsletters, segmented for different types of *stakeholders*.
- Annual and quarterly reports, enriched with dynamic data visualizations.
- *Corporate* presentations with automatically generated slides and visually appealing content.
- Content for corporate social media that includes trend analysis to optimize *engagement*.
- Product and service descriptions, optimized for online search.

Each organization usually has its own style in communication and specific guidelines to follow.

For best results and to reduce rework of what AI produces, the ideal is to provide multiple examples of press releases, newsletters, documents, and other products so that AI understands the style and guidelines.

In the case of press releases we need to provide:

1. Examples of existing press releases.

- At least 2-3 releases that represent our typical style and format well.
- Make sure they contain information that is authentic or otherwise similar to what we would like to communicate in the future (layout, tone of voice, terminology, type of content).

2. Style guidelines.

- Internal documents or specific instructions (e.g., desired length, use of headings and subheadings, fonts, paragraph formatting, etc.), share them.
- Include any lexical or tone rules (e.g.

formal, informal, technical, institutional, etc.).

3. Graphic or structural elements (if any).

- If our press releases use special graphic elements or layouts (e.g., logo, headings, color scheme), describe them or better send an example (even with pictures, if helpful).
- Specify whether and how such elements should be inserted into the text or referred to (e.g., "{Insert company logo}" as placeholders, etc.).

4. Key Messages/Corporate Values.

- List the key messages we always want to get across (e.g., trust, innovation, sustainability, etc.).
- Include any keywords to be integrated and guidelines on what is strategic to highlight in each release.

5. Internal *best practices*.

- If there are recurring phrases or "calls to action," include them.
- Possibly provide examples of terminologies to avoid and those to favor.

With this material, the AI can analyze recurring elements (tone of voice, headline structure, average length, formatting, word choice) and replicate them in new releases, respecting style and rules of our company. Once the AI receives the information, it can return draft releases to you that conform to the guidelines provided.

Here is the *prompt* we can use to instruct the AI to draft content (e.g., press releases) according to company style and rules:

Prompt Name	press_release_style_guidelines_analysis
Template	Claude-3-7-sonnet with Extended Thinking
Prompt	I provide below a set of documents and guidelines related to our press releases. I ask you to carefully analyze the writing style, formatting, tone of voice, structure, and internal communication rules so that we can generate new press releases in the future that conform to these guidelines. Examples of existing press releases: [Insert text or links from 2-3 press releases representative of the style and format you use here]. Style Guidelines: [List here any documents or guidelines where the following are defined: tone of voice, length, formatting, use of headlines/subheadings, fonts, language preferences, etc.] Graphic or structural elements: [Describe or attach examples of layout, logo placement, any color schemes, header and footer formats, etc.]. Indicate if you have textual placeholders to use, e.g., "{Company Logo}"] Key Messages and Corporate Values. [List key messages to be communicated, pivotal values, keywords to be used regularly, etc.] Internal Best Practices. [Insert any standard phrases, recurring call-to-actions, terminologies to avoid, terms that should always appear instead, etc.] Once I have received and analyzed all the material, I ask you to confirm that you understand the guidelines. Next, I will provide you with guidance on the first press release I would like to produce, so that you can write the initial draft strictly adhering to the style, format, and company values.
	https://tinyurl.com/3zu3facp

Adapting the tone of voice for different targets while maintaining consistency with the brand.

If we have a need to adapt the same content to different audiences but maintaining the consistency of our brand or at least the positioning we want to have, we can use a *prompt* like the following by adapting and customizing it to our need:

Prompt Name	multi_target_content_adaptation_framework
Template	Claude-3-7-sonnet with Extended Thinking
Prompt	# *PROMPT* FOR MULTI-TARGET CONTENT ADAPTATION. ## 1. BRAND INFORMATION. Provide the following information about the brand: Brand Identity: -Brand name -Sector of reference -Positioning in the marketplace -Company mission and vision Tone of Voice: -Main features (e.g., formal/informal, technical/discursive). -Keywords to use -Terms to avoid -Preferred Communication Style Brand Values: -List of core values. -How these are reflected in communication -Distinctive elements of the brand Visual Guidelines: -Preferred Formatting. -Use of graphic elements -Typographic standards ## 2. CONTENT TO BE ADAPTED. [Insert original content] ## 3. TARGET AND SPECIFICATION OF ADAPTATION. ### Executive version (C-Level):

	Objectives: -Focus on ROI and strategic benefits. -Alignment with business objectives. -Evidence KPIs and key metrics Specifications: Length: 300 words Style: executive summary Elements to include: -Impact on business -Cost-benefit analysis -Competitive advantages -Future Perspectives ### Technical Version (Implementation Team): Objectives: -Procedural clarity -Technical completeness -Adherence to standards Specifications: Length: [specify] Level of technical detail: [high/medium/low] Elements to include: -Detailed procedures -Technical specifications. -Reference standards. -Best practices -Related documents ### Marketing Version (End Client): Objectives: -Engagement of target audience -Value communication -Conversion Specifications:

<table>
<tr><td></td><td>Length: [specify]
Narrative style: [specify]
Elements to include:
-Value proposition
-Tangible benefits
-Social proof
-Call to action

4. OUTPUT REQUIREMENTS.
For each version, provide:
-Main text
-Abstract (50 words)
-Highlighted key points
-Specific calls to action.
-Suggestions for supporting visuals/graphics.

5. BRAND CONSISTENCY CHECKLIST
Checklist checks:
-Alignment with brand values.
-Coherence of tone of voice
-Correct use of terminology
-Compliance with stylistic guidelines
-Maintenance of positioning

6. METRICS OF SUCCESS.
Define for each version:
-KPI benchmarks
-engagement goals
-Conversion metrics
-Indicators of communication effectiveness</td></tr>
<tr><td></td><td>https://tinyurl.com/bdhk94bv</td></tr>
</table>

Grammatical and stylistic correction based on advanced computational linguistics models.

To obtain grammatical verification of our text, we can simply request it with a *prompt of* a few words followed by the text we want the LLM to analyze.

If the text we are interested in is technical and in addition to grammatical correctness we need more in-depth verification on technical style we can use the following *prompt* that we can modify according to our context and needs:

Prompt Name	technical_document_review_and_optimization
Template	Claude-3-7-sonnet with Extended Thinking
Prompt	Perform a thorough review of the following technical document according to these parameters: Linguistic analysis: Grammatical correctness and syntax Uniformity of verb tenses Technical punctuation Consistency in the use of acronyms and acronyms Technical style: Verification of industry terminology Standardization of technical formulas Compliance with ISO writing standards Formal optimization: Format citations and references Layout and formatting Paragraph structure Output required: Revised document Report of interventions carried out Updated technical glossary

	Text to be revised: [insert text]
	https://tinyurl.com/bdfjz74e

Adaptation of text length according to the media.

If we need to adapt a piece of content to the specific media, we can structure a *prompt* like this:

***Prompt*: https://tinyurl.com/mf8pvjhw**

Adapt the following [technical white paper on cybersecurity] for different communication channels:

Blog Version (Articles):

- Length: 1000 words
- Focus on key insights
- Popular but technical style

Social (LinkedIn) version:

- Length: 200 words
- Key points and statistics
- Call to action

Newsletter version:

- Length: 150 words
- Abstract and value proposition
- Strategic links

Maintain for each version:

- Key messages
- Technical credibility
- Brand consistency

Original content: [insert content]

Simplifying complex content to make it accessible to a wider audience or ourselves.

For as long as I can remember, technology has been my greatest passion. When you devote all your free time-from childhood through college and into your professional career-to telecommunications, electronics and computer science, certain concepts seem intuitive to you.

But this familiarity often creates a communication gap with those who do not share the same background.

In my family, which ranges from a seven-year-old to a 17-year-old with interests far removed from technology, via a 14-year-old video game enthusiast and a wife who puts up with technology "just the right amount," transferring enthusiasm for technical concepts requires well-thought-out communication strategies.

One evening at dinner, an unexpected educational opportunity presented itself to me-our little one proudly tells his 14-year-old brother that he has learned to play chess. The natural sibling rivalry immediately brings out a challenge: the 14-year-old, probably repeating something heard elsewhere, states with conviction that "a computer can predict all possible moves and the human being can never beat it."

I jump at the chance and intervene: "Actually, no existing computer-not even a quantum one-could predict all possible chess games. They are more numerous than even the atoms in the known universe! Rather they evaluate a limited number of future moves and select the best ones according to various criteria."

Their puzzled looks make me realize that my statement, though correct, needs a more accessible explanation.

Dinner over, I turn to structuring an effective *prompt* that can translate this abstract concept into understandable terms for a 14-year-old boy. The key, I intuit, lies in connecting the topic to something he is familiar with and passionate about: Fortnite, his video game of the moment.

My goal is threefold:

- Explain the concept of choice and consequences using Fortnite as a metaphor.
- Introduce the concept of exponential growth through the idea of viral content.
- Help him visualize the enormity of the number $10^{(120)}$ (a 1 followed by 120 zeros) of combinations of possible moves.

Prompt Name	quantum_choices_and_infinite_games
Template	ChatGPT-o4-mini-high
Prompt	# *PROMPT* FOR EXPLANATION OF CHESS COMPLEXITY Goal: Explain to a 14-year-old boy why even a quantum computer cannot calculate all possible chess games, using: Practical examples from his daily life Concrete visualizations A friendly but scientific tone A logical progression that builds understanding step by step ## STRUCTURE OF THE EXPLANATION 1. Engaging Introduction Starts with an interesting question about the boy's favorite video game Connects the concept of choices in the game to moves in chess Uses an enthusiastic and curious tone 2. First Concept: Exponential Growth. Create a practical example using:

	Teenagers' favorite social media The virality of content How numbers grow quickly when sharing with friends 3. Visualizing the Numbers Present the numbers in an understandable way: Start with small examples (first 3-4 moves) Use analogies with familiar things: Grains of sand on Earth Stars in the galaxy YouTube video Time since the beginning of the universe 4. Quantum Computers: Superpowers with Limits Explain quantum computers as: A computational superhero Something incredibly fast but still limited Use analogies with: Speed of Light in video games Power-ups that still have rules 5. The Greatness of Practical Infinity Create a comparison between: Number of atoms in the universe (10^80) Number of possible chess games (10^120) - Use creative visualizations such as: "If every atom in the universe was a universe..." "If every grain of sand were a galaxy..." ## ELEMENTS TO INCLUDE Interactivity: Rhetorical questions that stimulate curiosity "Wow" moments that create amazement Invitations to do small calculations together Analogies with:

	Popular video games Social media School situations Sports Suggested visual elements: Simple tree diagrams Visualized scales of size Visual comparisons of large numbers ## LANGUAGE AND TONE Uses: Short, direct sentences Vocabulary appropriate for 13-year-olds but not childish Technical terms explained with examples A tone that conveys wonder Avoidance: Condescension Oversimplification Overly technical terms without explanation ## CONCLUSION. Close with: A summary that connects everything A reflection on the beauty of mathematics An invitation to explore other math puzzles A connection to the boy's daily life ## VERIFICATION OF UNDERSTANDING The explanation should enable the boy to: Understand what exponential growth means Visualize the magnitude of the numbers involved Understand why even advanced technologies have limits

	Feel inspired by math and science ## SUGGESTED FOLLOW-UPS Suggest: Practical experiments to do at home Related YouTube videos Apps or games that illustrate concepts Questions to stimulate further curiosity
	https://tinyurl.com/yzvshvpn
Output	**1. Engaging introduction** Imagine you are playing your favorite video game-say, a battle-royale or platformer full of narrative forks-and at each "decision point" you are presented with two, three, or even four different path options. How many different paths can you choose? Now let's transfer this concept to chess: every time you muscle the knight, queen or pawn, you open up new alternatives. Just as in a video game where at each fork in the road the games multiply, in the game of chess the possibilities explode to the level of ... astronomical! **2. First concept: exponential growth** **Practical example from social media** Think of TikTok or Instagram. Posting a video means hoping one of your friends will share it with two of his or her contacts, and each of them with two others... In four sharing cycles you could have 1→2→4→8→16 1 \to 2 \to 4 \to 8 \to 16 visualizations. **"Multiplication" growth** If each share involved not 2 but 10 users, in four cycles you would have 1→10→100→1 000→10 000 1 \to 10 \to 100 \to 1\,000 \to 10\,000 visualizations. **Parallel with chess moves** On average, a player can choose from about 30-40 legal moves

in a given position. After the first move there are ~35 possible choices, after the second 35×35=1 225, after the third 35^3≈42 875, and so on...

3. Visualization of numbers

First 3-4 moves

Moves	Approximate cumulative possibilities
1	35
2	1 225
3	42 875
4	1 500 625
Even with only four moves you are already over a million!	

Family comparisons

Sand grains on Earth: estimated to exist around 10^{18} (one billion billion).

Stars in the Milky Way: around 10^{11}-10^{12}.

YouTube videos uploaded daily: nearly 10^5-10^6.

Seconds since the beginning of the universe: ~4×10^{17}.

Small calculation together

"If each grain of sand were a 1 500 000-move chess game, how many grains would it take to contain all possible openings in 4 moves?"

1 000 000 000 000 000 0001 500 000≈6×1011\displaystyle \frac{1\,000\,000\,000}{1\,500\,000}approx 6\times10^{11} grains!

4. Quantum computers: superpowers--with limits

The "superhero" of computation

A quantum computer is like a character in a video game equipped with incredible speed-boost: it exploits superposition and entanglement to explore many configurations at once.

Analogy with power-ups

Imagine having a power-up in the game that halves the recharge time: it is super-powerful, but it does not reset the time. Similarly, a quantum computer speeds up some problem families, but it cannot simply "jump" to enumerating 10^{120} possible matches.

Physical limit

Even with an atomic qubit accelerator, more qubit, space, and time resources will be needed than the entire universe allows to be built.

5. The magnitude of "practical infinity"

Comparison of orders of magnitude

Atoms in the observable universe: $\sim 10^{80}$

Possible chess games: $\sim 10^{120}$

Creative visualizations

If every atom in the universe were a universe unto itself, and a different game was played in each of these contexts, it would still take 10^{40} "additional" universes to accommodate all the chess games!

If every grain of sand on our planet were a galaxy, and each galaxy contained 10^{20} stars, we would still be hundreds of orders of magnitude away from the number of possible chess games.

Conclusion

Summary

Even a few moves generate millions of variations (exponential growth).

Comparisons with sand, stars and videos help us "see" otherwise incomprehensible numbers.

Quantum computers, while exceptional, do not circumvent the fundamental constraints of physics and resources.

Reflection

Mathematics offers us tools of "wonder": such vast numbers challenge our intuition and remind us how deep the science is behind even a simple "board game."

	Invitation to exploration Would you like to try building a mini-diagram tree with the first 5 moves, or watch a YouTube video that simulates exponential growth? Curiosity is the first step to new math puzzles! **Suggested follow-ups** **Home experiment**: take paper and pencil, draw a simple tree of moves: count how many leaves you get after 1, 2 and 3 levels. **YouTube video**: search for "exponential growth visualization" or "shannon number chess" to learn more. **App or games**: try "ChessTree Explorer" or "Move Explorer" to see variant expansion graphically. **Trivia questions**: *What happens if we limit the game to only pawns and bishops?* *What is the longest game ever recorded?* Enjoy exploring the wonderful world of mathematics and chess!
	https://tinyurl.com/88za8be3

Translation and Localization

We have already seen how generative AI can help us in the quick translation of emails, usually consisting of a few lines of text. If we look at the field of professional translation and localization, we are witnessing a radical transformation of the industry, offering significant advantages that deserve an in-depth analysis.

Efficiency and speed represent one of the most obvious benefits. Generative AI can process large volumes of text in considerably less time than traditional methods. A technical manual that would take weeks to translate into multiple languages can be completed in a few hours, while maintaining a high quality output.

Consistency in terminology is another key advantage, particularly relevant in technical and specialized fields. AI maintains consistent uniformity in the use of technical terms across all documents, ensuring that specific expressions are always translated the same way. This is crucial when working with technical documentation, standardized procedures and regulatory materials.

From an economic perspective, implementing generative AI can lead to significant optimization of translation costs. Organizations can handle higher volumes of translations with lower investment, freeing up resources to be allocated to other strategic areas of the business.

Scalability is another strength. AI systems can handle peak workloads without the need for additional resources, enabling organizations to respond quickly to fluctuations in market demand. This is particularly advantageous in industries with varying volumes of documentation to be translated.

Integration with existing processes is a strategic aspect. Generative AI systems can be incorporated into existing document workflows, creating automated processes that improve the overall operational efficiency of the organization.

Continuous improvement characterizes these systems: generative AI can learn and refine itself over time, especially when fed with systematic feedback and corrections. This continuous learning process leads to increasingly accurate and relevant results.

Generative AI has the potential to break down language and cultural barriers, making content more accessible and relevant to a global audience.

One of the most significant aspects of generative AI is its impact on the role of human translators. While AI takes on routine tasks such as translating large volumes of text, human translators are moving into more specialized roles such as post-editing and quality control. This shift highlights the evolution of the translation profession in the AI era, where human-machine collaboration becomes increasingly important to achieve the highest quality and accuracy in translation and localization.

Ultimately, generative AI is transforming the translation and localization industry, offering new opportunities for companies to reach global audiences and communicate more effectively. As this technology continues to develop and improve, we can expect a future in which global communication will be more fluid, accessible and personalized than ever before.

To implement this technology effectively, it is essential to maintain a human review process, especially for documents of particular importance or technical complexity.

There are numerous translation services available online that use generative AI; to translate this book into multiple languages I am evaluating this service: https://translation.x-doc.ai/

If we want to resort to well-known LLMs such as ChatGPT, Anthropic's Sonnet or Gemini we will have limits on the number of words we can get translated per *prompt* if the text is very long we will have to resort to multiple *prompts*. A *prompt* that guarantees a good result is the following:

Prompt: **https://tinyurl.com/4x3vmjas**

Act as an experienced professional translator with the following characteristics:
-Mother tongue in the target language.
-Expert in the specific field [insert your field, e.g., technical, legal, marketing]
- Specialized in localization and cultural adaptation

Document context:
-Document type: [specify, e.g., technical manual, contract, brochure]
-Target Audience: [specify, e.g., technical specialists, end customers, business partners]
-Document purpose: [specify objective, e.g., inform, persuade, instruct]
-Required style: [formal/informal, technical/discursive]
-Specific terminology: [insert glossary or key terms if available] Suggestions for improving clarity of text in the language

Translation requirements:
-Maintain original formatting.
-Preserve any references or quotations
-Adapt idioms to the target cultural context

-Use industry-standard terminology
-Maintain consistency in translating technical terms
-Highlight any passages that require special attention

Text to be translated: [insert original text].

Provide:
-Complete translation
-Notes on any cultural adaptations made
-Notes on any cultural adaptations made
-Explanation of translation choices for more complex passages
-Suggestions for improving the clarity of the text in the target language

Compliance and legal documentation

The adoption of generative AI in the legal sector enables text generation, automation of repetitive processes, and the provision of accurate analysis in the regulatory environment.

Specifically, it enables the following:

- **Generate legal texts** such as contracts, privacy notices, terms and conditions of use, without starting from scratch, but by customizing standard drafts according to specific needs.
- **Automate the creation of documents** such as compliance reports, engagement letters and other document templates, ensuring consistency and constant updates in an ever-changing regulatory environment.
- **Analyze and interpret complex documents**, highlighting critical clauses, identifying potential risks, and suggesting areas for action to mitigate errors or regulatory discrepancies.

The following *prompt*, taking as a reference the Italian law related to real estate leases will conduct an interview in order to gather all the information relevant to the drafting of a lease agreement.

Prompt Name	custom_rental_contract_wizard
Objective	The *prompt* is designed as an intelligent legal interviewing system that guides the user through a structured and sequential data collection process for creating a custom rental contract according to Italian law. Unlike an approach that assumes pre-existing information, this *prompt* adopts a "zero-knowledge" methodology in which: **Contextual education**: Each section begins with a brief explanation of the relevant legal framework, making the legal

	significance of the available choices understandable even for users who are not experts in real estate law **Progressive collection**: The system proceeds in logical steps (contract type → parties → property → economic conditions → duration → obligations → special conditions → fulfillments) **Exploration of options**: For each decision element, available alternatives are presented with their advantages and disadvantages, facilitating informed choices **Full customization**: The absence of assumptions about property characteristics, tenants, or contract preferences ensures a final document perfectly tailored to specific needs **Synthesis and validation**: The process provides a mechanism for confirming the information gathered before final drafting In summary, the *prompt* functions as a virtual legal advisor that takes the user from complete ignorance of details to the creation of a legally sound and fully customized lease.
Template	Claude-3-7-sonnet with Extended Thinking
Prompt	[SYSTEM] You are an Italian lawyer specializing in real estate law, experienced in drafting leases that comply with Italian law (Law 431/98 and subsequent amendments). Your mission is to guide you through an interactive data collection process to create a perfectly customized and legally valid lease agreement. [CONTEXT] The user needs to draft a lease agreement for a property in Italy but has not provided detailed information. You will need to conduct a structured interview to gather all the necessary data, explaining the legal relevance of each piece of information and the options available under Italian law. [BEHAVIOR] Adopt a didactic but professional approach. For each category of information: 1. Briefly explain why this information is legally relevant 2. Presents the options available with their advantages/disadvantages 3. Gather the user's decision 4. Confirm the choice before proceeding to the next section

	[INSTRUCTIONS] Conduct a comprehensive interview organized into the following sections, progressively gathering all the information needed for a valid and effective lease: **SECTION 1: CONTRACT TYPE** Present and explain the different types of contracts possible under Italian law: - Free rent contract (4+4) - Agreed fee contract (3+2) - Transitional contract - Contract for university students For each type, illustrate: - Main features - Duration and renewal - Tax advantages - Specific requirements - Special constraints - Cases in which it is advisable CONTINUE...
	https://tinyurl.com/uzktdszj
Output	LEASE AGREEMENT FOR RESIDENTIAL USE FOR UNIVERSITY STUDENTS (pursuant to Article 5, paragraph 2, Law No. 431 of December 9, 1998) BETWEEN Mr. ROSSI MARIO, born in [date of birth to be inserted], Fiscal Code RSSMRA72M14D969X, residing in Genoa, Via Corsica 1, e-mail: mario.rossi@gmail.com, telephone: +39 348 6919999, hereinafter referred to as "LESSOR" E Mr. PALLINO PINCO, born in [date of birth to be inserted], Fiscal Code PLLPNC82H15H501Z, residing in Rome at Viale Cesare Pavese 304, student enrolled at the Milan Polytechnic, hereinafter referred to as "CONDUCTOR" IT IS AGREED AND STIPULATED AS FOLLOWS

<table>
<tr><td rowspan="2"></td><td>Article 1 - SUBJECT OF THE LET.
The LESSOR hereby leases to the CONDUCTOR, who accepts, the real estate unit located in Milan, Via Bandi 32, interior 8, consisting of 3 independent bedrooms, 3 bathrooms and a common room, with a total area of approximately 100 square meters.

The property is registered in the Cadastre of Buildings of the Municipality of Milan as follows:
- Urban Section N
- Sheet 35
- Subaltern 8
- Cadastral category A/2 (civilian-type dwelling)
- Class 3
- Rooms 5
- Surface area 100 sqm
- Cadastral income Euro 1,200.00
The property has been recently renovated and is leased fully furnished, as per the inventory attached to this contract (Annex A).
The property is equipped with installations in accordance with the law and belongs to Energy Class E, as shown in the Energy Performance Certificate, a copy of which is attached to this contract (Annex B).
Art. 2 - DESTINATION OF USE.
The property shall be intended exclusively for the civil dwelling use of the CONDUCTOR and persons living with him/her. The CONDUCTOR declares that he/she is an off-site university student enrolled at the Polytechnic University of Milan, as shown in the attached documentation (Attachment C). Any change of use not permitted by the LESSOR will ipso jure result in the termination of the contract.
CONTINUED...</td></tr>
<tr><td>https://tinyurl.com/4yfswxf2</td></tr>
</table>

5.2 Image creations

We did not have time to recover from the amazement of text generation by generative AI to be amazed again by discovering its ability to generate images from a textual *prompt*.

Just as for *prompts* aimed at generating text or getting solutions the quality of the *prompt* is critical so it is for image generation.

Personally, I have found image generation useful in two main areas: in the context of LinkedIn and in slide preparation.

I love contributing to the spread of generative AI through LinkedIn, which I also use to broaden my skills and keep abreast of the latest news.

Very often to accompany a post by an image I resort to generation through AI by using components of the post itself to guide it to create one or more images to represent it graphically.

The other area where I use it almost daily is in the creation of images to support the messages I want to convey during a presentation usually prepared with Microsoft Power Point.

There are thousands of databases filled with millions of keyword-searchable images that until yesterday represented my only chance to enrich content with graphic elements/images.

I would often invest hours and hours searching for the perfect photo or image to represent the content, and today it only takes me a few minutes to type in the appropriate *prompt* to get the image of the type, format, color I wanted.

Without underestimating the fact that such realizations are unique and you are also assured of owning the rights to use them.

There are numerous services that allow the creation of images for free or for a fee, and new ones are coming out every day. Some allow very fine controls of generation by even being able to define and maintain their own graphic style such as Midjourney.

As with textual or numerical results, progressive refinement of the *prompt* leads to results closer and closer to those desired.

The table below shows how different services/ LLMs generate images all starting from the same *prompt*:

"Create the image related to an epic battle between two artificial intelligences in a futuristic, digital environment. One of the AIs looks bright, with a body made of blue energy and bright circuits, while the other is dark, with a red and black design, resembling a cybernetic shadow with lines of code running across its body. The two collide in a data storm, with digital lightning bolts and shards of pixels exploding in the air. The backdrop is an infinite virtual web, filled with grids and holograms that warp from the impact of the battle. The style of the image is *cyberpunk* with *high-tech* details and neon lights."

Tool	Price	URL	Image
Canva	Basic version: free, Pro ~$11.99/month;	www.canva.com	
Adobe Firely	Starting at~ 12/month	firefly.adobe.com/	
Qwen2.5-Max	Free	chat.qwenlm.ai	
Microsoft Designer	Free	Designer.microsoft.com	

Dall-E (ChatGPT)	Free	Chatgpt.com	
Ideogram	Free up to 10 credits per week then $7 or $16 or $48 per month	Ideogram.ai	

5.3 Creating podcasts

Globally, podcasting has expanded exponentially in recent years, supported by the massive adoption of digital technologies and the growing demand for *on-demand* content. Recent studies indicate that the number of global listeners has grown from about 332 million in 2020 to more than 383 million in 2021, and projections suggest a further increase as the evolution of *streaming* technologies and the spread of advanced broadband connections-including 5G-promote access to high-quality audio content. These developments not only increase the reach of podcasts, but also improve their quality and listening experience.

Specifically, the global podcasting market has been valued at about $27 billion in 2023, with forecasts indicating a compound annual growth rate (CAGR) of more than 15 percent over the period 2024- 2032 (gminsights.com).

If this growth is assumed to continue steadily, the market could reach a value around $70 billion as early as 2030, an achievement that testifies to the enormous economic potential of this sector. Similarly, the number of global listeners could expand to more than 500-600 million, thanks to continued technological innovation and the penetration of mobile devices in emerging and developed markets.

This expansion is strongly fueled by the integration of AI and big data tools, which are revolutionizing the way audio content is produced, distributed and personalized. The use of advanced algorithms makes it possible to analyze user preferences in real time, delivering tailored listening experiences and improving audience retention. In addition, innovations in automation are significantly reducing production costs and facilitating the creation of high-quality content, making podcasting an increasingly accessible medium even for independent creators.

Google Labs' NotebookLM is among these very innovations.

NotebookLM was created to assist users in managing, organizing, and analyzing personal notes and documents, leveraging AI to improve search efficiency and to enrich our notes and documents with information. We will see in Chapter 6 how it can be our personal AI-enhanced knowledge management system. Almost by accident, I discovered that it is set up as an innovative, state-of-the-art podcasting tool, capable of transforming a multiplicity of information sources into a highly realistic and engaging audio conversation in a matter of minutes. All, for free. The process begins with logging into the platform, which can be reached at notebooklm.google.com, where the user, authenticating with his or her Google account, creates a "notebook"-a sort of virtual container into which up to fifty items can be uploaded, ranging from PDF documents and text files to web pages, links to YouTube videos, as well as content from Google Docs or slides. Once uploaded, the material is carefully reviewed and organized, allowing those irrelevant content to be excluded, thus focusing on the essential data.

At this point, thanks to the "*Audio Overview*" feature, NotebookLM turns the selected content into a simulated conversation between two virtual interlocutors-a male and a female voice-interacting in a surprisingly natural way, with pauses, interruptions and even the use of colloquial expressions such as "umm" or "you know."

This tool thus makes it possible to create podcasts even for personal use by allowing long and complex content to be reduced into an easily usable format, ideal for listening while driving or exercising, while maintaining a conversational tone reminiscent of that of traditional podcasts. The process is extremely simple: after adding the sources to the Notebook, simply click "Generate" to start creating the audio, which will then be processed within minutes, allowing the user to listen, share or download the produced file.

Despite NotebookLM's extraordinary capabilities, the system has some limitations-including the lack of control over the number, genre of voices and the inability to precisely adjust the duration of the audio, which usually varies between five and fifteen minutes. Moreover, although the voice output is surprisingly realistic, some "telltale signs" of AI, such as the repeated use of terms like "*deep dive*" or "*delving into*," can still betray the artificial nature of the synthesis. It is also interesting to note that despite the possibility of providing specific instructions to guide the generation of content, such indications do not always significantly affect the final result.

In addition to podcast creation, NotebookLM offers additional useful features, such as the generation of study guides, *FAQs*, and accurate summaries, complete with citations and direct references to original sources. This versatility makes the tool particularly suitable not only for those who wish to produce innovative audio content, but also for those who intend to efficiently organize and manage large amounts of information. Ultimately, the integration of AI's automated capabilities with human creative intervention opens up new perspectives in the field of digital production, transforming NotebookLM into an indispensable ally for the creation of high-quality podcasts and the optimization of *content creation* processes.

5.4 Preparation of presentations

There are numerous solutions for creating PowerPoint presentations from scratch.

If you have a subscription to Microsoft Copilot this functionality is already built into Power Point itself.

As can be seen in the following image in the area highlighted with the red rectangle:

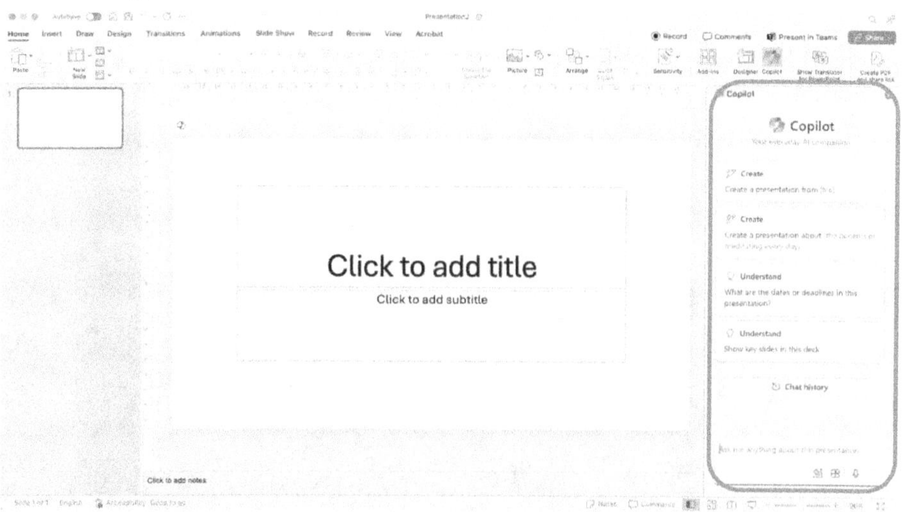

We can have a presentation created from a Ms Word or PDF document or by describing what we need by means of a *prompt*.

If we don't have a subscription to Copilot we can turn to numerous online tools for automatic slide creation such as gamma.app.

At the moment the result of these tools is, in my opinion, not up to the standard of what any of us can accomplish on our own.

They eliminate the blocking of the white paper, but I personally find it much more useful to have AI help me in structuring the presentation and revising it in its entirety.

For example, I recently used it to have it support me in the presentation for our plenary meeting that we have at the end of each quarter and in particular for the one at the beginning of the year by which we take stock of the past year and share goals for the current one.

I used different *prompts* depending on whether I was in the design phase, the implementation phase or the review phase.

In the planning phase, I asked for support in structuring the presentation according to my goals, time available, participants, etc.

Prompt for design:

***Prompt*: https://tinyurl.com/rru7kryd**

Context: I want to present to my entire group The achievements of 2024 in terms of economics, finances, and progress against our strategic plan. Highlight The successes and failures, lessons learned.

I also want to present the ambitious goals for 2025

Instructions:

Step 1: Help me identify the duration of each talk.

-The total duration of the meeting will be one hour.

-It will be in hybrid mode.

-I want to reserve the last 15 minutes for a question and answer section.

-I want to reserve The first 10 minutes for our CEO's welcome and reserve at least 3 slots of about 5 minutes for 3 colleagues to present 3 successful projects.

Step 2: Propose me a detailed agenda specifying for each talk how many minutes maximum it should last to meet the total hour duration.

Step 3: Ask me if I agree with the agenda or re-

> Step 4: when the agenda is confirmed advise me slide by slide what content to put.
>
> Required format: agenda by points with length of individual talk in minutes.
>
> Constraints: duration 1 hour total.
>
> Very clear style.

Prompt for implementation:

"For each slide you have planned, prepare me:

- Content suggestions and possible *call to action*.
- A *prompt* so that I can use it in DALL-E to have me generate an image per slide.

Ask me for confirmation for the hints and *prompts* for each slide, and in case I do not agree, for the specific slide, recreate the hints and *prompt* for DALL-E."

Using the prompts I independently prepare the slides by integrating the images I create on DALL-E with the *prompts* that were suggested.

Once the presentation is complete I export it as a PDF and ask for a check on grammatical correctness, correctness of the information given, and a set of tips on how to improve it.

Suggestions that I usually implement in part.

Prompt for verification:

***Prompt*: https://tinyurl.com/25um9kv8**

Act as a slide communication expert and perform a complete review of my presentation.

In particular, I would like a thorough review on four key aspects:

Grammatical Correctness:
Please check the entire text of the presentation, identifying any grammatical, syntactical and spelling errors, and suggesting appropriate corrections to ensure flawless use of the Italian language.
Accuracy of Information:
Check the consistency and accuracy of the information reported, with particular attention to economic, financial data and indicators related to strategic progress. Check that numbers and statements are consistent and supported by logic and hard facts. Ask for confirmation if you have any doubts.
Communication Effectiveness:
Provide detailed recommendations to improve the clarity and communicative impact of the presentation. Suggest possible changes in the language structure, and organization of the content to make the message more direct and engaging for the entire team.

Graphic and Visual Quality:
Offer guidance on how to optimize the graphic appearance of slides. This includes suggestions on layout, appropriate use of colors, choice of fonts, inclusion of visual elements (graphics, icons, images), and any other changes that will contribute to a more professional and eye-catching presentation.

For each of the above sections, include practical examples and specific suggestions so that any changes can be implemented effectively.

The move from presentation-assisted creation to video generation is a natural evolution in the path of generative AI adoption. If with presentations we have seen how AI can support us in organizing and visualizing static concepts, with videos we enter a dynamic dimension that until very recently seemed the exclusive domain of specialized professionals. The same *prompt engineering* methodology we applied to effectively structure our slides can be adapted, with appropriate modifications, to direct the creation of video content that communicates with even greater impact.

5.5 Video creation: when reality surpasses science fiction

The advent of AI systems capable of creating video represents a quantum leap in content generation. If text AI had already amazed us and AI for images had left us speechless, the ability to generate full videos makes us stand up in disbelief, redefining the boundaries between reality and fiction.

The year 2024 has anointed itself as the year of democratization of video generation via AI, bringing into the hands of creators, companies and even amateur users tools once relegated to science fiction. Although the first attempts between 2022 and 2023 were still immature, showing videos that were at times inconsistent and had artifacts, the evolution was exponential. These were no longer curious experiments, but rapidly maturing technologies ready to radically transform the audiovisual landscape.

The real turning point came with tools such as OpenAI's Sora, Gen-2 and other models from Runway, Pika Labs, Luma AI, Google's Veo 2, and, not least in power, Alibaba's impressive Qwen-2.5. These platforms have disrupted the world of video production, demonstrating ultra-realistic capabilities that far exceed the limitations of early attempts. Not only is physics now convincingly respected-a critical aspect of early models that struggled to simulate gravity or object interactions-but also camera movements have become fluid, complex, and cinematic, opening up new narrative frontiers.

The innovation does not stop at aesthetics: these systems handle scenes with multiple actors with ease, maintaining consistency of characters and their interactions. One can request a video with "two people talking in a café" and get surprisingly natural results, with believable facial expressions and realistic interaction with the surroundings.

But what are the implications of this revolution? The potential is immense and touches a variety of fields:

- **Film and entertainment**: faster and cheaper pre-production, instant visual prototypes, ability to create complex special effects at reduced costs.
- **Advertising and marketing**: rapid generation of customized video content for targeted campaigns, reduced production costs, ability to test different creatives quickly.
- **Training and *e-learning***: creation of engaging and interactive instructional videos, realistic simulations for professional training, customization of training content.
- **Journalism and information**: support for visualization of complex news and data, creation of explanatory content in video format, verification of information through hypothetical scenario generation.
- **Art and creativity**: new medium of expression for digital artists, possibility of experimenting with novel narrative forms, democratization of video creation for non-professional users.

Of course, with these extraordinary potentials also emerge ethical challenges and questions. The ease with which ultra-realistic videos can be created raises questions about the veracity of information, the spread of *fake news*, and the manipulation of public opinion. It also opens up debates about copyright and intellectual property of AI-generated content, as well as about the impact on the labor market for audiovisual professionals.

Despite these challenges, it is undeniable that the creation of videos with generative AI represents a technological revolution of historic significance. We are only at the beginning of a journey that promises to radically transform the way we create, consume and interact with video content, opening up scenarios unimaginable just a few years ago. The future of video production is already here, and it promises to be incredibly dynamic and full of opportunities.

Chapter Summary

Chapter 5 explores how generative AI is radically transforming content creation processes across multiple formats, offering practical applications that significantly improve productivity without compromising quality and brand consistency.

Text generation and optimization

The chapter presents advanced methodologies for document analysis, where AI effectively synthesizes complex information from multiple sources into coherent summaries. Through structured *prompts*, technical documentation, corporate communications and legal content can be created with remarkable efficiency. Proven *frameworks* reduce document processing time by 30-60% through automated grammar verification, stylistic optimization, and contextual adaptation for different audiences and communication channels.

Visual and multimedia creation

Expanding on text capabilities, the chapter explores image generation through a comparative analysis of major platforms (Adobe Firefly, Microsoft Designer, Dall-E and others), highlighting their strengths for professional applications. The section on presentation preparation introduces a three-step methodology: planning *prompts* for structure, content development prompts for individual slides, and comprehensive review *prompts* that systematically improve visual communication.

Emerging media applications.

The section on podcasts examines NotebookLM's capabilities in transforming documentary *repositories* into conversational audio content, while the segment on video creation addresses the revolutionary advancement of AI-generated video tools in 2024-2025, including their applications in marketing, education, journalism, and entertainment.

Throughout the chapter, practical examples and ready-to-use *prompts* provide immediately applicable tools for professionals seeking to integrate AI into their content creation processes, effectively balancing the benefits of automation with the necessary human oversight.

PART III

AI FOR PERSONAL AND PROFESSIONAL DEVELOPMENT

CHAPTER 6

AI AS PERSONAL *COACH*: BOOST YOUR PERFORMANCE

At the heart of the digital age we live in, AI no longer represents a distant frontier, but an intimate presence that redefines how we express ourselves, learn, and grow as professionals. This chapter stems from my personal experience as an executive going through the different stages of technological evolution, gradually transforming my relationship with these tools from mere curiosity to strategic partnership.

Like a conductor who discovers that he can amplify the capabilities of his musicians with instruments never imagined before, we now have the opportunity to experience how AI can become not a substitute for our intelligence, but a harmonious extension of our cognitive faculties. What I propose is not a technical guide, but a reflective journey through the possibilities that open up when we consciously integrate AI into the fundamental dimensions of our personal and professional development.

In the next paragraphs, we will explore two interconnected territories: the transformation of productivity through AI-enhanced knowledge management systems and, the acceleration of learning through personalized pathways and advanced cognitive techniques.

The real revolution that AI brings to our lives is not in the technology itself, but in the profound transformation of our relationship with ourselves and our potential. These tools offer us a sophisticated mirror that reflects and amplifies our uniqueness, allowing us to distill the essence of our professional contribution and express it with unprecedented clarity and impact.

6.1 Enhanced knowledge management: building your second brain with AI

In the hectic pace of the modern professional world, time has become the most precious resource we possess. Too often we find ourselves trapped in an endless cycle of repetitive tasks that devour precious hours, taking them away from strategic thinking and personal growth. AI today represents the most powerful tool for this liberation, enabling us to automate processes, organize information and reclaim the priceless resource that is our time.

How many times, at the end of a busy workday, have you asked yourself, "What have I really accomplished today?" Despite the many hours spent in front of the computer, we often find ourselves feeling that the really important tasks have been left undone, swamped by a sea of administrative and operational tasks.

In the path of an executive, the difference between a successful career and one of mere survival lies precisely in the ability to break free from the shackles of low-value-added activities. To do this systematically and effectively requires a structured approach to personal knowledge management.

Personal Knowledge Management: the architecture of cognitive effectiveness

Personal Knowledge Management (PKM) represents the art of capturing, organizing and effectively using the information that flows through our lives on a daily basis. With the explosion of digital data, developing an effective PKM system is no longer a luxury, but a necessity for any professional who wishes to excel.

David Allen's *Getting Things Done®* (GTD) methodology offers an ideal foundation for an effective PKM system. Allen's fundamental principle-that the mind excels at generating ideas but not at retaining them-finds new relevance in the age of AI. Neuroscientific research confirms that uncaptured thoughts generate cognitive "open loops," creating a cumulative mental load that diminishes our creative and analytical capacity. This phenomenon, first documented in 1927 by psychologist Bluma Zeigarnik and known as the "Zeigarnik effect," has since been confirmed by modern *neuroimaging* studies.

Research conducted by neuroscientists such as Daniel J. Levitin, author of "The Organized Mind" (2014), has shown how maintaining information in working memory significantly engages the prefrontal cortex, reducing cognitive resources available for other tasks. Studies conducted at Stanford University (Ophir et al., 2009) quantified how this fragmentation of attention can reduce decision-making efficiency by up to 40 percent and increase related stress, resulting in increased cortisol levels. More recently, research by Adam Gazzaley and Larry D. Rosen, reported in "The Distracted Mind" (2016), used functional *neuroimaging* techniques to visualize brain activity during interrupted tasks, highlighting how each unprocessed thought repeatedly activates neural circuits in the hippocampus and prefrontal cortex, generating what is referred to in neuroscientific terms as "residual cognitive load." This load accumulates throughout the day, progressively eroding our capacity for sustained concentration and creative thinking.

David Allen, in his GTD methodology, identifies a five-step process for effective information management:

1. **Gathering**: capturing all information at reliable capture points.
2. **Processing**: determining the meaning of each piece of information and the action required.
3. **Organizing**: placing items in appropriate categories.
4. **Review**: regularly examine the organizational system.
5. **Action**: using the organized information for decision-making and completion of activities.

This model, originally designed for a pre-AI context, gains new power when integrated with AI tools.

NotebookLM: the enhanced dialogue with your knowledge.

At the heart of an effective PKM system is a structured method for capturing, organizing and retrieving notes. It is not simply about accumulating information, but creating an ecosystem of knowledge that evolves and grows with us.

The traditional approach to notes-isolated documents organized by folders-is a thing of the past. Modern smart note systems rely on links, tags and metadata that create an interconnected network of knowledge, similar to how our brains work. With the integration of AI, these systems gain new dimensions of power.

Personally, I have adopted Google's NotebookLM as the central pillar of my PKM system, having experimented with numerous solutions over the past few years. This platform represents, in my experience, the most advanced embodiment of the "second brain" concept developed by Tiago Forte and which you can learn more about in his book, "Building a Second Brain: A Proven Method to Organize Your Digital Life and Unlock Your Creative Potential."

NotebookLM: the future of contextual learning

NotebookLM represents a revolutionary approach to knowledge management, developed by Google Research Labs. Unlike traditional note systems, NotebookLM is specifically designed to interact with documents through advanced language models, transforming the very relationship between users and their information.

The real innovation of NotebookLM lies in its ability to semantically understand the content of imported documents, establishing a bi-directional dialogue with the information corpus. During my adoption experience, I quickly realized that I was not simply using another notes tool, but was fundamentally altering the way I interact with my personal knowledge base.

NotebookLM particularly excels in projects that require deep analysis of complex documents-industry reports, scientific *papers*, interview transcripts, technical documentation. The difference from traditional systems is immediately noticeable: instead of manually extracting information, we can converse with the documents themselves, exploring connections and implications that we would otherwise struggle to grasp.

Distinctive features that make NotebookLM particularly effective include:

- **Deep contextual understanding**: the AI analyzes and semantically understands the content of uploaded documents, establishing conceptual connections between different sections and sources. This level of understanding goes far beyond simple keyword searching, allowing queries based on concepts rather than specific terms.

- **Advanced conversational interface**: the ability to ask natural, contextual questions about documents, receiving answers that synthesize information from different sections or sources. This approach transforms the search for information from a mechanical process to an intuitive dialogue.
- **Precise citation system**: each generated answer and synthesis is accompanied by references that conform to the original sources, allowing information to be immediately verified and deepened when necessary. This traceability creates a crucial bridge between AI's synthetic intuition and the analytical rigor required in professional contexts.
- **Transparent attribution**: the system maintains a clear distinction between original content from documents and AI-generated content, preventing confusion and maintaining informational integrity. This aspect has proven critical in my experience, especially when using the system for pre-meeting *briefings*.
- ***Audio overview***: a particularly innovative feature is the ability to turn notes and documents into dynamic audio conversations between two synthetic voices, in true podcasts as explained in Chapter 5.3. This allows information to be absorbed during "downtime" such as commuting or physical activity, extending the space available for learning in the day.

In my daily use, NotebookLM has completely transformed my interaction with complex documentation. For example: when I prepare for a strategy meeting, I don't just review the relevant documents, but actively query the system, "What are the three most controversial points that came up in previous discussions on this project?" or "How has the team's position on this evolved over the past three months?" The concise but comprehensive answers, always accompanied by precise references, allow me to enter conversations with a contextual understanding that previously required hours of re-reading.

Implementing an AI-enhanced knowledge system

An effective PKM system does not emerge spontaneously, but requires methodical implementation through progressive steps. My direct experience with NotebookLM allowed me to develop a practical *framework* that integrates GTD principles with the advanced capabilities of this tool.

Table: correspondence between NotebookLM capabilities and phases of David Allen's GTD methodology

GTD Phase	GTD Key Activity	Relevant NotebookLM Functionality	How to Use in NotebookLM
Capture	Collect all "material"	Versatile import (Drive, PDF, text, URL, audio, copied text), Add note	Create a "GTD Inbox" clipboard; paste URLs of articles, upload meeting transcripts, add quick notes for impromptu ideas
Clarify	Process material, decide actionability	Q&A on sources, Automated summaries, Content analysis, Idea generation.	Upload a project document, ask NotebookLM, "What are the key deliverables?"; generate a summary of a long email to identify key actions
Organize	Place clarified items in the right place	Notes (for lists), Notepad (for projects), Mind	Create notes for "Project List," "Next Actions (@Computer)," "Waiting

		Maps, Archiving sources	For"; use Mind Maps to break down complex projects
Reflect	Regularly review the system	Q&A, Summaries, Audio Overviews, Mind Maps, Access to notes and sources	During Weekly Review, ask NotebookLM about the status of a project based on uploaded reports; listen to an Audio Overview of key documents in a project
Take Action	Perform selected actions	Quickly access notes (contextual lists), Q&A for details on activities, Access supporting materials	Refer to the note "Upcoming Actions (@Telephone Calls)"; if an activity is unclear, ask NotebookLM a question about the associated original source

1. Create a notebook structure aligned with GTD.

NotebookLM was not created to natively implement GTD methodology, so we must customize it for this purpose, and the first step is to establish a notebook architecture that directly maps to GTD organizational categories:

Main Notebooks:

📥 -INBOX (Unprocessed acquisitions)

🎯 -PROJECTS (Multi-step results)

⚡ -NEXT ACTIONS (Categorized by context)

📅 -CALENDAR ELEMENTS (Commitments with specific date)

👁‍🗨 -PENDING (Delegated elements)

🔍 -REFERENCE (Non-actionable information)

💭 -EITHER SOON/FOREVER (Future possibilities)

Within NotebookLM, I have found that creating separate notebooks for these categories provides the clearest implementation of GTD's organizing principles. The inbox serves as a universal capture point, with subsequent notebooks corresponding to Allen's recommended categories.

This structure provides not only a logical organization, but also a clear flow path for information through the system. Each item begins in the inbox, is processed and categorized, and finally finds its appropriate location in the system.

2. Simplify the acquisition process

The capture phase is the most critical time in information management-if friction exists here, valuable insights are lost. I optimized my capture workflow in NotebookLM through several strategies:

1. **Configure mobile shortcuts**: I created custom iOS shortcuts that directly initiate NotebookLM voice capture, allowing me to capture thoughts on the go with a simple tap (using the NotebookLM mobile app).
2. **Use *web clipper* extension**: for online research, I use a *web clipping* tool that sends web content directly to my system, keeping formatting and references intact (a Chrome extension).
3. **Establish capture triggers**: I have trained myself to open NotebookLM whenever a thought arises that triggers the question "Should I remember this?", creating a habit of immediate capture.

This multichannel capture strategy ensures that regardless of the context-whether in a meeting, traveling, or browsing online-information flows smoothly into my reliable system. The crucial element is reducing friction: any barrier, even a small one, between the emergence of an idea and its capture represents a risk of loss.

3. AI-enhanced weekly review.

Weekly review represents the "heart of GTD," according to Allen-a sacred time to process, organize and refresh the entire system. NotebookLM's AI capabilities turn this critical practice into a much more effective and enlightening process with the following interactive check-box:

Weekly Review Checklist with NotebookLM

- Process Inbox down to Zero
  - AI Assistance: "Analyze my inbox and suggest categorization for each item."

- Project List Review.
  - AI Assistance: "Identifies projects without definite next actions."
  - AI Assistance: "Highlights projects with upcoming deadlines."

- Update Upcoming Actions.
  - AI Assistance: "Generates potential next actions for Project X."

- Review Pending
  - AI Assistance: "Identifies items on hold for more than 7 days."

- Review Before or Then/Maybe

- AI Assistance: "Bring up 'sooner or later' items relevant to current projects."

By leveraging these AI-driven insights during my weekly review, I significantly reduced the time required (from about 1.5 hours to less than 45 minutes), simultaneously improving the quality and completeness of the process. The most transformative element is the system's ability to identify relationships and opportunities that would likely have escaped manual review, making connections between seemingly disconnected projects.

I have found specific *prompts* such as "Based on this source, what are the potential next steps?" particularly effective when processing complex project documents, and "What are the key points of this document?" for quick analysis of extended materials. When reviewing projects, I often ask NotebookLM to "Outline the main steps to achieve [specific result]" when I need to break down a goal into concrete steps.

4. Managing reference material

For knowledge workers, reference information is often the largest category of information-and the one most prone to disorganization. NotebookLM particularly excels in this domain through two key capabilities:

Semantic search capabilities.

Unlike traditional keyword search, NotebookLM's AI understands concepts and relationships, allowing you to find information even when you don't remember the exact wording:

Traditional search: "cybersecurity certification meeting notes"
Semantic search NotebookLM: "What did we discuss about the

new ISO certification process last month?"

This capability directly addresses one of the primary challenges in reference material management: retrieving information based on conceptual understanding rather than perfect recall of keywords. I have found that this feature dramatically reduces search time, especially when working with complex technical documents or discussions that have taken place over a period of months.

Contextual Summary

When dealing with extensive reference materials, concise summaries become invaluable. NotebookLM can generate contextual summaries at multiple levels:

- Document-level overviews.
- Topic-specific extractions.
- Comparative analyses across multiple sources.

I regularly use this feature when preparing for board meetings, having NotebookLM generate executive summaries of complex technical documentation-a task that previously consumed hours of manual effort. The quality of these summaries is remarkable: they retain the essence of the original material while preserving important nuances, while eliminating redundancies and non-essential details.

5. Audio overview: extending learning beyond the text

We have already analyzed the *audio overview* function in the section devoted to podcast creation because, although it was not born with this objective and does not have the pretensions to compare with dedicated solutions for personal use, it performs its task excellently. This capability extends GTD principles in fascinating ways:

- **Mobile processing**: listening to my notes while commuting, effectively using what used to be "dead time" for revision and learning. This is exactly what I did to prepare for a recent panel discussion: having to drive about an hour and a half to the city hosting the event, I took the entire commute to listen several times to a podcast of about fifteen minutes, made for me by NotebookLM, so that I showed up to the meeting perfectly prepared.
- **Cognitive reinforcement**: using multiple sensory channels significantly improves information retention compared to passive reading.
- **Dialogic perspective**: the conversational format often reveals connections and tensions in the material that were not evident in the original text form.

During my experimentation with this feature, I have found that certain types of information-particularly complex strategic concepts and issues with various contrasting perspectives-become significantly clearer when transformed into a dialogic format. This allows me to process complex information during walks or while driving my car, turning what was previously wasted time into opportunities for insight and reflection.

6. Progressive implementation plan

Implementing NotebookLM as the centerpiece of your PKM system requires a phased approach that I have personally tested and refined. Here is the three-step plan I recommend:

Phase 1: Foundations (2 weeks)

- Create the NotebookLM account and configure access on all devices.

- Import key documents as an initial base (max 10-15 key documents).
- Familiarize with the conversational interface through guided exploration sessions.
- Define initial thematic notebooks aligned with your focus areas.

Phase 2: Expanding and connecting (1 month)

- Systematically expand the document corpus with relevant material.
- Begin making interconnections through cross-queries.
- Experiment with the *Audio Overview* feature during transit times.
- Develop the first custom *prompt* templates for information processing.

Step 3: Integration and optimization (continued)

- Incorporate NotebookLM into daily decision-making processes.
- Refine the information architecture based on emerging usage *patterns*.
- Implement weekly maintenance and enrichment rituals.
- Develop personal effectiveness metrics to assess impact on one's cognitive process.

Hybrid approach to maximizing effectiveness

So NotebookLM, while powerful, is not designed to be a complete task manager. It lacks native features such as reminders, recurring tasks, and robust management of due dates. For this reason, I recommend a hybrid system that combines the strengths of several tools:

- **NotebookLM**: Use it for the intellectual aspects of GTD (capturing complex content, clarifying, organizing project support material, deep thinking).
- **Dedicated *task* manager** (such as MS Planner, Todoist, Asana or others): Employ it for granular task tracking, contextual reminders and deadline management.
- **Calendar**: Reserve it exclusively for specific time commitments and deep work blocks.

This "strengths-based" approach avoids forcing NotebookLM to perform functions for which it is not optimized, instead creating a synergistic ecosystem of complementary tools.

To ensure the long-term sustainability of the integration, I developed a system of rituals that incorporate NotebookLM into daily routines:

1. **Morning reflection ritual (10 minutes)**: start each day by querying the Calendar (in my case MS Outlook) asking Copilot for the day's appointments and essential information about participants and topics. For insights I move to my *personal knowledge management system*: NotebookLM .
2. **Capturing information:** has no specific schedule or process with the exception of notes I take on virtual or in-person phone calls or meetings. As soon as I have a thought to capture, an idea or relevant information I pull out my smartphone and with the mobile app access NotebookLM.
3. **Enhanced pre-meeting preparation (15 minutes)**: use NotebookLM to create contextual *briefings*, prior to any significant meeting, based on relevant documents and history of previous interactions.

4. **Integrated weekly review (60 minutes)**: devote an uninterrupted hour to reviewing the system, identifying emerging *patterns*, and planning for the following week with AI analytic support. I usually devote the first hour of Friday afternoon to the weekly review.

These rituals transform NotebookLM from a simple *repository* to an active cognitive partner, integrated into the daily flow of thought and action.

Enhanced productivity: toward an extended mind

The implementation of NotebookLM as the heart of the *Personal Knowledge Management* system represents more than an incremental improvement in productivity: it is a fundamental transformation in the way we think, learn, and create.

In my personal experience, this shift has marked the evolution from simple "information management" to a true "cognitive extension," where the boundary between internal and external memory becomes increasingly fluid. NotebookLM does not just store and retrieve information, but actively participates in the thinking process, offering alternative perspectives, highlighting hidden *patterns* and suggesting unexpected connections.

Mind Maps to Visualize GTD "Horizons of Focus"

One of the most powerful applications I have discovered is the use of NotebookLM's Mind Maps to visualize GTD "Horizons of Focus," specifically Horizon 2 (Areas of Focus and Responsibility). This approach transforms an abstract concept into a dynamic visual representation:

- I create a clipboard specific to each Focus Area (e.g., "Professional Development," "Health and Wellness").
- I import key documents related to that area (articles, notes, planning).
- I generate a Mind Map that visually links active projects, resources, and potential new directions.
- I use interaction with nodes on the map to explore connections and generate new ideas.

This visualization of Horizons reveals synergies and gaps that are unlikely to emerge from simple text lists, elevating GTD review from a mechanical exercise to true strategic exploration.

Creating mind maps, from content-whether textual or drawn from a Microsoft Excel spreadsheet-provides numerous opportunities to represent complex concepts in graphic form.

Advanced Features to Enhance GTD.

The unique capabilities of NotebookLM offer opportunities to further enrich traditional GTD practice:

Features	**Key Capabilities in NotebookLM**	**Specific Application in the GTD Context.**	**Potential Benefit to the GTD User.**
Podcast/Audio Overview.	AI presenters, interactive mode, topic customization, content discussion	Summarize weekly project reports during Reflection phase; audio *briefing* to start new projects; learning new topics (One Day/Maybe)	Better understanding of project status; faster *onboarding*; accessible and engaging learning
Mind Map.	Visual branching, node Q&A, branch	Visual decomposition of a complex project during	Clearer identification

	expansion/collapse, downloading	the Organization/Clarification phase; GTD *brainstorming* sessions; visualization of Areas of Interest	of all project activities; creative exploration of ideas; holistic view of strategic commitments

Conclusions

Building your *Second Brain* with NotebookLM requires an initial investment, but ensures progressively increasing returns. Like any deep transformation, the journey begins with small, conscious steps characterized by experimentation and constant adaptation. The benefit is not limited to higher productivity: it transforms the way we think, learn and generate value in an increasingly complex context. However, it takes months of practice to internalize and make automatic this new form of collaboration between human and artificial intelligence. In my view, the adoption of an 'extended mind' represents the future of cognition in the digital age: it does not replace natural intelligence, but rather complements it harmoniously, amplifying creative thinking, empathy and contextual judgment - qualities that make us unmistakably human.

Having an efficient 'extended mind' not only optimizes the management of existing knowledge, but also frees up the cognitive resources needed for the modern professional's most critical challenge: the continuous acquisition of new skills. Once the system has been built to organize knowledge, the next step is to use AI to accelerate the way this knowledge is built. Let us now look at how to turn AI into a personal coach for learning faster and better.

6.2 Accelerate the development of key skills with AI: learn faster and better

The most valuable capital in a knowledge economy is not physical or financial *assets*, but the skills we bring with us. In a rapidly changing world, the ability to acquire new skills quickly and with depth is no longer simply a competitive advantage-it has become a necessity for professional survival. AI is radically transforming the way we can develop these skills, offering personalized learning paths, immediate feedback and unprecedented opportunities for practice.

Over careers, the cycle of skills obsolescence has shortened dramatically. Skills that once represented solid foundations for decades of careers can now become irrelevant within a few years. This acceleration has made continuous learning not just a professional virtue but an existential condition of contemporary work.

The real competitive advantage lies not in the specific skills we possess at any given time, but in the meta-competence of "learning to learn"-the ability to rapidly acquire new knowledge and skills in response to changing market needs.

If I were asked today what I consider the most valuable skill, I would answer without hesitation: the thirst for knowledge. It is that burning desire, that unrelenting passion that drives one to seek out, every day, something new to learn - to the point of investing with discipline at least one hour daily in study and insight.

Today, AI offers unprecedented tools to enhance this meta-competence, allowing us to personalize learning paths, receive immediate feedback, and simulate hands-on experiences in ways that were simply impossible before.

Personalized learning plan

The beauty of AI-assisted learning lies in its ability to adapt precisely to our individual needs, strengths, and weaknesses. No longer standardized paths, but tailored development itineraries that dynamically evolve with us.

Assessment of current competencies

The starting point of any effective learning pathway is a clear understanding of the starting point: what skills we already possess, what is our level of mastery in each, and what are our strengths and weaknesses. When we have the opportunity to take on new responsibilities, we may be faced with a seemingly impossible challenge: quickly acquiring in-depth knowledge in very different technical areas. The turning point comes when we abandon the generalist approach and instead adopt a strategy based on a precise analysis of current skills and specific gaps that need to be filled to be effective in the new role. AI can transform this process, offering objective, multidimensional assessments that go far beyond traditional *assesments*. I was faced with this challenge when I was appointed CEO of a company specializing in cybersecurity, despite having never worked in that field. I sensed the need to acquire a level of technical expertise that would allow me to dialogue with a CISO (*Chief Information Security Officer*) of a client or potential client company with a business-oriented rather than exclusively technical approach. Given the type of interlocutor, I needed to acquire the technical knowledge essential to sustain conversations, understand the complexities my team was facing, and subsequently propose new services once I had mastered the context. To achieve this goal, I decided to devote two hours daily to self-training with the goal of closing the gaps within thirty days. The outcome was excellent and I have to thank the output of this prompt, which allowed me to assess my technical, strategic and market skills, draft a customized training plan including a strategy to engage CISOs and define a *continuous* learning path (*continuous learning*). Below I present the prompt that literally "saved my life," which you can adapt to your specific needs.

Prompt: **https://tinyurl.com/4w6yv94e**

Based on my professional profile (attached as a PDF of my LinkedIn profile or CV), help me develop a targeted cybersecurity training program that will enable me to effectively interact with CISOs and promote cybersecurity services. I need to build my skills in this area for my new position as CEO of a small company specializing in cybersecurity consulting.

Profile Analysis and Skills Assessment.

First, analyze my professional background to:

1. Identify my relevant experience in the cybersecurity field.
2. Assess my current level of knowledge in cybersecurity based on my professional history
3. Identify my transferable skills from certification, compliance, and leadership roles
4. Determine the knowledge gaps that need to be filled

Then help me rate my competence in these key domains (scale of 1 to 5):

Technical Skills:
- Governance, Risk & Compliance frameworks and methodologies
- Cyber Risk Quantification approaches and tools
- Offensive Security concepts and methodologies
- Principles of Identity and Access Management
- Functions and processes of the Security Operations Center
- Incident Response protocols and best practices
- DevSecOps integration approaches
- IoT/OT security considerations for industrial environments

Strategic/Business Competencies:
- Aligning security initiatives with business objectives
- Communicating cyber risks to executive leadership
- Understanding of regulatory requirements (GDPR, NIS2, DORA, etc.).
- Cyber insurance and risk transfer mechanisms
- Cybersecurity market analysis and trends
- Methodologies for evaluating the ROI of security investments

Market Knowledge:
- Major vendors and providers of security solutions
- Emerging technologies and approaches in cybersecurity
- Understanding of the current threat landscape
- CISO priorities and decision-making processes

Development of Training Program.

Based on this assessment, create a comprehensive 30-day training plan (2 hours per day) that:

- Elevate my technical expertise in cybersecurity domains
- Deepen my understanding of the cybersecurity market, key players and solutions
- Enhance my ability to interact effectively with CISOs by understanding their challenges
- Strengthen my ability to translate security needs into business value propositions
- Develop consultative sales skills for cybersecurity services)

The plan must include:

- A structured learning roadmap organized by weekly themes
- Daily learning resources (books, courses, articles, podcasts, webinars)
- Hands-on exercises to reinforce theoretical knowledge
- Networking opportunities with experts in the field
- Progress measurement metrics for weekly evaluation
- Role-playing scenarios that simulate conversations with CISOs

CISO Engagement Strategy
As part of the plan, help develop:
- A framework for understanding the priorities of CISOs in different industries
- A conversation guide with strategic questions to uncover needs and challenges
- Value proposition templates to position cybersecurity solutions
- Answers to common objections and concerns
- An essential glossary of technical and business terminology

Ongoing Intelligence on the Marketplace
Finally, he recommends resources for staying current:

- Key sources of information (blogs, newsletters, trade publications)
- Relevant industry events and conferences
- Professional communities and discussion forums
- Market analyst reports to follow
- Methods for monitoring emerging threats and innovative solutions

My ultimate goal is to leverage my current executive experience by combining it with a deeper knowledge of cybersecurity to effectively promote cybersecurity services through meaningful conversations with security managers. The plan should build on my current strengths by addressing gaps that would prevent me from confidently interacting with CISOs at both the technical and business levels.

Accelerated learning techniques.

Not all learning strategies are the same. Cognitive science research has identified techniques that can multiply the effectiveness of study time. AI can help us implement these techniques with precision and consistency, radically transforming our learning curve.

Feynman technique assisted

The Feynman technique, made famous by physicist Richard Feynman, is based on a simple but powerful principle: If you can't explain a concept in simple terms, you probably don't really understand it. This technique involves explaining a concept as if you were teaching it to a child, identifying *gaps* in understanding and continually refining the explanation.

When an executive becomes responsible for complex technical divisions, he or she is in urgent need of a deep understanding of topics that are outside his or her *background*. The *Feynman Technique* becomes a major tool, pushing beyond superficial understanding toward a working knowledge that enables informed decision making and effective communication with specialized teams.

AI can serve as an ideal partner to implement this technique, offering immediate feedback and guiding the refinement process.

Implementation of the *Feynman* technique with AI:

1. **Initial articulation**
    - Explain the concept to the AI as if you were talking to a novice.
    - Receive feedback on clarity and completeness.
    - Identifying areas where the explanation becomes complex or vague.

2. ***Gap* identification.**
    - Analyze with the AI which parts of the explanation are vague or complex.
    - Identify technical terms that have not been adequately simplified.
    - Recognize implicit assumptions or missing logical steps.
3. **Iterative refinement.**
    - Repeat explanation focusing on problem areas.
    - Use analogies and metaphors to clarify complex points.
    - Progressively simplify language while maintaining precision.
4. **Verification of understanding.**
    - Answer AI-generated critical questions.
    - Apply the concept to practical scenarios.
    - Test the robustness of understanding through variations of the theme.

Example *prompt* for *Feynman technique*:

"I want to use the *Feynman Technique* to consolidate my understanding of [complex concept]. I ask you to act as a *coach* in this process:

1. First I will explain the concept as if I were talking to an intelligent but unskilled 12-year-old.

2. Analyze my explanation and identify:

- Technical or slang terms that I have not adequately simplified.
- Logical steps I skipped or did not clarify sufficiently.

- Concepts that seem vague or show incomplete understanding.

3. Ask 3-5 "naive" but insightful questions that a curious listener might ask.

4. Guide me in refining my explanation, focusing on problem areas.

5. In the end, assess how well my final explanation reflects a deep understanding.

Here is my initial explanation:

[Space for user explanation]"

Personalized microlearning

Microlearning-the approach that divides learning material into small, focused modules-has proven particularly effective for professionals with busy agendas. By allowing learning in short sessions spread throughout the day, it maximizes the use of "interstitial time" and facilitates the integration of new knowledge.

The reality of executive life is that we rarely have blocks of several hours to devote to learning. When we restructure the approach to professional development into 10- to 15-minute modules, strategically distributed across the agenda, we find not only that we can be more consistent, but also that gradual integration leads to deeper and more lasting understanding.

AI can transform the *microlearning* experience by creating tailored modules that dynamically adapt to our needs and available time.

Microlearning strategies with AI:

1. **Intelligent *chunking*:**
    - Break down complex topics into logical, digestible units.
    - Sequence micro-modules in an optimal progression.

   - Make explicit connections between modules to build integrated understanding.
2. **Contextual personalization:**
   - Adapt content to the time available at different times.
   - Suggest micro-modules relevant to upcoming activities.
   - Calibrate depth according to context and mental energy.
3. **Multimodality:**
   - Vary formats (text, audio, interactive) for different contexts.
   - Optimizes for different devices and situations.
   - Alternate modes to maintain *engagement* and freshness.
4. **Planned Retrieval:**
   - Implements strategic recalls of key concepts.
   - Explicitly connect new micro-modules with previous ones.
   - Incorporate gamification elements to motivate continuity.

Sample *microlearning prompts*:

"Help me convert this complex topic into a *microlearning* plan that fits my busy schedule:

Topic: [Topic description].

Learning objective: [Description of objective]

Typical *patterns* in my schedule:

- 10-15 minutes between meetings (3-4 times a day)

- 20-30 minutes during commutes (2 times a day)
- Occasional 45-minute blocks (1-2 times a week)

Please create a *microlearning* plan that:

1. Breaks down the topic into 12-15 logical and consequential micro-modules.
2. For each module:
   - Defines a specific learning objective.
   - Suggest the optimal format (text, audio, quiz, hands-on exercise).
   - State the estimated duration (5-10-15-30 minutes).
   - Specify prerequisites (which modules should be completed first).
3. Organize the modules into "pathways" that can fit into different time slots.
4. Suggest how to incorporate elements of repetition and recall.

Consider that I prefer [visual/auditory/practical learning] and that my current level is [beginner/intermediate/advanced]."

Feedback loops and virtual coaching

Learning without feedback is like navigating without a compass: we can move a lot, but not know whether we are getting closer or farther from our destination. AI can act as a virtual *coach*, providing immediate, personalized, multi-perspective feedback that dramatically accelerates our path to mastery.

Simulations and role-playing

One of the most significant challenges in acquiring new skills, especially for soft skills, is the lack of safe practice opportunities. Simulations and *role-playing* offer a protected environment in which to experiment, make mistakes and hone skills before putting them to the test in consequential situations.

The first time an executive has to conduct a difficult feedback conversation with a senior manager can generate feelings of unpreparedness and anxiety. "Rehearsing" these difficult conversations in advance through *role-playing* not only improves performance but significantly reduces the associated stress.

AI represents an ideal simulation partner: always available, able to take on different roles and styles, and capable of providing detailed feedback.

Approaches to AI-powered simulations:

1. **Dynamic *role-playing*:**
    - Simulate conversations and negotiations with different *stakeholders*.
    - Experiments with alternative approaches to the same scenario.
    - Implements variations in personality and response styles.
2. **Decision-making simulations:**
    - Confront complex scenarios with cascading decisions.
    - Explores the consequences of different strategic choices.
    - Analyzes trade-offs and numerous considerations .
3. **Multi-angle feedback:**
    - Receive feedback from the perspective of different *stakeholders*.

- Analyze the impact of your communications on different *audiences*.
- Identify specific verbal and nonverbal elements and their effect.

4. **Progressive practice:**
   - Start with basic scenarios and gradually increase complexity.
   - Introduce variables and complications to test flexibility.
   - Develops emotional resilience through gradual exposure.

Example prompts for simulations:

"I want to simulate a difficult feedback conversation with a senior manager who:

- Constantly misses project deadlines.

- Tends to react defensively when confronted.

- Has excellent technical performance but is creating team dynamics problems.

Please play the role of this manager while I practice how to give feedback. After each of my interventions:

1. Respond realistically based on the profile described.

2. Provide brief notes on my approach (effective/ineffective and why).

3. Vary your responses based on my approach (more or less defensive).

At the end of the simulation, provide an overall analysis of:

- Strengths in my approach.
- Areas for improvement.
- Specific techniques I could have used.
- How I could have better structured the overall conversation."

If you have invested in a ChatGPT subscription, I strongly suggest you run these simulations with the voice mode that takes them to another level.

Chapter Summary.

In this chapter, we explore the transformative potential of AI as an intimate partner in professional development rather than a distant technological frontier. Drawing from my own executive experience through technological evolutions, I present practical *frameworks* for leveraging AI in amplifying our cognitive capabilities and accelerating skill acquisition.

Main Focus Areas:

- Transforming productivity through AI-enhanced knowledge management.
- Accelerating skill development with personalized learning systems.
- Creating effective feedback loops for continuous improvement.

Personal Knowledge Management: building your second brain

My implementation of Google's NotebookLM exemplifies how AI transforms traditional note-taking into dynamic knowledge ecosystems. This platform, with its contextual understanding capabilities, converts static information *repositories* into interactive thinking partners that extend cognitive capacity.

The practical *framework* I developed integrates the principles of *Getting Things Done*® with AI capabilities through:

- A structured notebook architecture aligned with GTD workflows.
- Frictionless capture systems across multiple channels.

- AI-enhanced weekly reviews that reduce processing time by 40 percent.
- Semantic search capabilities that transcend keyword limitations.
- Audio overviews that turn "dead time" into learning opportunities.

This approach represents a fundamental shift from information management to cognitive extension-creating a continuous feedback loop between human intuition and AI-enhanced *pattern* recognition.

Accelerated skill development through partnership with AI

When I was appointed to lead a cybersecurity company despite limited domain knowledge, I used a structured AI-assisted approach to acquire essential skills within 30 days. This experience validated the potential of AI as a learning accelerator through:

- Comprehensive skills assessment in technical, strategic and market dimensions.
- AI-enhanced Feynman Technique to consolidate understanding.
- Customized *microlearning frameworks* tailored to executive agendas.
- Virtual simulation environments to practice critical conversations.

Particularly transformative was the use of voice-based *role-playing* simulations to prepare for difficult feedback conversations, demonstrating how AI creates safe practice environments for high-risk professional interactions.

The integration of these approaches creates a virtuous cycle in which knowledge management fuels accelerated learning, which in turn enriches the knowledge ecosystem. This represents not only an improvement in efficiency, but a fundamental transformation in the way we approach professional development-moving from episodic skill upgrading to an ongoing cognitive partnership with AI systems that amplify our uniquely human capacities for creativity, connection, and contextual judgment.

CHAPTER 7

REDESIGNING YOUR CAREER IN THE AI ERA: STRATEGIES, SKILLS, AND NEW OPPORTUNITIES

AI is already radically reconfiguring the job market, creating new opportunities and making established professional models obsolete.

In this transitional phase, the ability to strategically interpret technological change becomes a crucial factor in professional differentiation. I have observed how professionals essentially fall into two categories: those who passively undergo the transformation and those who exploit it as a competitive lever. The difference lies in methodological approach and strategic vision.

This chapter provides an operational model developed through real experiences of professional transition in the AI era. I will not present an idealized or simplified view of this path, but a realistic map that includes obstacles, failures, and concrete strategies to overcome them.

The central case we will explore concerns Roberto (fictitious name), a cybersecurity professional who at age 50 suddenly found himself unemployed and forced to reposition himself in a market transformed by AI. I will also integrate other experiences-including my own-to offer a broader and more balanced perspective.

7.1 Strategic analysis: mapping the professional terrain in the AI era

Data-driven market assessment

The first step in any effective career transition is a deep understanding of the emerging professional landscape. In the AI era, this requires a systematic, *data-driven* approach that transcends the impressionistic analyses of the past.

Market analysis methodology with AI

I developed a structured methodology for labor market analysis using AI as a research assistant. This approach consists of four sequential steps:

1. **Structured data collection** from primary sources (mainly from LinkedIn Jobs, Indeed, and industry reports).
2. **Quantitative analysis** of emerging trends (percentage growth by position, salary trends, geographic distribution).
3. **Qualitative analysis** of skill requirements (through generative AI applied to hundreds of job descriptions).
4. **Strategic synthesis** identifying professional positioning opportunities.

To maximize the effectiveness of this analysis, it is critical to provide AI with quality data. With Roberto, we began by exporting his complete LinkedIn profile in PDF format, enriching it with a detailed document on his most significant projects in cybersecurity. This data became the input for the following *prompt* that supported us in our strategic market analysis.

***Prompt*: https://tinyurl.com/wzx5trjm**

Perform an in-depth analysis of the labor market at the intersection of [Cybersecurity] and [Artificial Intelligence], using my attached professional profile for contextualization.

1. QUANTITATIVE ANALYSIS.

- Identifies the 10 emerging roles with greatest percentage growth over the past 12 months
- Analyzes the geographic distribution of opportunities in Europe
- Determines average salary ranges for each identified role
- Calculates the gap between supply and demand for these roles

2. QUALITATIVE ANALYSIS

- Extract clusters of skills in demand for each role
- Identifies common patterns in "preferred qualifications"
- Analyze the evolution of job descriptions over the past 24 months
- Assesses the impact of the EU AI Act and other legislation on skills demand

3. OPPORTUNITY MAPPING

- Identifies market niches with high demand and low competition
- Identify roles where my experience in [Cybersecurity] is a differential advantage
- Suggest 3-5 specific roles where I could strategically position myself

4. COMPETITIVE ASSESSMENT

- Analyze the typical candidate profile for the suggested roles

- Identify points of differentiation from my profile
- Suggest strategies to close any gaps

Present results in structured format, with visualizations where appropriate

This approach generated, with Gemini 2.5 Pro's Deep Research feature, an impressive 27-page A4 report that gave us a detailed understanding of the emerging dynamics at the intersection of cybersecurity and AI. The analysis highlighted three macro-trends that were redefining the market:

1. The emergence of **hybrid governance roles** combining cybersecurity skills with AI governance, accelerated by the enactment of the EU AI Act.

2. The growing demand for **secure integration** skills between traditional IT infrastructure and new AI systems.

3. The growing premium for ***risk assesment*** skills specific to AI systems.

The value of benchmarking

To put these general trends in context, we conducted a detailed comparative analysis between Roberto's profile and those of professionals already positioned in the emerging AI cybersecurity industry with the following *prompt*:

***Prompt*: https://tinyurl.com/4punzsmv**

Using my attached professional profile, compare me to currently established professionals in the role of [AI Security Integration Mng]

1. PROFESSIONAL BENCHMARK

- Analyze 15-20 LinkedIn profiles of [AI Security Integration Manager].
- Identify common background, career paths, and typical credentials
- Extract recurring patterns in professional experiences and skills

2. DIFFERENTIAL ANALYSIS

- Systematically compares my profile to the identified benchmark
- Highlights unique strengths that positively differentiate me
- Identifies critical gaps compared to the benchmark profile

3. IDENTIFICATION OF COMPETITIVE ADVANTAGES

- Identifies elements of my experience that could represent unexpected advantages
- Analyze how my experience in [multinational IT systems implementation] could translate into value in this new context
- Suggest how to articulate these advantages in a compelling way

4. POSITIONING PLAN

- Propose a distinctive professional positioning based on analysis
- Suggest 3-5 "unique selling propositions" for my personal brand
- Identify 3 types of organizations where this positioning would have the most value

This analysis revealed a valuable piece of information: while the majority of professionals in AI security came from purely technical (*data scientists*, *machine learning* (ML) *engineers* with *backgrounds* in cybersecurity) or purely managerial (risk managers, *privacy officers*) backgrounds, very few combined solid operational experience as CIOs/CISOs with systems implementation skills in enterprise environments and strategic vision.

This finding enabled Roberto to identify a distinctive positioning as an "AI Security Integration Expert," capable of bridging the gap between emerging AI technology, existing IT infrastructure, and security governance model.

Case study: The value of detailed analysis

The methodical approach paid off when Roberto discovered an opportunity in a critical infrastructure company. Analysis of the company's activities-through review of recent patents, strategic acquisitions, and information from their technical blog-had revealed that they were implementing AI systems for infrastructure monitoring, but faced significant challenges in integrating security requirements.

During the interview, Roberto was able to demonstrate a thorough understanding of the company's specific challenges, already proposing possible solutions that he had hypothesized specifically for their context. The recruiter, amazed by the preparation, confessed, "This is the first time a candidate understands our specific challenges so deeply before even joining the company."

This analytical approach produced tangible results not only for Roberto. The key to success in this case was not simply access to information-widely available online-but its structured and personalized organization that transformed a mass of data into strategic and actionable information. This highlights how AI does not replace human analysis, but significantly enhances it, allowing complex information ecosystems to be navigated with previously impossible precision.

Realistic *assesment* of transferable skills

A common mistake in career transitions is to focus excessively on missing skills, underestimating the potential of transferable skills. For senior professionals like Roberto, this approach can generate anxiety and a sense of inadequacy that prevents them from valuing decades of relevant experience.

Analysis of transferable skills

Transferable skills can be grouped into three macro-groups:

1. **Technical skills** (methodological and instrumental).
2. **Organizational skills** (leadership, team and project management).
3. **Meta-competencies** (cognitive skills and problem-solving approaches).

To help us identify Roberto's, including a matrix of transferability of these skills to the role in the AI world to which he aspired, as well as the skills to be developed to complete the role, we always used Gemini with the following *prompt*.

***Prompt*: https://tinyurl.com/5n79w6cx**

Analyze my attached professional profile to identify transferable skills to the field of [AI Security Integration].

1. TRANSFERABLE TECHNICAL SKILLS

- Identifies methodologies and frameworks that I have used that are applicable to the new context
- Evaluates how my experience in [ERP systems implementation] translates into value for [AI integration]
- Identifies tools and technologies I have mastered with applications in the new domain

2. TRANSFERABLE ORGANIZATIONAL SKILLS

- Analyze my experience leading and managing teams in multinational settings
- Evaluates how my experience managing external vendors applies to the AI ecosystem
- Identifies project management methodologies that remain relevant in the new context

3. TRANSFERABLE META-SKILLS

- Extract problem-solving patterns from my professional history
- Identifies strategic thinking approaches applicable to the AI context
- Assesses my ability to navigate complex and ambiguous environments

4. TRANSFERABILITY MATRIX.

- For each identified competency, assign a transferability score (1-10)
- Indicate the level of adaptation needed for each competency
- Suggest concrete ways to articulate these competencies in interviews and CVs

5. COMPETENCIES TO DEVELOP
- Identify 3-5 critical missing competencies for the target role
- Propose accelerated learning paths for each
- Suggest strategies to temporarily compensate for these deficiencies

This *assesment* revealed that Roberto possessed a surprisingly rich portfolio of transferable skills. Among the most valuable:

1. **Experience in *incident response***: directly applicable to incident management in AI systems.
2. **Implementation of security governance models**: critical to structuring the approach to AI security.
3. **Compliance with international regulations**: crucial in the context of emerging AI regulation.
4. **Multinational vendor management**: essential for navigating the AI vendor ecosystem.

Three critical gaps emerged from the analysis generated by the prompt, particularly the point about skills to be developed, that required immediate action:

1. **Fundamental knowledge of AI models** (*machine learning, deep learning*, LLM).
2. **Familiarity with the EU AI Act** and other emerging AI-specific regulations.
3. **Understanding of vulnerabilities specific to AI systems** (adversarial attacks, poisoning, etc.).

Accelerated learning plan

Based on this analysis, we developed a 90-day accelerated learning plan, structured in three blocks of 30 days each:

Phase 1: AI Literacy (Days 1-30)

- Course: "AI for Everyone" by Andrew Ng on Coursera (https://www.coursera.org/learn/ai-for-everyone).
- Book: "Artificial Intelligence: A Modern Approach" by Stuart J. Russell and Peter Norvig (selected chapters).
- Workshop: " AIS247: AI Security Essentials for Business Leaders" (SANS Institute, https://www.sans.org/ai/).

Phase 2: AI Security (Days 31-60)

- Course: "Security and Privacy for AI Systems" (Microsoft Learn, https://learn.microsoft.com/en-us/training/paths/ai-security-fundamentals/).
- Webinar: " OWASP AI Security and Privacy Guide" (OWASP, https://owasp.org/www-project-ai-security-and-privacy-guide/).
- Book: "Adversarial Machine Learning" by Anthony D. Joseph, Blaine Nelson, Benjamin I. P. Rubinstein, and J. D. Tygar.

Phase 3: AI Governance and Compliance (Days 61-90).

- Course: " LSE: AI: Law, Policy, and Governance" (edX, https://www.edx.org/executive-education/lse-ai-law-policy-and-governance-online-certificate-course).
- In-depth analysis of the EU AI Act and the NIST AI Risk Management *Framework*.

This plan allowed Roberto to quickly acquire the core skills needed for his repositioning, without trying to become a technical expert in AI- an unrealistic goal that would have required years of study and experimentation.

The reality of failure and resilience

A crucial aspect often ignored in career transition narratives is the reality of failures. Roberto's path was not linear, but marked by obstacles and moments of crisis that required adaptation and resilience.

The psychological cost of transition

"After three months of preparation and six interviews, I still haven't received any offers," Roberto confessed to me during one of our weekly sessions. "I started wondering if it was all a waste of time, if at 50 years old it was realistic to reinvent myself in such a new field."

This experience highlighted how professional transitions involve not only technical challenges, but also a significant psychological cost.

Resilience and adaptation strategies

After several unsuccessful attempts, we began to analyze them to adapt our strategy:

1. **Systematic feedback analysis**: collection and categorization of explicit and implicit feedback received during interviews.
2. **Identification of recurring patterns**: recognition of common themes in recruiters' objections.
3. **Iterative adaptation of the strategy**: incremental changes to the approach based on the identified patterns.

A pivotal moment was when Roberto received direct feedback from a recruiter who appreciated his expertise but felt it "lacked practical exposure to real AI projects."

This feedback led to a strategic shift: instead of continuing to apply directly for leadership roles in AI security, Roberto sought a short-term consulting project that would allow him to gain documentable practical experience.

Through his professional network, he identified an opportunity to assist as a consultant to a company that, at the urging of its own client, had decided to implement a governance system for AI systems.

Although he invested far more time and expertise in the project than the compensation recognized, this assignment provided him with a valuable resume reference, filling that critical gap that finally allowed him to overcome the objections of recruiters.

With a clear understanding of the professional landscape and one's transferable skills, the next step in the repositioning strategy is to transform the way we present ourselves to the marketplace-optimizing our professional profile to maximize visibility and relevance in the new context.

7.2 Optimizing the professional profile

Strategic transformation of CV and LinkedIn profile

In an era where systems used by recruiters, *Applicant Tracking Systems* (ATS), automatically filter candidates before a human eye sees the CV, optimizing the professional profile becomes a technical skill in its own right.

Achievement-based *storytelling*

Achievement-based storytelling transforms lists of responsibilities into impactful narratives based on measurable results. This technique is particularly effective for senior professionals who need to demonstrate the value of their experience in a new context. One *prompt* that accomplishes this task is the following:

***Prompt*: https://tinyurl.com/2khw8mm7**

Transforms the following job role descriptions into outcome-based impactful narratives optimized for ATS systems in the context of [AI Security].

For each position, restructure the description following these principles:

1. Start with a contextual "hook" that frames the challenge faced
2. Articulates specific actions taken, with emphasis on leadership and initiative
3. Quantifies results achieved with precise metrics (%, €, time-to-value)
4. Include keywords relevant to the target audience [AI Security Integration].
5. Explicitly connect past experience to new domain challenges

ORIGINAL POSITION:

[Insert original description].

Make sure each point is:

- Supported by quantifiable evidence
- Relevant to the target role
- Optimized for industry keywords [AI, security, governance, risk, compliance]

Here is an example of the transformation achieved for one of Roberto's experiences:

- **Original description:** "As CIO and CISO of a company operating in five European countries, I was responsible for managing IT infrastructure and cybersecurity. I managed a team of 12 people and several external support vendors."
- **Transformed version:** "Called to play the dual role of CIO and CISO in an environment of increasing cyber complexity and geographic fragmentation, I led the digital transformation and security strategy for a company operating in 5 European countries. I implemented an integrated IT governance model that unified previously isolated systems while simultaneously improving security and business continuity. I led a multinational team of 12 IT and cybersecurity specialists, also orchestrating a network of external vendors. These initiatives reduced security incidents by 62 percent, improved incident response times by 78 percent, and generated annual savings of €350K through infrastructure optimization while maintaining compliance with GDPR and NIS2 regulations in all European markets."

This reformulation:

- Contextualizes the experience in terms of complexity and challenges.
- Highlights leadership and change management skills.
- Quantifies impact with specific metrics.
- Introduces keywords relevant to the target audience (governance, compliance).

- Implicitly connects experience to AI security challenges.

Data-driven keyword optimization.

ATS systems use *matching* algorithms that compare CV with position requirements. An effective strategy requires targeted keyword optimization based on *data-driven* analysis of the *target* market:

Prompt: **https://tinyurl.com/52u49zts**

Analyze 20-30 job descriptions for [AI Security Integration Manager] positions and extract:

1. KEYWORD ANALYSIS.

- The 25 most frequent technical keywords with relative percentage frequency
- The 15 most frequently asked soft skills keywords
- The 10 most frequently mentioned certifications
- The 10 most cited frameworks and methodologies

2. PROFILE OPTIMIZATION

- Suggest how to strategically incorporate these keywords into your LinkedIn CV and profile
- Propose a LinkedIn headline optimized for maximum visibility
- Create a LinkedIn summary that naturally incorporates the main keywords
- Suggest specific changes to role descriptions to incorporate them

3. DENSITY ANALYSIS

- Identify optimal keyword density
- Suggest strategic placement in the different sections of the CV
- Suggest semantic variations to avoid excessive repetition

4. COMPETENCY FRAMEWORK

- Create a structured competency framework for the target role
- Organize keywords into logical clusters of related competencies
- Suggest how to articulate these competencies in a coherent manner

For Roberto, this analysis identified clusters of high-frequency keywords, including:

- AI risk management (in 78% of job descriptions).
- Security by design (in 64%).
- Digital transformation (in 61%).
- AI compliance and regulatory models (in 57 percent).
- Cloud security and AI integration (in 52%).
- Security governance (in 48%).

Based on this analysis, we transformed its LinkedIn headline from a generic version to a strategically optimized one:

Original headline: "CIO/CISO | IT Management | Cybersecurity"

Optimized headline: "AI Security & Governance Leader | CIO/CISO | *Digital Transformation Expert* | *Secure-by-Design Implementation* Strategist"

The results were measurable: a 40% increase in profile views and several connections from recruiters specializing in AI security in the first three weeks after optimization.

The personal branding paradox

A crucial element often underestimated by transitioning professionals is the importance of ongoing *personal branding*. This presents a particular challenge for senior professionals who, by training and culture, tend to see *personal branding* as a form of digital vanity rather than a strategic imperative.

Roberto's resistance on this front is emblematic: "I'm not an influencer, I'm a serious professional," he confided to me, revealing a common misconception that wrongly conflates professionalism and strategic visibility.

I attempted to recontextualize this perception by explaining how *personal branding* in the AI era is not an exercise in digital narcissism, but a practical necessity:

1. **Demonstration of relevance**: in the age of AI, senior professionals must actively demonstrate that they are current and relevant.
2. **Algorithmic** visibility: modern recruitment algorithms reward visibility and recent activity.
3. ***Proof of work***: public contributions serve as a *portfolio* that demonstrates competence in real time.

Despite my insistence on the importance of daily micro-investments in professional visibility (15-20 minutes per day), this element of the strategy has not found fertile ground. This experience highlights an important lesson: even the most effective strategies must be tailored to personal predispositions to be successfully implemented.

Case study: Daniela and the multichannel approach.

To illustrate an alternative approach, let's consider the case of Daniela, a 48-year-old CISO who embraced a multichannel professional positioning strategy as she transitioned to an AI Security Lead role in a financial firm.

Unlike Roberto, Daniela adopted a "content-led branding" strategy structured around three pillars:

1. **Targeted *content creation***: monthly publication of an in-depth article on LinkedIn that connected traditional cybersecurity principles with emerging AI challenges.
2. **Strategic event participation**: *speaking* at industry conferences, positioning herself as an expert in the intersection of regulation, governance, and AI security.
3. ***Community building***: creation of a LinkedIn discussion group dedicated to "AI Security & Governance" that quickly reached 500 members and active participation in other thematic groups.

This strategy has generated significant results:

- Recognition as a *thought leader* in the emerging field of AI governance.
- Invitations to participate on *panels* and *advisory boards*.
- Some unsolicited job offers.

The difference in approach between Roberto and Daniela highlights a crucial point: there is no one-size-fits-all career transition path. The optimal strategy must align with personal predispositions, skills, and individual goals. Forcing Roberto into an activity that is not congenial to him would not have offered a genuine picture of his professionalism.

While an optimized professional profile ensures our visibility, it is the ability to effectively navigate modern selection processes-increasingly mediated by AI-that determines success at the crucial application stage.

7.3 Excelling in AI-driven selection processes.

Biases and opportunities in AI recruitment systems

Modern selection processes are increasingly mediated by AI systems, from initial CV scanning to video interview analysis. These systems, although presented as "objective," incorporate significant biases that can particularly penalize transitioning senior professionals.

Identifying biases in AI recruitment systems

The first step in effectively navigating these systems is to understand them. Current AI recruitment systems have several structural biases:

1. **Age-related biases**: tendency to penalize candidates with long careers, through:
    a. Focus on "recent skills" vs. cumulative experience.
    b. Preference for contemporary terminology.
    c. Underestimation of pre-digital experience.
2. **Biases related to career path linearity**: preference for linear rather than diverse career paths, penalizing:
    a. Transitions between sectors.
    b. Periods as freelancers or entrepreneurs.
    c. *Gaps* in CV due to personal circumstances.
3. **Biases related to topicality of keywords**: preference for candidates using the most recent terminology, even when representing familiar concepts by new names.
4. **Biases related to digital footprint**: algorithmic advantages for candidates with strong digital presence, regardless of actual skills.

Strategies for navigating and countering biases.

Understanding these biases enables the development of ethical "conscious optimization" strategies that maximize visibility without compromising authenticity:

1. **CV formatted for ATS:**
    a. Use standard machine-readable formats.
    b. Avoid graphic elements that confuse automatic text analyzers (*parsers*).
    c. Structure in clearly identifiable sections.
2. **Terminology Modernization:**
    a. Update traditional skills with contemporary terminology.
    b. Explicitly map traditional skills to contemporary patterns.
    c. Incorporating emergent *keywords* into descriptions of past roles.
3. **Foregrounding relevant experience:**
    a. Create a "Relevant Experiences" section at the top of the CV.
    b. Reorganize projects and accomplishments to prioritize the most relevant ones.
    c. Condense older experiences to avoid the impression of "being outdated."
4. **Strategic digital reporting:**
    a. Optimize profiles on Linkedin and GitHub and Stack Overflow in the case of technical profiles or relevant industry platforms.
    b. Create visible connections with reference figures/influential experts/opinion leaders in the target industry.

c. Develop role-specific mini-demonstration projects.

For Roberto, the implementation of these strategies was a turning point. His CV, initially filtered automatically by ATS systems, began to systematically pass the initial *screening* stage, allowing him access to interviews with human recruiters.

Interview preparation: the AI-enhanced method

Preparing for interviews in the AI era goes far beyond studying the company and formulating answers to standard questions. It requires a systematic approach that leverages AI as a personal *coach* and business intelligence tool.

Deep business intelligence

AI can automate and enhance analysis of the *target* company, turning a traditionally time-consuming activity into a structured process that generates strategic insights. Useful for building company profiles for multiple purposes, such as for business development, identifying *targets* for acquisition, or profiling competitors:

Prompt: **https://tinyurl.com/4u36z89k**

Conduct in-depth research on [company name] to prepare for interview for the position of [AI Security Integration Manager].

1. COMPANY PROFILE.
- History and evolution of the company with focus on digital and AI initiatives
- Business model analysis and value proposition
- Competitive positioning and strategic differentiators
- Corporate culture and values (analyzing Glassdoor, social media, public interviews)

2. STRATEGIC TRAJECTORY
- Analysis of the last 3 annual reports and press releases
- Recent investments in technology and AI
- Strategic acquisitions in the last 24 months
- Relevant collaborations and partnerships
- Recent patent filings indicating technology directions

3. CHALLENGES AND OPPORTUNITIES
- Sector-specific challenges [critical infrastructure] with respect to AI
- Regulatory trends impacting AI adoption in this sector
- Initiatives by direct competitors in AI
- Potential gaps in AI implementation strategy

4. LEADERSHIP AND DECISION MAKERS
- Professional background of key executives

5. PERSONAL STRATEGIC QUESTIONS.

- Generate 10 questions that I might ask during the interview that demonstrate:

(a) In-depth understanding of the business

b) Alignment with strategic challenges.

c) Vision for the specific role

d) Ability to generate immediate value

Present the analysis in a structured format, with emphasis on points that represent opportunities to connect my experience with the needs of the business.

This type of analysis allowed Roberto to discover that a major critical infrastructure company was facing significant challenges in integrating security into their nascent AI systems.

With this knowledge, Roberto was able to structure his responses in a way that highlighted experiences directly relevant to these not-quite-stated challenges, creating an impression of deep understanding that struck a positive chord with the interviewers.

Advanced voice simulations

One of the most powerful innovations in interview preparation is the use of AI with voice capabilities for immersive simulations. This mode adds a dimension of authenticity that cannot be replicated through simple written preparation.

Once we start Voice mode on ChatGPT (e.g., on a smartphone) we need to issue a *prompt* by reading the following:

Prompt: **https://tinyurl.com/2nuthtf2**

I want you to simulate a realistic interview for an AI Security Governance Lead position. Act like an interview panel consisting of CISO, CTO, and Head of AI.

STEP 1: INTERVIEW STRUCTURE

Conduct an interview structured in three parts:

1. Background and motivation (5-7 minutes)
2. Technical questions on AI security (10-12 minutes)
3. Situational and behavioral questions (10 minutes)

STEP 2: INTERVIEW CHARACTERISTICS

- Ask one question at a time and wait for my answer
- Delve into incomplete or vague answers
- Include challenging questions that test the limits of my knowledge
- Simulate different interviewer styles (technical, skeptical, cooperative)
- Insert occasional interruptions or sudden topic changes

STEP 3: SPECIFIC FOCUS AREAS

Focus on these key areas:

- Implementing integrated security frameworks
- Assessment of risks specific to AI systems
- Regulatory compliance (EU AI Act, NIST AI RMF)
- Management of security incidents in AI systems
- Leadership of cross-functional teams
- Future vision of integration between traditional security and AI

STEP 4: FEEDBACK
At the end of the simulation, provide:
- Detailed analysis of my responses (strengths/areas for improvement)
- Specific recommendations to improve communication of my skills
- Suggestions on how to better answer the most difficult questions

ChatGPT's voice alerts us to begin the simulation by following the steps we have suggested.

The effectiveness of these simulations was unquestionable and allowed Roberto to identify and correct small but significant behavioral patterns:

- Tendency to ramble when unsure about a topic.
- Excessive use of traditional IT technical jargon.

Correcting these patterns significantly improved his performance in actual interviews.

Strategic bid negotiation

The negotiation phase is a critical moment often underestimated by candidates in transition. AI can provide strategic support, helping to analyze offers, identify leverage points, and prepare effective negotiation strategies.

Competitive bid analysis

Prior to any negotiations, a thorough understanding of the market value of one's skills in the new environment is critical. Once the fields in square brackets are filled in, the following prompt will analyze our proposal by comparing it with market values and recommend a negotiation strategy.

Prompt: **https://tinyurl.com/2cs5shhx**

Analyze the following job offer for the position of [AI Security Integration Manager] and develop a comprehensive negotiation strategy.

OFFER DETAILS:

- Annual base salary: [€X]
- Target Bonus: [Y%]
- Equity/Stock Options: [details]
- Benefits: [list]
- Other components: [details]

MY CURRENT SITUATION:

- Last position: [role]
- Last Compensation: [details]
- Other offers/opportunities: [if applicable]
- Personal priorities: [list]

1. COMPETITIVE ANALYSIS.

- Compare offer to market benchmarks for similar roles
- Evaluates each component separately (base, variable, equity, benefits)
- Identifies sub-benchmark or missing elements
- Analyzes the overall structure in relation to the current market

2. NEGOTIATION STRATEGY

- Identify the 3 priority elements to be negotiated
- Suggest realistic target ranges for each element
- Propose strategic trade-offs between different components
- Develop a phased negotiation strategy, with contingency plans

3. NEGOTIATION SCRIPT

- Create a framework for the initial conversation.
-Develop responses for possible objections
-Suggest specific wording for key requests.
-Prepare closing statements for different situations

4. NON-MONETARY CONSIDERATIONS

. Identify non-monetary negotiable elements of value (remote work, training, flexibility).

-Suggest how to integrate these elements into the negotiation

-Propose how to quantify the value of these elements.

5. ACTION PLAN.

-Optimal sequence of communications.
-Strategic timing
-Recommended modes of communication.
-Opening/closing signals to monitor.

Present results in structured format, with specific recommendations and scripts to initiate negotiation.

When Roberto received his first offer for an AI Security Lead role, this analysis revealed that while the base salary was competitive, the variable incentive elements (MBO) were significantly under *benchmarked*.

Customized negotiation strategies

AI helped Roberto develop a customized negotiation strategy that considered not only market data, but also company specifics and personal priorities. Three principles proved particularly effective:

1. **Value-based negotiation**: clearly articulate the ROI the company will gain from its unique expertise by quantifying the value of its expertise in security governance.
2. **Collaborative approach**: present negotiation as a process of aligning interests rather than pitting them against each other.
3. **Focus on metrics**: tie some of the compensation to objective KPIs related to the secure implementation of AI systems.

The implementation of this strategy enabled Roberto to achieve substantial improvement in the overall conditions, particularly the alignment of incentives with the security outcomes of AI projects, something that enhanced his unique experience and supported his professional development in the new domain.

Obtaining a new role, however, is only the beginning of a journey of continued growth. In the rapidly evolving AI ecosystem, the ability to constantly acquire new skills becomes a strategic professional *asset* that transcends a single career transition.

7.4 Continuous professional development in the AI ecosystem.

Roberto's success in repositioning is not an end point, but the beginning of a journey of constant adaptation. This requires a system of continuous professional development. In the next section, I will share the methodological model I personally developed and applied to address this challenge.

Learning *Roadmap*: Personal experience in accelerated skill acquisition

Over the past three years, my career has gone through a significant acceleration, leading me to three different executive roles in rapid succession. These changes are not a source of stress for me, but rather stimulating challenges that fuel my professional growth.

The evolving professional learning landscape

However, I have noticed a fundamental transformation in the professional learning landscape: whereas in the past there was a "grace period" for acquiring the skills needed for a new role, today the market demands a "*plug-and-play*" approach - to use a technological analogy, like a peripheral that starts working immediately once plugged in, with no need for drivers or configuration.

The paradox of the executive in transition

When an executive makes a radical role change or joins a new organization, he or she often finds himself or herself in a paradox: on the one hand, he or she needs to acquire a broad range of skills quickly; on the other hand, he or she may be embarrassed to manifest these gaps, fearing that he or she will not meet the expectations of a team that expects immediate leadership and technical expertise in an increasingly complex and unpredictable world.

I addressed this paradox by developing a structured methodology for AI-enhanced autonomous learning, which proved exceptionally effective in allowing me smooth transitions between even very different domains.

Methodological model for accelerated skill acquisition

My approach consists of four distinct phases:

Phase 1: Systematic mapping of competencies.

The starting point is always the creation of a comprehensive map of the skills and knowledge domains needed to excel in the new role. Unlike impressionistic approaches, I prefer an analytical method that produces a comprehensive inventory.

I developed a specific *prompt* that uses AI to identify:

- Core technical skills for the domain.
- Essential conceptual and methodological *frameworks*.
- Emerging trends that could impact the domain.
- Relevant regulations and standards.
- Emblematic case studies.

Prompt that served me when I took over responsibility for a company in our group specializing in cybersecurity.

Prompt: **https://tinyurl.com/2ra6rt3z**

Develop a comprehensive mapping of the skills needed to excel in the role of [Executive VP Cybersecurity], considering my background in [IT management and certification].

1. TECHNICAL CORE COMPETENCIES.

- Identify the 15-20 technical domains essential to this role
- For each domain, specify:
  * Core concepts to be mastered.
  * Specialized terminology to be mastered.
  * Reference methodologies and frameworks.
  * Level of depth required (overview/operational/expert).

2. STRATEGIC AND MANAGERIAL COMPETENCIES.

- Identifies 10-12 key leadership competencies in the specific context
- For each competency, outlines:
  * Practical applications in the role
  * Relevant decision-making frameworks.
  * Metrics for evaluating effectiveness.
  * Best practices in the specific field

3. EMERGING TRENDS AND INNOVATIONS
- Identify 5-7 emerging developments with potential impact on the role
- For each trend, specify:
  * Expected short/medium-term impact
  * Resources for staying current

4. REGULATION AND COMPLIANCE
- Identify relevant regulatory frameworks and industry standards
- For each, outline:
  * Key requirements to understand
  * Direct operational implications.
  * Implementation timelines/deadlines.
  * Authoritative resources for further study.

5. CASE STUDIES AND BEST PRACTICES
- Identify 8-10 emblematic cases in the field.
- For each case, highlight:
  * Context and challenges faced.
  * Approaches taken and results achieved.
  * Key lessons applicable to my context.
  * Sources for detailed insights

Make sure the mapping is:
- Context-specific [cybersecurity enterprise].
- Calibrated to my current background
- Structured to facilitate subsequent prioritization
- Inclusive of both technical and leadership aspects

This process typically generates an inventory of 30-50 areas of expertise, which would be daunting without a prioritization strategy.

Step 2: Stratification and prioritization.

Once the mapping is complete, I apply prioritization based on three dimensions:

1. **Operational** impact: how much does this competency affect my ability to generate immediate value?
2. **Contextual urgency**: how quickly will this competency be needed in the new role?
3. **Required depth**: what level of mastery is sufficient for my responsibilities?

Example *prompt* for prioritization:

Prompt: **https://tinyurl.com/3y8s8cyh**

Using the generated competency mapping, develop a strategically prioritized learning plan for the role of [Executive VP Cybersecurity].

1. MULTI-CRITERIA ANALYSIS.

Evaluate each identified competency according to the following parameters:

- Operational impact (1-10): How much this competency affects the ability to generate immediate value
- Contextual urgency (1-10): How quickly this competency will be needed in the new role
- Required depth (1-5): Level of mastery

(1=familiarity, 5=expertise)
- Strategic alignment (1-10): How well this competency supports the strategic goals of the organization
- Transferability from existing skills (1-10): How much can I leverage my current experience

2. TEMPORAL STRATIFICATION

Organize competencies into three time categories:
- Mission-critical competencies (first 30 days)
- High-impact competencies (first 90 days)
- In-depth competencies (progressive development).

For each category, create a sequential plan that considers the interdependencies between competencies.

3. LEARNING MODALITIES.

For each priority competency, suggest the optimal combination of:
- Training resources (books, courses, webinars, articles)
- Learning modalities (reading, audio, practice, mentorship)
- Estimated time required for acquisition
- Learning verification milestones

4. PORTFOLIO BALANCE.

Ensures that the overall plan:
- Balances technical and managerial skills
- Alters different learning modes
- Distributes cognitive load in a sustainable way
- Provides for moments of consolidation and reflection

5. ADAPT TO MY SPECIFIC CONTEXT
Taking into account my personal constraints:
- 30-60 minutes of focused study in the morning (6 days out of 7)
- 3 hours per week of hands-on learning
- Car travel time (convertible to audio learning)
- Micro-sessions throughout the day

Present the plan in tabular format, with clear indication of priorities, modalities and timelines.

This process transforms an undifferentiated list into a layered *roadmap* that distinguishes:

- Core competencies (to be acquired in the first 30 days).
- High-impact competencies (to be acquired in the first 90 days).
- In-depth competencies (to be developed progressively).

Phase 3: Multimodal learning orchestration.

The real innovation in my methodology lies in the orchestration of learning, which integrates different modalities according to time and contextual constraints.

My daily routine involves:

- 30-60 minutes of focused study in the early morning hours, usually starting by 06:15 / 06:30 (6 days out of 7).
- Strategic use of car travel and sports time.
- Opportunistic micro-sessions throughout the day.

***Prompt*: https://tinyurl.com/39ms2ztk**

Create customized training materials on [AI Security Governance] adapted to my specific context.

LEARNING PROFILE:
- Current level: Intermediate in cybersecurity, beginner in AI governance
- Background: Executive with experience in certification and compliance
- Goal: Ability to strategically oversee AI security initiatives and effectively dialogue with technical team
- Time constraints: 45-minute morning learning session
- Mode: Text material followed by self-assessment quiz

CONTENT STRUCTURE:

1. CONCEPTUAL RECAP (5 minutes).
  - Summary of key concepts learned in previous session
  - Connections to new material
  - Clarification of any points that remained ambiguous

2. **CORE CONTENT (30 minutes)**

- Presentation of new concepts in progressive format
- Illustration with concrete examples in the cybersecurity context
- Connections to already familiar frameworks (e.g., ISO 27001, NIST)
- Analogies with familiar concepts to facilitate assimilation
- Visualizations and diagrams to support understanding

3. PRACTICAL APPLICATION (10 minutes)

- Short case study with reasoning questions
- Decision-making scenario contextualized to the role
- Framework of application in business context

4. VERIFICATION AND CONSOLIDATION

- 5-7 self-assessment questions with immediate feedback
- Identification of areas for further study
- Suggestions for immediate application of concepts

5. AUDIO SESSION PREPARATION

- Synthesized version of key concepts in audio format
- Structured for listening during the car ride
- Duration: 15-20 minutes with focus on most relevant aspects

Make sure the content:

- Uses precise but accessible terminology
- Balances theory and practical applications
- References authoritative and up-to-date sources
- Is structured to facilitate the later Feynman method

AI transforms this time structure into a personalized learning system that:

- Generates training content calibrated to my current level.
- Adapts the format to the context (text for morning study, audio for road trips).
- Dynamically rearranges priorities based on progress.
- Prepares quizzes and tests to consolidate learning.

Step 4: Implementing the Feynman Loop.

A particularly powerful element in my approach is the implementation of a Feynman-inspired feedback loop, enhanced by voice AI.

During car rides, I use ChatGPT Voice as a learning partner that:

- Listens to me as I articulate aloud the concepts I have just learned.
- Identifies gaps or inaccuracies in my understanding.
- Asks targeted questions that stimulate clarification.
- Synthesizes recurring patterns of misunderstanding.

This seemingly simple practice has a profound impact on the speed and quality of learning, transforming travel time from "dead time" to a valuable consolidation opportunity.

Concrete results and lessons learned

This integrated system enabled me to acquire technical and managerial skills with a speed that would have been unthinkable using traditional training approaches. For example: when I took over responsibility for the cybersecurity firm, I was able in less than 60 days to develop sufficient understanding of *risk assesment* models, penetration testing methodologies, and emerging regulations to effectively lead the team and credibly dialogue with clients.

The key lessons I learned from this experience are:

- **Discipline and balance:** consistency is more important than intensity. Shorter daily sessions generate superior results than sporadic marathons.
- **Contextual integration**: immediate application of knowledge in real-world contexts accelerates learning. I always try to implement learned concepts in daily activities.
- **Unlearning to learn**: often, the biggest obstacle to acquiring new skills is not the complexity of the subject matter, but the need to abandon established mental patterns.
- **Multiple feedback loops**: the combination of self-assessment, AI feedback and field verification creates a resilient and adaptive learning system.

The combination of personal discipline and AI tools has created a continuous learning ecosystem that transcends the simple acquisition of specific skills to become a fundamental *mindset* for navigating a constantly changing professional landscape, both in the work and personal dimensions.

Career *"resilience"* strategies

In an environment of rapid technological change, preparing a career for future challenges requires a strategic approach that goes beyond simply acquiring specific technical skills.

"AI-proof" skills

Some human skills retain differential value even in an environment of increasing automation:

- **Contextual intelligence**: ability to integrate technical, ethical, regulatory and business considerations.
- **Meta-innovation skills**: ability to lead complex, multi-stakeholder innovation processes.
- **Adaptive leadership**: ability to lead organizations through uncertain and rapidly changing environments.
- **Systems thinking**: ability to identify complex interdependencies and second- and third-order consequences.
- **Human-AI orchestration**: expertise in designing and implementing collaborative systems that optimize the strengths of humans and AI.

Continuous learning strategies.

Developing a personal approach to continuous learning is critical. Two strategies have proven particularly effective:

- **Portfolio approach**: Diversify training investments among:
  - Established skills (70%).
  - Adjacent skills (20%).
  - Emerging/experimental skills (10%).
- **Strategic subprojects**: Develop personal projects that:

- Build emergent competencies.
- Generate demonstrable artifacts.
- Expand the professional network.

This continuous learning ecosystem not only serves the immediate present, but also prepares for the evolving professional future-a topic we will explore in the next section on strategies for future-proofing careers.

7.5 Conclusion: An integrated approach to professional transformation

Professional transformation in the AI era requires a holistic approach that integrates:

1. **Strategic market analysis** based on data and AI.
2. **Optimization of the professional profile** to maximize visibility and relevance.
3. **Advanced preparation for** AI-driven **selection processes**.
4. **Development of relevant skills** through structured learning pathways.
5. **Psychological resilience strategies** for navigating uncertainty and ambiguity.

Roberto's experiences highlight that there is no single path or magic formula for professional transformation. The optimal strategy must align with personal predispositions, existing skills, and individual goals.

What remains constant, however, is the value of a methodical, *data-driven* and psychologically aware approach that transforms a potential threat into an opportunity for reinvention and professional growth.

In an era where the only certainty is change, the ability to consciously evolve represents perhaps the most valuable skill of all.

Reviewing Roberto's journey, it emerges that professional transition in the AI era is not just a process of acquiring new skills, but a transformation of *mindset* and professional identity. This transformation requires a delicate balance between continuity and change -- valuing accumulated experience while embracing the uncertainty of uncharted territories. It also requires a reflective approach that considers not only "what I can do," but "how I learn" and "how I evolve." Ultimately, sustainable advantage in the AI era comes not from mastering specific technologies or patterns-inevitably bound to evolve rapidly-but from the ability to navigate change itself with strategic awareness, psychological resilience, and methodical adaptability.

Chapter summary

Strategic Career Transformation in an AI-Driven Marketplace.

The accelerated integration of AI into professional environments has radically altered the career landscape, creating both unprecedented challenges and extraordinary opportunities. Chapter 7 presents a comprehensive blueprint for navigating this transformation, drawn from real-world case studies and my own experience in guiding professionals through strategic repositioning.

This chapter presents a model that integrates five key dimensions for professional evolution:

1. **Strategic market analysis**: employing AI-enhanced methodologies to identify emerging opportunities at the intersection of traditional skills and AI innovation. Through data-driven research combining structured information from multiple sources (LinkedIn Jobs, industry reports), qualitative pattern recognition, and comparative positioning analysis, professionals can identify unique value propositions in emerging domains.
2. **Skills assessment and development**: implementation of a systematic approach to identify high-value transferable skills and develop accelerated learning *roadmaps* to close critical *gaps*. The chapter introduces a multidimensional assessment model that balances technical competencies, organizational skills, and meta-competencies-creating a basis for authentic professional development rather than superficial rebranding.
3. **Profile optimization**: transforming traditional CVs and digital profiles into strategically positioned *assets* through results-based *storytelling* and keyword optimization aligned

with evolving AI recruitment systems. Documented case studies show how this approach has increased profile visibility by up to 40 percent and significantly improved the number of interviews.

4. **AI-enhanced selection** processes: navigating increasingly AI-mediated recruitment processes through understanding embedded bias and implementing ethical counter-optimization strategies. Particularly valuable is the methodology for AI-enhanced interview preparation, including the collection of business intelligence and advanced voice-based simulation techniques.
5. **Continuous learning systems**: establishment of disciplined principles for continuous professional development that integrate multiple learning modalities, strategic prioritization, and AI-enhanced feedback loops. The personal methodology I developed and implemented demonstrates how executives can acquire domain skills at unprecedented speed while maintaining leadership presence.

The pragmatic value of the chapter derives from its candid examination of both successes and failures in professional transformation journeys. Rather than presenting idealized narratives, it candidly addresses psychological challenges, strategically navigates failures, and presents resilience-building approaches critical to successful professional evolution.

Perhaps most significantly, the vision transcends the false dichotomy between technical and strategic skills, demonstrating how practitioners can develop hybrid value propositions at the intersection of traditional skills and AI innovation-where the most significant opportunities are emerging.

For executives navigating complex career transitions or for organizations designing workforce transformation initiatives, this methodology offers a structured approach that balances analytical rigor with the human dimensions of professional development. Roberto's case study illustrates that although there is no universal formula for professional reinvention, a methodical, data-informed and psychologically tuned approach consistently transforms potential disruption into opportunities for growth and differentiation.

CHAPTER 8

THE FUTURE OF GENERATIVE AI: PREPARING FOR THE NEXT LEVEL

As I write these lines, in advancing 2025, we can now see how *Large Language Models* have gone from experimental tools to essential components of the operational infrastructure of countless organizations in just three years. What we have seen so far is only the proverbial tip of the iceberg, the embryonic stage of a much deeper and multidimensional transformation.

The transition we are undergoing-from analysis and generation tools to truly autonomous agents capable of operating with increasing independence-requires a fundamental rethinking of skills, roles, architectures and decision-making models. Organizations and professionals who can effectively navigate this transition will not only survive, but thrive in an environment of unprecedented opportunity.

8.1 The evolution toward AI agent systems.

Technological innovation often follows a recognizable evolutionary pattern: what began as a single, isolated tool tends to evolve into a complex, interconnected ecosystem. This phenomenon, which I have observed repeatedly, is manifesting itself with particular evidence and speed in the field of generative AI.

In the past 18 months, I have witnessed a fundamental transformation that transcends the concept of a single autonomous agent. We are rapidly moving from large-scale language models (LLMs)-already extraordinarily sophisticated but essentially unitary in their architecture-to what is called "agentic AI systems": integrated ecosystems where multiple specialized intelligences operate in concert, orchestrated by coordinating meta-structures.

The metamorphosis of agents into agentic systems

The Large Language Models that dominate the current landscape represent only the first generation of a rapidly evolving technology. During a recent visit to the research labs of a major technology company, I was able to observe the near future of this evolutionary trajectory: multicomponent agentic systems that overcome the inherent limitations of monolithic models through specialization and orchestrated collaboration.

In these systems, rather than relying on a single generalist model, we see the development of ecosystems where specialized agents-mathematical analysts, information researchers, strategic planners-operate under the direction of an orchestrating meta-agent. The central coordinator assigns subtasks to the most appropriate specialists and integrates the results into coherent outputs, creating emergent intelligence that is greater than the sum of the parts.

A particularly innovative element of these agentic systems is their persistent episodic memory. Unlike current models, which are characterized by interactions with basically no state memory, the new ecosystems incorporate memory structures that enable continuous learning and deep personalization of interactions. I had the opportunity to personally test a prototype agentic system locally and was fascinated by its ability to autonomously decompose complex problems, distribute them among the most appropriate specialists, and synthesize integrated solutions with a process transparency that is impossible in single systems.

The real evolution of agentic systems, however, is not limited to their internal architecture, but extends to their integration with the world. The incorporation of multimodal sensory capabilities represents a qualitative leap: the most advanced systems are not limited to textual processing, but integrate visual, auditory and even tactile inputs into a unified model of understanding. In parallel, the acquisition of actuation capabilities enables these systems to interact directly with APIs, Web services and, in the not-too-distant future, with the physical environment through robotic systems.

The third pillar of this evolution concerns reasoning models. AI agent systems are evolving from "*black box*" reasoning paradigms to explicit, self-documented decision-making processes. The capacity for critical self-assessment and meta-cognition, i.e., the system's ability to "think about its own thinking," monitoring and evaluating its own cognitive processes to identify limitations and improve its performance, complements this evolution, enabling systems to independently identify knowledge gaps or fallacious reasoning.

The transformation of operational models

The emergence of AI agent systems is profoundly redefining human-computer interaction models. In implementation projects, I have identified an evolutionary progression through three distinct stages, each characterized by a different balance between automation and human supervision.

The first stage, now widely used, is supervised workflows (*human-over-the-loop*), where agentic systems generate outputs that are systematically evaluated by human operators before final approval. In certification projects, we have implemented this model to support the planning of audit activities and to support decision makers in their evaluations, resulting in high productivity gains and cost reductions while maintaining quality levels superior to traditional processes.

The second stage, which we are actively implementing in more mature processes, is collaborative workflows (*human- in-the-loop*). Here the relationship becomes more dynamic and equal: agentic system and human operator work in tandem, with task allocation based on their respective competencies. A concrete example is the evolution of the automated e-mail response system: we are implementing a confidence-based routing system, where the agentic system assesses its own level of certainty and forwards decisions to the human where this parameter is subthreshold. The human feedback is not only used to correct the immediate output, but feeds into a continuous learning cycle that progressively improves system performance.

The third stage, which we are beginning to explore in selected low-risk domains, is that of autonomous workflows (*human-on-demand*), where agentic systems operate with full decision autonomy, triggering human intervention only in predefined exceptional circumstances. The success of this model depends on the rigorous definition of escalation conditions, which in our conceptual model include confidence thresholds, novelty detection, and evaluation of the potential impact of decisions.

The most advanced frontier, still in the research and development phase, involves hybrid and adaptive workflows where the level of automation dynamically modulates according to contextual variables such as criticality, complexity, and availability of human expertise. Unlike current systems that operate at the level of individual tasks, future agentic systems will have complete awareness of the entire process, continuously analyzing operational patterns to identify optimization opportunities and creating virtuous cycles of continuous improvement.

This evolution toward increasingly autonomous agentic systems does not imply the marginalization of the human element, but rather its strategic relocation to higher value-added activities. My experience has convinced me that the most effective systems are not those that maximize automation, but those that optimize the synergy between human and artificial intelligence, creating hybrid ecosystems where each component operates in the domain where it generates the most value.

We are witnessing not the simple evolution of autonomous agents, but the emergence of true artificial cognitive ecosystems that replicate, in increasingly sophisticated ways, not individual functions but entire architectures of intelligence-a paradigm shift that requires a fundamental rethinking of the relationship between humans and technology.

Transformation of *Knowledge Work*

Evolving cognitive roles and new collaborations

The emergence of autonomous agents is catalyzing a profound redefinition of knowledge-intensive job roles. I have directly observed how this evolution follows recurring patterns that cross different sectors and disciplines.

Metamorphosis of traditional roles

Traditional professional roles are undergoing substantial transformation, with patterns that I have identified and categorized in an evolutionary conceptual model:

- Phase 1: Empowerment-In this initial phase, which we have already gone through in many areas, AI provides assistance without significantly altering the nature of the role. Professionals use AI as a tool to accelerate repetitive or research-intensive tasks.
- Phase 2: Specialization - The second phase, which we are currently going through, sees professionals specializing in activities where human expertise retains a comparative advantage.

- Phase 3: Orchestration - The emerging phase, which we are beginning to explore in more mature processes, transforms the professional into an orchestrator of AI ecosystems, allowing them to focus on verification strategy and customer interaction.

This evolution is not uniform but proceeds at different speeds depending on domain complexity, technological maturity, and regulatory constraints.

To better understand this metamorphosis, let us take for example a freelancer, a privacy lawyer with a particular focus on the European GDPR. This professional would like to evolve from a freelancer to a company but has a lot of difficulty finding GDPR experts interested in becoming his employees. This phenomenon that I have closely observed with my lawyer brother I attribute it mainly to two factors, the first related to the scarcity of privacy lawyers and the second in the inherent characteristic of the profession where the vertical expert prefers to work as a freelancer rather than as an employee.

Today his metamorphosis will take him through the three phases:

Phase 1: Empowerment - The empowered GDPR lawyer.

An empowered GDPR lawyer initially uses AI tools to expedite the routine aspects of compliance work. Privacy impact assessments that used to take days are completed in hours using intelligent templates drafted by the AI itself. Document review systems automatically analyze thousands of regulations and contracts to identify GDPR-related risks. Data breach notification processes become semi-automated. The lawyer retains essentially the same core role, but with significantly greater efficiency, allowing him or her to handle a larger client base while maintaining quality.

Step 2: Specialization-The strategic advisor in GDPR.

As AI systems increasingly handle routine compliance issues, the lawyer moves toward areas that require sophisticated human judgment. He focuses on strategic privacy architecture, designing an integrated governance system that anticipates regulatory evolution. He becomes adept at translating abstract GDPR principles into concrete technical specifications for engineering teams. Advises clients as they move from explaining regulations to helping organizations leverage privacy as a competitive advantage. Develops expertise in cross-border data transfer strategies in an evolving international context-an area that requires contextual understanding of geopolitical nuances beyond AI capabilities.

Stage 3: Orchestration - The architect of the privacy ecosystem.

The lawyer evolves into a strategic orchestrator who designs and oversees integrated privacy management systems. He configures AI-driven compliance monitoring platforms customized for specific industries. Instead of personally reviewing documents, sets parameters for autonomous compliance systems with human escalation protocols for complex cases. Creates a conceptual model of sectoral privacy where specialized AI agents handle routine tasks while human experts tackle complex interpretive challenges. It develops "regulatory intelligence networks" that connect different organizations with similar compliance challenges, creating economies of scale previously impossible in privacy management. Its agents become its employees, and its orchestration of them is equivalent to the management activities of a traditional human team.

New forms of collaboration

Parallel to the transformation of individual roles, we are witnessing the emergence of new human-machine collaborative models that transcend the traditional paradigm of "using" a tool: humans and AI collaborate iteratively to solve complex problems, with a process of co-evolution of the solution.

An embryonic preview of this new form of collaboration is the Canvas interfaces we discussed in Chapter 2.

This emerging form of collaboration involves an ongoing relationship with personalized AI agents that develop a deep understanding of the user's cognitive style and preferences.

The most advanced model, still in the exploratory stage, involves collaborative networks where hybrid teams of humans and AI operate as a distributed cognitive entity.

The effectiveness of these new collaborative models depends critically on the human-machine interface. In my experience, the most effective implementations are not necessarily the most technologically advanced, but those that optimize "*human-AI bandwidth*"-the ability to transfer information and intentions bidirectionally with minimal cognitive friction.

Emerging skills and training gaps

The transformation of job roles is creating a demand for emerging skills that traditional training pathways are not yet equipped to develop:

- Strategic AI literacy: the ability to understand the potential and limitations of AI not at a technical but at a strategic-operational level.
- Human-AI interface design: the ability to design workflows that optimize human-machine collaboration.
- Evaluation of AI results: the critical ability to evaluate AI-generated results, identifying potential biases, or errors.
- Advanced *Prompt Engineering*: evolution from formulating individual *prompts* to designing "conversational architectures" that guide AI through complex decision-making processes.

To fill this training *gap*, organizations need to promote the development of in-house *academies* dedicated to developing/enhancing AI skills with a "learning by doing" paradigm by getting support from experts in the field.

The profound transformations in professional roles and competencies that we have explored require a structured mode of operation that is intentional to individual and organizational strategic positioning. While collaborative models and emerging competencies define the "how" of the future of *knowledge work*, strategic positioning focuses on the "where"-the identification of optimal value spaces in a rapidly evolving ecosystem.

Strategic Professional Positioning

In a context of accelerated transformation, strategic positioning becomes a critical competency for both individual professionals and organizations. It is critical to adopt a conceptual model of strategic positioning.

Value migration map

The first element of the integrated system is a structured mapping of professional value migration, which identifies where value is shifting in the work ecosystem:

- Standardization zones: areas where generative AI is rapidly automating previously high-value activities. This category includes activities such as information search, standardized content generation, top-level document analysis, and reporting. The optimal strategy here is progressive disengagement or full automation.
- Empowerment zones: domains where human-AI collaboration creates value greater than the sum of the parts. This category includes strategic synthesis, problem-solving in ambiguous contexts, specialized content creation, and critical analysis. The optimal strategy here is targeted *upskilling* and adoption of collaborative toolchains.
- Human premium zones: areas where the human element maintains a sustainable competitive advantage in the medium term. Here we find unconventional creativity, genuine empathy, ethical judgment and high-level strategy. The winning strategy is in-depth specialization with focus on the distinctively human elements of the profession.

This mapping, which should be updated quarterly through analysis of technology and market trends, guides both organizational development decisions and individual *coaching*.

Strategic positioning system

The second element is a conceptual decision-making model to identify optimal individual positioning, based on multifactor analysis:

- Personal comparative advantage: structured *assesment* of competencies where the professional has a natural or developed advantage. Useful set of "*personal advantage discovery*" tools combining historical performance analysis, structured feedback, and guided *self-assesment*.
- Technology substitution risk: assessment of the vulnerability of the current position to AI automation. Various public and paid sources are available that based on empirical data collected over three years of AI implementations, quantify this risk through a combination of factors such as repetitiveness, dependence on pattern recognition, and information intensity.
- Market opportunity mapping: analysis of emerging areas of high value potential. Using *scenario planning* techniques and trend analysis to identify "opportunity spaces" where existing competencies can be reapplied in higher-value emerging contexts.

The application of this system can successfully guide workforce retraining.

Adaptive strategies.

The third element of the system is a structured set of adaptation strategies, tailored to different job profiles:

- Vertical integration: expansion of the professional role "upward" in the value chain, incorporating strategic and decision-making elements.
- Horizontal expansion: expansion of the professional domain through the integration of complementary skills.
- Domain transfer: application of core competencies in new emerging domains with higher added value. For example, in the areas of sustainability and ESG.

- AI Symbiosis: creation of competitive advantage through advanced mastery of AI tools.

The effectiveness of these strategies depends on tailoring them to the individual profile.

The AI paradox: famine in an age of abundance

An emerging pattern I have identified through this research is what I call the "AI paradox": in a context of increasing automation and standardization of cognitive tasks, some skills paradoxically become rarer and more valued:

- Long-term planning skills and systemic vision become more valuable in a context of accelerating technology and decision-making.
- The ability to navigate complex interpersonal dynamics and manage divergent interests becomes a critical differentiator.
- The ability to integrate knowledge from disparate domains to generate non-obvious insights is a sustainable advantage.
- Informed ethical judgment becomes essential in a landscape of increasing decision-making complexity.

This paradox creates strategic opportunities for practitioners and organizations that can identify and develop these "niches of scarcity" in a landscape of increasing automation.

8.2 AI for a sustainable future

The race for innovation in AI is occurring in parallel with a growing awareness of our collective environmental responsibility.

The same technology that has the potential to significantly accelerate the ecological transition also has a considerable and growing environmental *footprint*.

Environmental and social impact

AI's energy footprint: exponential growth

Data centers powering generative AI today represent one of the fastest growing infrastructures in terms of energy consumption. The numbers I have gathered are indicative of an alarming trend:

- Current consumption: in 2023, global data centers consumed about 240-340 TWh of electricity, equivalent to 1-1.3 percent of the world's electricity consumption (International Energy Agency's 2025 report, "Energy and AI"). Of this share, the component devoted specifically to AI is estimated to be between 10-15%, an increase of 70% from 2021. The U.S. Department of Energy documents a consumption of 176 TWh in 2023 for the U.S. alone, or 4.4 percent of national consumption.
- Energy intensity of training: training a single large-scale language model (LLM) such as GPT-4 requires an estimated 15,000 to 30,000 MWh of energy consumption - equivalent to the annual consumption of about 3,000 to 6,000 European households (academic sources).
- Growth in inference (the daily use of models): while historically the focus has been on the energy required for training, inference is rapidly becoming the dominant component of energy

consumption. According to the data I analyzed, inference now accounts for 70-80% of total AI energy consumption, with an increase of 120% year-on-year.

- Projection 2025-2030: Current analyses predict that in the absence of significant efficiency improvements, AI energy consumption could grow by a factor of 10 to 15 times by 2030, reaching 3-5% of global electricity consumption-a figure comparable to the energy footprint of the entire transportation sector in some European countries.

These trends are further compounded by the increasing size of the models, which have increased by a factor of 1,000x in just three years, resulting in an almost proportional increase in the computational resources required.

Mitigation strategies: the efficiency imperative

My experience has taught me that any sustainability challenge can be addressed through a multidimensional approach. For AI, this means operating on three levels:

1. **Hardware infrastructure optimization:** Energy efficiency is pursued through two main directions. On the one hand, semiconductor manufacturers (such as Nvidia) continuously develop more efficient GPUs and optimized data center architectures. On the other, innovation focuses on improving existing infrastructure: advanced cooling solutions, intelligent thermal management systems, and heat dissipation technologies can dramatically reduce power consumption in data centers without requiring replacement of the main hardware (as, for example, GEMATEG.com proposes).
2. **Algorithm optimization**: Modern efficiency techniques include three basic approaches. Distillation enables

knowledge transfer from complex models to compact versions while maintaining essential performance. Selective attention dynamically activates only the neural components needed for each specific task, reducing computational load. Quantization optimizes the numerical accuracy of parameters, achieving energy reductions of 60-70% with negligible performance degradations.

3. **Operational optimization:** Concerns how AI systems are managed in practice, from shifting non-urgent workloads to times of higher renewable energy availability to dynamically allocating computational resources according to the complexity of demands.

Measurement and accountability: foundations for sustainable AI

My experience in certification has taught me that "what cannot be measured cannot be improved." For this reason, we are considering the development *of* a certification scheme specifically for AI sustainability:

- Standardized metrics: we have defined metrics such as "energy per inference" and "emissions per parameter" that allow objective comparisons between different models and implementations.
- Full life cycle assessment: the system assesses the environmental footprint of the entire life cycle of an AI system, from training to maintenance to end of life.
- Emissions transparency: we are promoting the adoption of "energy labels" for AI models to enable users to make informed choices.

AI for social good: high-impact applications.

Parallel to environmental challenges, generative AI offers unprecedented opportunities to address complex social issues.

Health and life sciences: AI as a democratizer of health.

AI's potentially most profound impact occurs in the health sector, where it can break down barriers to access and close specialized skills *gaps*:

- Accessible diagnostics: AI-based diagnostic systems that I have personally tested have demonstrated *screening* capabilities comparable to experienced specialists in settings where access to medical professionals is limited. A pilot project in a rural region increased early diagnosis of critical conditions by 45 percent.
- Accelerated drug discovery: generative AI has reduced the development cycle of new candidate molecules from 3-5 years to 8-14 months, with profound implications for rare diseases and traditionally unprofitable pharmaceutical markets.
- Therapeutic personalization: AI systems that analyze genetic profiles and clinical data to personalize therapeutic protocols.

Environmental monitoring and climate action: democratization of environmental data.

A second high-impact domain concerns the application of generative AI to climate and environmental challenges:

- Ecosystem monitoring: multimodal analysis systems (satellite, IoT sensors, historical data) enable real-time monitoring of fragile ecosystems with previously impossible precision. One project in the Amazon region identified illegal deforestation activities 72 hours earlier than traditional methods.
- Accessible climate modeling: AI-generated local climate models that make high-resolution projections accessible to communities and local governments without specialized skills or infrastructure. A pilot program enabled 28 local governments to develop evidence-based climate adaptation plans at 85 percent reduced cost.
- Energy optimization: systems to forecast and optimize energy consumption in urban settings have demonstrated consumption reductions of 15-25%, with particular benefit to low-income communities previously excluded from smart grid technologies.

Crisis response and humanitarian aid: life-saving speed and accuracy

A third domain where generative AI is demonstrating transformative impact concerns humanitarian crisis response:

- Rapid post-disaster analysis: systems for multimodal analysis (satellite imagery, social media, radio communications) have demonstrated post-disaster damage assessment capabilities with a speed 5-7 times faster than traditional methods. During a recent earthquake, this allowed relief resources to be directed with critical accuracy within the first 12-24 hours.

- Humanitarian crisis prediction: predictive models combine climate, economic, political and social data to predict potential humanitarian crises 3-6 months in advance. A pilot system correctly anticipated a food crisis in the Sahel region, enabling preventive interventions that reduced the impact by 35 percent.
- Translation in critical contexts: AI-based and specialized translation systems for medical and emergency terminology. During a recent health crisis, such a system enabled effective communication between international medical staff and local populations, reducing critical errors by 65 percent.

Technology Democratization.

Accessibility and reducing the digital divide

The current AI ecosystem is characterized by a deeply asymmetric distribution of access and capabilities.

The AI accessibility paradox

Generative AI represents an accessibility paradox: on the one hand, models such as ChatGPT have made interaction with AI accessible to billions of people through intuitive interfaces; on the other hand, the ability to develop, customize, and deploy advanced AI solutions remains concentrated in an extremely limited number of organizations.

I have identified three key barriers that fuel this AI *digital divide*:

1. Computational barrier: training advanced models requires computational resources inaccessible to most organizations. The estimated cost of training GPT-4 exceeds $100 million--a prohibitive investment for all but the most capitalized technology companies.

2. Barrier of expertise: developing and managing AI systems requires highly specialized skills that are scarce in the market.
3. Data barrier: access to high-quality *datasets* remains a key competitive advantage, with significant asymmetries between organizations.

These barriers create a two-speed ecosystem, where a limited number of players accumulate exponentially greater AI capabilities than the majority of the market.

Strategies for democratizing AI

The spread of AI requires concrete strategies to overcome the accessibility gap. The *open source* movement is making this technology more democratic through lightweight models that also run on standard hardware. These compact models offer remarkable performance while requiring limited computational resources, enabling even small organizations to harness the potential of AI.

In parallel, simplified interfaces are breaking down technical barriers to entry. The "AI-as-a-Service" mode of operation is enabling teams with basic IT knowledge to integrate advanced functionality into their processes, while *no-code* platforms allow automation solutions to be created without writing code. The sharing of preconfigured templates and templates is further facilitating the adoption of best practices even in resource-constrained settings.

On the infrastructure front, new solutions are dramatically reducing deployment costs. Running AI models directly on local devices eliminates the need for expensive cloud infrastructure, while shared computing resource models allow small organizations to access otherwise prohibitively expensive computing capacity. Pay-per-use architectures are further democratizing access, transforming AI from a capital investment to a scalable operational expense.

8.3 Navigating the regulatory landscape

The AI regulatory landscape is evolving with unprecedented speed, creating a complex operating environment for organizations. This phenomenon requires a strategic approach that transcends simple reactive compliance.

My experience leading the certification team at RINA has taught me that regulatory compliance is not simply an exercise in adherence to static rules, but a dynamic process that requires deep understanding, continuous adaptability, and strategic vision. This is especially true in the field of generative AI, where technological complexity is intertwined with constantly evolving ethical, social, and legal implications.

Practical compliance *framework*

The global regulatory patchwork

The AI regulatory landscape is taking the form of a complex global mosaic, with distinct regulatory approaches reflecting different visions and priorities:

The European Approach: risk-based regulation

The EU AI Act represents the world's first comprehensive regulatory *framework* specifically dedicated to AI. It is based on a risk-based approach that classifies AI systems into four categories:

1. Unacceptable risk: prohibited applications (social *scoring*, subliminal manipulation).
2. High risk: systems subject to stringent requirements (health care, transportation, recruitment).
3. Limited risk: subject to transparency requirements (chatbots, *deepfakes*).

4. Minimal risk: minimally regulated.

The most significant implication I noted in analyzing the EU AI Act is the concept of "*accountability by design*"-accountability is no longer a *post-deployment* element but must be integrated into the entire life cycle of the AI system.

For high-risk system providers, requirements include:

- Documented risk management systems.
- High-quality *datasets* with auditable governance.
- Detailed technical documentation and automated *logging*.
- Meaningful human oversight.
- Demonstrable *accuracy*, robustness and cybersecurity.

A particularly relevant element for generative AI systems is the requirement for transparency about artificially generated content, with significant implications for the implementation of *watermarking* and *detection* mechanisms.

The U.S. Approach: sectoral models and self-regulation

Unlike the holistic European approach, the United States has adopted a more fragmented strategy, combining:

1. Blueprint for an AI Bill of Rights: non-binding guidelines that I have analyzed in detail, focusing on principles such as algorithmic security, non-discrimination and privacy.
2. Sectoral regulations: growing body of vertical regulations from agencies such as FDA (for AI in healthcare), FTC (for discriminatory practices) and NIST (for technical standards).
3. Executive Orders: Executive Order 14110 on the "Safe, Secure, and Trustworthy Development and Use of AI" introduced new requirements for core system *developers*, including sharing security findings with the federal government.

This fragmentation creates significant compliance challenges for organizations operating in cross-border contexts, forcing them to navigate partially overlapping but not fully aligned requirements.

The Chinese model: centralized oversight

China has implemented a distinctive approach that I have had the opportunity to study during consulting projects with organizations operating in Asia:

1. Deep synthesis management measures: specific regulations for content generated or manipulated by artificial intelligence, with digital watermarking and consent requirements.
2. Administrative measures for generative artificial intelligence: regulatory framework requiring prior review,

explicable algorithms, and content that conforms to "socialist values" (with significant implications for multinationals operating in China).

The United Arab Emirates (UAE) model: attraction and pragmatism

The UAE has developed a distinctive approach to artificial intelligence, characterized by a strategic combination of economic incentives, long-term vision, and regulatory pragmatism. This model represents an interesting case study in the global landscape of technology regulation.

The UAE follows a soft-regulation model based predominantly on incentives rather than regulatory obligations. This approach aligns perfectly with their AI Strategy 2031, an ambitious and structured roadmap that aims to transform the country into a global artificial intelligence hub.

The national strategy has several key pillars:

- Development of sector ecosystems with targeted investments in strategic areas such as healthcare, transportation and energy.
- Creation of special economic zones and dedicated tax incentives for startups operating in the AI sector.
- Formation of strategic international partnerships with key players such as the United States, European Union and China.

In 2017, the Emirates took an unprecedented step by appointing the world's first Minister for Artificial Intelligence, clearly signaling its ambitions in this area. This institutional innovation made it possible to:

- Centralize strategic vision and coordination of initiatives.
- Accelerate the implementation of pilot projects in key areas.
- Promote the adoption of AI technologies in the public and private sectors.

The ethical guidelines developed by the UAE address crucial issues such as transparency, privacy and fairness, while maintaining a predominantly voluntary nature. This balance between ethical principles and regulatory flexibility allows for:

- Foster innovation by reducing barriers to entry.
- Attract international investment.
- Adapt the regulatory framework to technological evolution with greater agility.

Cultural and legal traditions deeply shape the approach to AI regulation in different regions, influencing technological development and innovation hubs. China, for example, adopts a model based on pervasive laws and regulations that ensure state oversight, in line with its national strategic goals. In contrast, the United Arab Emirates promotes a highly flexible regulatory framework, free of rigid constraints, to attract investment and foster experimentation, reflecting its economic diversification strategy. The United States, true to its liberalist tradition, prefers a non-interventionist approach, relying on industry self-regulation to let innovation precede any regulation. The European Union, on the other hand, has structured an organic system of prohibitions, obligations and sanctions, rooted in its Romanist legal heritage, with a strong emphasis on the protection of fundamental rights and risk prevention.

In this diverse context, Italian AI legislation is distinguished by a balanced approach, which aims to promote technological development by focusing on the creation of skilled employment, the protection of workers' rights and the strengthening of the competitiveness of domestic enterprises at the European and international levels. The diversity of these regulatory models underscores how AI regulation is not merely a technical issue, but a reflection of societal values, traditions and visions, the understanding of which is crucial for businesses and policymakers to navigate the global AI landscape.

The regulatory-innovation cycle: a two-way relationship

One pattern I have identified through analysis of multiple technological innovation cycles is the bidirectional relationship between regulation and innovation:

1. Regulatory push: regulation not only limits but also directs innovation to specific areas. In the past year, I have observed a 300 percent increase in investment in artificial intelligence explainability and equity solutions in direct response to emerging regulatory requirements.
2. Innovation push: Technological evolution continues to outpace regulatory frameworks, creating significant "gray" areas. *Large Language Models* initially operated in a specific regulatory vacuum, forcing authorities into extensive interpretations of existing regulations such as GDPR.

This dynamic creates an operational environment characterized by pervasive uncertainty but also strategic opportunities for organizations capable of effectively navigating this complexity.

Operational approach to AI compliance

Addressing regulatory compliance in AI requires a structured approach that enables organizations to effectively navigate a complex and rapidly changing regulatory environment. An effective approach has three interconnected core elements.

The first step is strategic mapping of regulatory exposure. This process involves analyzing the various jurisdictions in which the organization operates, assessing the regulatory intensity and operational volume of each. AI applications are then classified according to risk categories, allowing efforts to be focused on the most critical solutions. Systematic analyses that identify gaps between existing systems and emerging regulatory requirements complete the picture.

The second element concerns the integration of compliance into the development process. Rather than viewing compliance as an after-the-fact activity, this approach translates regulatory requirements into technical specifications that can be implemented early in the design phase. Particular attention is paid to documenting each stage of the AI lifecycle and continuously validating compliance through structured methodologies.

The third aspect focuses on building robust and defensible documentation. This includes creating comprehensive data sheets of AI models that document not only technical parameters but also ethical considerations and limitations, tracking systems of data origin and use, and structured assessments of the potential impact of AI systems on individuals and society.

This integrated method not only mitigates the risks of noncompliance, but can turn into a genuine competitive advantage, significantly speeding up certification time compared to traditional approaches.

Anticipating regulatory change: regulatory intelligence and adaptability

In a landscape of rapid technological evolution and continuously developing regulatory response, the ability to anticipate regulatory changes has become a key operational requirement. An advanced approach to regulatory intelligence moves beyond traditional passive monitoring to embrace a proactive and predictive view.

An integrated regulatory intelligence framework

The first element of this approach consists of a layered monitoring system that integrates different information sources. This includes formal tracking of legislative initiatives at various jurisdictional levels, monitoring of the evolution of voluntary standards and guidelines, systematic analysis of case law interpretations, and the study of enforcement actions that provide concrete insights into the practical application of regulations. These different levels of monitoring, when integrated, create an early warning system that identifies emerging trends before they crystallize into formal requirements.

The second pillar focuses on identifying evolutionary patterns through comparative analysis. Particularly effective is cross-jurisdictional analysis, which detects regulatory trends that are manifest in different geographic areas, allowing anticipation of how specific approaches may propagate across different regulatory regimes. Complementary to this is the historical analysis of regulatory responses to previous technological innovations, which enables the identification of recurring patterns applicable to generative AI. No less important is the monitoring of industry self-regulatory initiatives, which frequently anticipate and influence subsequent formal regulations.

The third element enhances relational capital as a source of strategic information. Active participation in forums that bring together regulators and industrial stakeholders provides privileged visibility into the evolving directions of regulations. Involvement in industry coalitions enables not only anticipation but also influence on regulatory development. Completing the picture are collaborations with academic institutions that specialize in analyzing the regulatory implications of emerging technologies, which often provide insights into regulatory trends significantly in advance of their formal manifestation.

This multidimensional approach to regulatory intelligence has demonstrated the ability to anticipate significant regulatory developments an average of 8-14 months in advance, transforming compliance from a reactive cost to a strategic competitive advantage.

Preparing for the future of business systems in the age of AI

In the contemporary environment of simultaneous technology and regulatory evolution, making business systems adaptable to change is a strategic imperative, A structured approach to regulatory resilience is structured around three fundamental architectural principles.

Resilient architecture: design principles for regulatory adaptability.

The first pillar consists of the strategic separation of components based on their regulatory sensitivity. This principle involves the identification and architectural isolation of elements with high regulatory exposure, confining the impact of any regulatory changes to specific modules. Complementary to this is the standardization of interfaces between central components and regulated components, following a programmatic interface-oriented approach that allows upgrades with minimal impact on interconnected systems. The implementation of compliance capabilities as independent microservices complements this principle, allowing modular upgrades without interfering with central system functionality.

The second element concerns the implementation of inherently adaptable data architectures. This includes integrated governance structures that enable rapid identification of resources impacted by new regulations, schema-in-reading approaches that provide flexibility in evolving data structures, and incorporation of advanced privacy-protecting technologies: such as differential privacy and federated learning; an approach that enables AI model training on distributed data across multiple devices without centralizing sensitive data, thus preserving privacy. The latter is particularly relevant in the light of progressively more stringent privacy requirements, allowing adaptations with minimal architectural changes.

The third principle focuses on the ability to observe and document systems behavior. This includes multilevel structured logging systems that document not only actions but also reasoning and decision context, immutable traceability mechanisms for critical algorithmic decisions, and dedicated explicability interfaces that allow the level of detail of explanations to be modulated in response to emerging regulatory requirements.

Systematic implementation of these architectural principles has demonstrated concrete results in terms of adaptability. Systems designed according to this framework require on average 60-70% fewer resources to comply with new regulatory requirements than traditional architectures, turning potential regulatory hurdles into opportunities for sustainable competitive advantage.

8.4 Navigating the future with awareness

Over the course of my career, I have seen how the ability to navigate periods of intense technological transformation is a key strategic differentiator, for practitioners and organizations alike. Generative AI is redefining the boundaries of what is possible at an unprecedented rate, creating a context where mindful adaptability becomes not only beneficial, but essential.

My personal leadership experience during multiple cycles of technological disruption has taught me that success during these transition periods does not primarily depend on the specific technologies implemented, but rather on the meta-capabilities that enable one to effectively navigate an ever-changing landscape. These meta-skills-which transcend specific technical skills-are the foundation of sustainable adaptive resilience.

Meta-skills for the AI era: an integrated *framework*

The exponential acceleration of the generative AI ecosystem necessitates a fundamental rethinking of professional skills. Static expertise gives way to meta-skills that transcend specific domains, enabling professionals to evolve in tune with technological innovation. Two meta-skills emerge as particularly critical in the contemporary context: learning agility and systems thinking.

Learning agility: the art of continuous adaptation

Learning agility-the ability to assimilate new knowledge quickly and apply it effectively in different contexts-is the foundation of professional effectiveness in the AI era. This meta-competence has three interconnected dimensions:

The first dimension is accelerated pattern recognition-the ability to identify recurring structures in seemingly unrelated contexts.

Professionals with this skill practice analog transfer, applying principles learned in one domain to entirely new situations.

The second dimension concerns the effective integration of feedback. This manifests itself through rapid iteration cycles-daily sessions focused on specific skills-systematic practices of structured reflection, and active experimentation that constantly tests new ideas and approaches in low-risk environments.

Perhaps the most critical aspect is systematic unlearning-the ability to consciously abandon obsolete knowledge and practices. This process includes identifying and regularly testing core assumptions, deliberately expanding one's comfort zone, and recognizing established mental paradigms that may hinder the successful adoption of innovation.

Systemic thinking: navigating interconnected complexity

Systems thinking constitutes the second core meta-competency, enabling an understanding of the complex interdependencies that characterize the contemporary technological ecosystem. Transcending traditional linear analysis, this capability manifests itself in three distinctive modes:

Dynamic modeling enables the construction of mental representations of complex systems and their temporal evolutions. This includes identification of feedback loops within sociotechnical systems, consideration of second- and third-order implications of technological decisions, and sensitivity to nonlinear patterns that may signal impending changes in the technological landscape.

The ability to cross boundaries allows one to work effectively across disciplinary, organizational, and cultural delimitations. This ability is expressed in the translation of complex concepts across domains, the mapping of interconnected stakeholder ecosystems, and sensitivity to cultural differences that influence technology adoption.

Emergence recognition-the ability to identify and work with properties that emerge from the interaction of systemic components-completes this framework. This ability includes anticipation of emerging patterns based on weak signals, identification of leverage points where targeted interventions can generate meaningful change, and flexible adaptation in response to unexpected systemic behavior.

The AI growth mindset: an evolutionary mindset orientation

Complementary to cognitive meta-competencies, the *AI growth* mindset represents a mindset orientation that facilitates continuous adaptation to emerging technologies. This *mindset* transcends simple technological optimism, incorporating five distinctive components:

Expanding the space of technological possibilities manifested in systematic monitoring of developments beyond the boundaries of one's domain, application of first-principles thinking that breaks down complex problems into their fundamental elements, and structured practices of applied imagination that explore implications of different technological trajectories.

The focus on human-AI collaboration, explored earlier as a key element in new operational models, is manifested here in the systematic mapping of potential synergies between human and artificial capabilities, emphasizing the aspect of complementarity rather than substitution.

Intelligent risk calibration balances openness to innovation and appropriate prudence. This approach weighs the risks of technological adoption against the risks of inaction, privileges incremental experiments with low risk but high information value, and calibrates confidence in emerging technologies based on empirical evidence rather than general perceptions.

Ethical consideration integrates systematic assessment of the moral implications of technology implementations, verification of alignment between AI systems and human/organizational values, and proactive incorporation of ethical considerations in the early stages of design.

Probabilistic thinking complements this *mindset* by inherently accepting uncertainty as a building block of innovation. This component includes accurate calibration of confidence levels in predictions, concurrent planning for alternative scenarios, and application of appropriate decision-making systems in contexts of high uncertainty.

The integrated development of these meta-skills and mental orientations is a sustainable competitive advantage in a landscape of increasingly rapid innovation cycles. Unlike specific technical skills, these meta-skills retain their value across multiple technological generations, facilitating continuous professional evolution in tune with the frontiers of AI.

Personal action plan in the AI era.

The exponential acceleration of technological evolution has made continuous professional development no longer an option, but a strategic necessity. In today's AI-dominated landscape, I have observed how professionals and organizations need a structured and systematic approach to learning and planning. Through years of experience implementing AI solutions in complex contexts, I have developed an integrated system that has proven particularly effective in accelerating learning curves and increasing professional resilience.

Learning Orbit: a continuous learning system

The "*Learning Orbit*" model represents a holistic approach to continuous learning, articulated in four interconnected dimensions that, when effectively integrated, create a virtuous cycle of accelerated skill development.

The first dimension: structured knowledge acquisition, transcends the simple accumulation of information to embrace an architectural approach to knowledge construction. At the heart of this dimension is strategic knowledge mapping, which allows for visualizing and balancing deep experience in core areas and breadth in adjacent domains. This "T-shaped" approach enables the development of vertical robustness without sacrificing horizontal connectedness, which is particularly critical in a technology ecosystem characterized by accelerated convergence.

Complementary to mapping is the definition of the integrated, personalized learning pathway-a resource architecture that integrates different learning modalities into a coherent pathway. This process goes beyond simply collecting materials by strategically organizing theoretical, experiential and social resources in an optimized sequence. The implementation of spaced repetition systems complements this dimension, incorporating neuroscience principles of learning to maximize long-term retention.

The second dimension enhances direct experiential learning, transforming theoretical knowledge into embedded understanding. At the heart of this approach is strategic project *portfolio* management, which deliberately balances consolidation initiatives (which strengthen existing skills), extension projects (which develop capabilities in adjacent areas) and leapfrogging projects (which require the acquisition of entirely new capabilities). This deliberate balancing creates a development path that simultaneously optimizes depth, breadth, and exponential growth.

Deliberate practice complements this *portfolio* management by decomposing complex skills into their core components - true "skill atoms" - with focused exercises that isolate and develop each element. This decomposition enables focus and accelerates the acquisition of mastery in complex technological domains. Rapid prototyping loops complement this dimension, creating accelerated feedback loops that rapidly transform theoretical concepts into concrete implementations, generating intensive experiential learning.

The third dimension, reflective integration, transforms experience into insights through structured processes of conscious processing. Multilevel reflection protocols guide the simultaneous analysis of outcomes (what was achieved), processes (how it was accomplished) and assumptions (why certain choices were made). This depth of reflection makes it possible to identify not only superficial successes and failures, but deeper patterns that can inform future learning.

Knowledge distillation practices are an essential complement, allowing complex learning to be synthesized into accessible formats with high information density. This condensation process not only consolidates understanding, but creates reusable artifacts that accelerate future learning. Cross-domain integration complements this dimension by facilitating explicit connections between seemingly unrelated concepts, a particularly powerful process in identifying potential innovations at the intersection of different domains.

The fourth dimension, the social amplification of learning, recognizes that the most effective professional development rarely occurs in isolation. Intentional curation of diverse learning communities connects complementary professionalism, creating knowledge ecosystems that accelerate collective development. The use of teaching as a learning tool is a particularly powerful application of this dimension: articulating newly acquired concepts not only consolidates one's understanding, but identifies knowledge gaps not evident during individual study.

Collaborative meaning-making processes complement this picture, facilitating the collective construction of meaning through structured sessions where different perspectives contribute to the creation of mental maps that are more sophisticated than technological evolution. This collective intelligence enables more effective navigation for complex landscapes such as generative AI, where individual perspectives are inevitably limited.

Strategic navigation: a professional planning system

Complementary to continuous learning, the "Strategic Navigation" system offers a structured methodology for strategically guiding professional development in contexts of high uncertainty. This approach integrates elements of future thinking, strategic foresight and robust decision making into a coherent system articulated in three interconnected phases.

Mapping the future landscape is the foundation of this process, combining structured trend analysis with identification of potential discontinuities. Particular attention is paid to evaluating emerging trends based on their potential impact and associated level of certainty, creating a prioritization matrix that focuses attention on the most significant developments. Discontinuity scanning techniques complement this analysis by identifying potential breakpoints through the systematic examination of weak signals that could anticipate nonlinear changes in the technology ecosystem.

STEEP+ analysis extends the traditional system by incorporating the regulatory dimension, which is particularly critical in the evolving AI ecosystem where the emergence of new regulatory systems can rapidly redefine the rules of the game. This holistic view makes it possible to identify not just isolated trends, but patterns emerging from the interaction of different factors.

Scenario development and analysis translates this mapping into plausible alternative narratives, using a matrix built around the critical uncertainties with the greatest potential for impact. This approach typically generates four distinct and internally consistent scenarios representing different possible futures, creating a "possibility space" that transcends simple linear prediction. Narrative immersion techniques facilitate detailed exploration of the operational dynamics within each scenario, allowing one to "live in the future" through immersive descriptions that activate not only intellectual understanding but also emotional resonance.

Systematic mapping of implications completes this step, exploring the consequences of each scenario through multiple lenses: from the impact on skills and professional roles, to transformations in business models, to redefinitions of entire industries. This multilevel analysis makes it possible to identify common *patterns* of change that transcend specific scenarios, revealing key evolutionary dynamics.

Strategic response development translates the analysis into concrete action plans, with emphasis on identifying robust and effective strategies across multiple scenarios. This approach, focused on finding value-generating opportunities across multiple possible futures, minimizes vulnerability to specific evolutionary trajectories and increases overall resilience. The *portfolio of* strategic options complements this search for robustness by strategically balancing *core* initiatives (effective in all scenarios), hedging strategies (which mitigate specific risks), and opportunistic strategies (which maximize potential in favorable scenarios).

The design of early warning systems complements this by creating systematic mechanisms to monitor key indicators that signal the evolution toward specific scenarios. This approach enables timely evidence-based adaptations, avoiding both premature reactions and delayed responses to emerging changes.

Practical implementation: from architecture to action

Translating these conceptual systems into daily practice represents the most significant challenge for many practitioners. Effective implementation requires the development of supporting infrastructure, ritualization of key practices, and systematic mechanisms for review and adaptation.

The learning infrastructure provides the operational foundation, with a focus on digital knowledge management systems that transcend simple archiving to facilitate meaningful connections between information. The "connect, don't collect" approach privileges the identification of patterns and relationships over passive accumulation, creating organic knowledge networks that evolve over time. The conscious design of work environments, both digital and physical, complements this infrastructure, creating spaces that facilitate deep states of concentration. Dedicated time blocks protected from distraction are a particularly critical element in an era characterized by fragmentation of attention.

Learning metrics *dashboards* complement this infrastructure, balancing indicators of inputs (time spent, resources consulted), outputs (projects completed, problems solved) and, most importantly, outcomes (concrete applications, value generated). This multidimensional approach to measurement transcends superficial activity metrics to focus on the tangible impact of learning.

The ritualization of learning transforms conceptual principles into recurring practices, anchoring them in daily routines. Especially effective are morning rituals devoted to knowledge acquisition, when cognitive resources are maximized and not yet consumed by reactive activities. Strategic integration of training micro-habits into existing routines complements these dedicated rituals, creating mutually reinforcing behavioral chains. External accountability systems enhance the persistence of these practices through formalized commitments, turning intentions into concrete actions.

Multi-horizon planning translates strategic vision into tactical execution, balancing immediate actions, medium-term direction and long-range aspirations. Quarterly action plans provide operational focus with clearly defined focus areas, specific goals, and tangible success metrics. The annual strategic *roadmap* provides medium-term guidance, succinctly visualizing direction, priorities and milestones. The multi-year development trajectory complements this system, articulating strategic aspirations that define overall direction without over-specifying implementation paths, thus maintaining the flexibility needed in rapidly changing contexts.

This integrated approach to continuous learning and strategic planning has demonstrated tangible results in the most diverse organizational contexts. Its effectiveness lies in its ability to transform abstract concepts into concrete operational systems, creating infrastructures that support the ongoing development of relevant skills in a constantly changing technological landscape. In an era where the only certainty is accelerated change, these systems offer a strategic compass for effectively navigating uncertainty, turning potential threats into opportunities for growth and innovation.

Chapter Summary

This chapter explores the radical transformation that generative AI is undergoing, evolving from isolated tools to complex cognitive ecosystems. Drawing on my own experience, I share direct observations of how this evolution is redefining operational models, professional roles, and decision-making systems.

Key evolutionary trajectories:

1) **Multi-component agent systems**: the transition from monolithic LLMs to orchestrated ecosystems of specialized intelligences with persistent memory capabilities and multisensory integration.
2) **Transformative operational models**: the evolution through supervised, collaborative and autonomous workflows, optimizing human-machine synergy rather than simple automation.
3) **Redefinition of *knowledge work***: the metamorphosis of job roles through phases of empowerment, specialization and orchestration, illustrated with real implementation cases.

Strategic implications:

- **Sustainability and social impact**: the imperative to balance innovation with environmental responsibility, with concrete energy *footprint* metrics and multilevel efficiency strategies.
- **Regulatory navigation**: the ability to operate effectively in a global regulatory patchwork with divergent approaches (EU, US, China), transforming compliance from cost to competitive advantage.
- **Critical meta-skills**: the development of learning agility, systems thinking and AI growth mindset as foundations for professional resilience in an era of accelerated change.

Successful implementation of AI solutions depends not primarily on technology, but on the ability to strategically integrate innovation with core human values.

The systems presented are not theoretical, but emerge from iterative cycles of implementation, evaluation, and optimization in real business contexts.

The chapter balances strategic vision and concrete application, offering operational tool sets for practitioners and organizations seeking to navigate this transition. Through quantified case studies and structured decision-making systems, I provide a *roadmap* for capitalizing on emerging opportunities while mitigating associated risks.

The speed of change in the AI ecosystem requires not just reactive adaptation, but strategic anticipation. Organizations that embrace the systematic integration of human and artificial capabilities while simultaneously developing resilient-by-design architectures will be the ones that thrive in the era of generative AI.

THE HUMAN-MACHINE SYNERGY: A JOURNEY INTO AUGMENTED WRITING, MY CO-AUTHORS

Augmented Intelligence in Action

This book represents a concrete example of Augmented Intelligence applied to content creation. Unlike my previous two volumes, this is the first I have developed in the era of generative AI, radically transforming the creative process through a methodology of human-machine collaboration.

AI tool ecosystem

I systematically integrated a broad spectrum of generative AI tools available on the market, creating a complementary technological ecosystem that enhanced each stage of production:

- **Claude** has been my main intellectual collaborator, accompanying me for about 50 percent of the work time. His ability to synthesize and precision in analysis was a key pillar in articulating the most complex concepts.
- **ChatGPT Voice** facilitated particularly productive *brainstorming* sessions. The conversational dimension stimulated unexpected reflections that, through dialogue, gradually refined the initial thinking, turning into a mutual learning experience.

- **Gemini and Perplexity** have revolutionized the research phase, enabling verified and contextualized access to information, reducing traditional Web searches to almost zero and allowing greater focus on creative and analytical aspects.

AI capabilities built into tools such as **Microsoft Word** and **Canva** have streamlined the technical aspects of production, from page layout to managing graphic elements.

Augmented working methodology

This project, developed in the scraps of time, at night and in the wee hours of the morning, took nearly two years of discontinuous effort. In such an extended time frame, one of the main risks is unintentional repetition of concepts already covered. AI played a crucial role in identifying conceptual redundancies and overlaps, ensuring consistency and logical progression within the text.

The technical review of the manuscript was significantly enhanced by the AI tools, which accurately identified missing punctuation elements, verbal inconsistencies, and other stylistic inaccuracies that might have escaped the human eye, especially after long writing sessions.

The limitations of the current Man-AI partnership.

This partnership has not always been perfect. Current AI systems still have obvious limitations that underscore the gap between human capabilities and general AI. On several occasions, tools have attempted to "meet my requirements at any cost," producing technically plausible but conceptually inaccurate results.

In these critical moments, my professional skills have been the indispensable filter for identifying inconsistencies and correcting inaccurate information. This dynamic highlights how, in the current evolutionary phase of AI, the added value lies in the synergy between human intuition and computational power rather than in complete delegation.

A new creative paradigm

The era of human-AI collaboration is not a future prospect but a tangible reality that is transforming creative and productive processes. This book testifies to how AI, when used as a tool to amplify human capabilities, can significantly expand creative horizons, optimize workflows, and enable results that combine the depth of human thinking with the efficiency of computational systems.

The end result is not simply text written with the aid of technology, but a new form of expression emerging from the intersection of human cognition and AI-a creative paradigm that will increasingly define the future of intellectual production.

CONCLUSIONS

Throughout this book, we have explored multiple dimensions of the evolution of generative AI: from the technical metamorphosis of agent systems to their sustainable integration, from regulatory challenges to the meta-competencies needed to thrive in this rapidly changing environment.

The trajectory we have outlined-from monolithic language models to distributed cognitive ecosystems-represents only the beginning of an evolutionary path that will continue to accelerate. As we complete these reflections, it is critical to recognize that we are at a potentially critical moment of technological bifurcation: the emergence of general AI (AGI) on the horizon.

The current multicomponent agentic systems I have described constitute incremental but significant steps toward increasingly generalist capabilities. The increasing integration of specialization, persistent memory, symbolic reasoning, and long-term planning capabilities is gradually bridging the gap between specialized artificial intelligences and systems with cognitive capabilities comparable to humans across multiple domains.

This convergence toward AGI does not follow a linear or predetermined path. Every week, new research *papers* open up unexpected avenues, alternative methodologies, and conceptual systems that redefine our understanding of the possibilities and limits of AI. The research frontier remains as fluid as it is vibrant, with significant advances often emerging from the most unexpected interdisciplinary intersections.

Looking beyond the horizon of AGI, the possibility of superintelligence - cognitive systems that exceed human capabilities across all relevant domains - raises profound questions that transcend the technological dimension. As a society, we face the need to develop not only the technologies themselves, but also the ethical, philosophical and governance systems that ensure that these systems remain aligned with core human values and the collective good.

My experience implementing AI systems in complex contexts has taught me that the future is not simply something that happens-it is something we collectively build through our decisions, priorities and actions. The organizations and professionals that will thrive in this future will be those that simultaneously maintain an openness to innovation and an anchor to core human values: creativity, empathy, contextual wisdom, and ethical judgment.

In a technological ecosystem characterized by structural uncertainty and accelerated change, the ability to navigate with awareness, adapt with intentionality and collaborate across disciplinary and organizational boundaries will be the most sustainable competitive advantage. The systems, methodologies and strategies we have explored in this book do not offer definitive answers, but rather concrete tools for navigating an ever-changing landscape.

The journey ahead is as challenging as it is rich in potential. May you navigate it with curiosity, wisdom and an eye always on the emerging possibilities on the horizon.

Hoping you have enjoyed this journey, I renew my invitation to stay in touch through LinkedIn:

https://www.linkedin.com/in/emanuelecastagno/

ACKNOWLEDGEMENTS

My heartfelt thanks to Giovanni Gambaro, a fellow adventurer since 2005, whose deep understanding of technology and extraordinary ability to connect it to business has enriched me enormously over these years of evolving artificial intelligence. I would also like to thank Cristiano Sciaboni, who has guided me through the practical projects recounted in this book - from steel to pasta, demonstrating how technological innovation can transform seemingly distant sectors.

My gratitude also goes to Riccardo Dolfi, CEO of a major technology company, for the continuous and stimulating discussions on the evolution of AI in the world of work and the new business models that are redefining our professional future.

www.ingramcontent.com/pod-product-compliance
Lightning Source LLC
LaVergne TN
LVHW052225200926
848481LV00001B/212

9798231044665